AF283998

FROM EPSOM
TO TRALEE

A Journey Round the Racecourses of the British Isles

Medina Publishing

From Epsom to Tralee
A Journey Round the Racecourses of the British Isles

Published by
Medina Publishing Ltd
310 Ewell Road
Surbiton
Surrey KT6 7AL
medinapublishing.com

ISBN: 978-1-909339-07-1

Designer: Kitty Carruthers
Editor: Martin Rickerd
Assistant Editors: John Slusar, Doug Sutton, John Pinfold
Printed and bound by Toppan Leefung Printers Ltd, China

CIP Data: A catalogue record for this book is available from the British Library.

FROM EPSOM TO TRALEE

A Journey Round the Racecourses of the British Isles

ROY GILL

Scotland

Perth
Hunt

Hamilton
Park
Musselburgh
Ayr
Kelso

Hexham
Newcastle
Carlisle
Sedgefield
Redcar
Catterick
Bridge
Thirsk
Ripon
York
Cartmel
Wetherby
Beverley

Northern
Ireland

Down
Royal
Sligo
Downpatrick
Dundalk

Ballinrobe
Roscommon
Navan
Laytown
Bellewstown
Fairyhouse
Kilbeggan
Galway
Naas
Leopardstown
The Curragh
Punchestown

Haydock
Park
Pontefract
Market
Rasen
Aintree
Doncaster

Chester
Southwell
Bangor-
on-Dee
Uttoxeter
Nottingham
Fakenham

Ireland

Wolverhampton
Leicester
Yarmouth

Limerick
Thurles
Gowran
Park
Ludlow
Huntingdon
Newmarket
Listowel
Warwick
Tralee
Tipperary
Clonmell
Wexford
Worcester
Towcester
Tramore
Hereford
Stratford-
on-Avon
Killarney
Cork

Wales

Cheltenham
England

Chepstow
Windsor
Kempton
Park
Bath
Newbury
Sandown Park
Ascot
Epsom
Folkestone
Salisbury
Lingfield
Park
Taunton
Fontwell
Park
Wincanton
Goodwood
Plumpton
Brighton
Exeter
Newton
Abbot

Key

Flat only

National Hunt only

Both Flat & National Hunt

4

CONTENTS

Spectators flock to see the Epsom Derby in 1913 on foot, by car, by motor bus and by horse-drawn coach. Little did they know what dramas would unfold that memorable day.

FOREWORD
by Frankie Dettori MBE

I was thrilled to be asked to contribute the Foreword for Roy Gill's book since, although I don't ride on all of these racecourses, I do spend most of my life on one course or another! The main difference between racing in the UK and Ireland compared with the rest of the world is the huge variety of our racecourses and the fact that we change venues on an almost daily basis. Every course has different features that make up the challenge for owner, trainer, jockey and punter, and these include undulating tracks like Epsom that are left handed and stiff tracks that are right handed like Sandown or Ascot.

The number and variety of tracks also has the downside in terms of the hours that we jockeys have to spend travelling. The mileage involved is as arduous as anything else in the job and, now that racing is so established on an international stage, we could be racing on a different continent every weekend.

I obviously have my favourite tracks and these include Ascot – you just cannot beat the Royal meeting which, for me, is the best and most competitive racing of the year. I also, of course, had a life-changing experience there in 1996 when I went through the card and won all seven races. For that reason, whenever I walk through the gates on Ascot High Street I get a real buzz that I don't get anywhere else. I also love riding at Newmarket, York and the other feature meetings of the summer season – like Goodwood, which beats them all in terms of location.

This book is testament to the rich variety of our racecourses and the heritage and history that wrap them all together. I think it is these behind-the-scenes stories that make it such a special compilation.

Naturally, many horses and people I've known feature here, but also a great many I had never heard of. I enjoyed reading about the chap who won the Irish Grand National in 1929 with a wooden leg and a few fingers missing, and the race that was awarded to a dead horse at Tralee. There are heroes and villains aplenty and it was interesting to me to learn the background to some of the greatest riders of years gone by, like Frank Buckle who won 27 Classic races (including five Derbys) and the biggest ringers in racing history, like Francasal and Flockton Grey.

I hope that you enjoy *From Epsom to Tralee* as much as I did. It is thoroughly researched and entertainingly told and is the ultimate guide to all of our individual racecourses.

Frankie Dettori

PUBLISHER'S ACKNOWLEDGEMENTS

Roy Gill appeared on our doorstep in the late summer of 2012, weighed down with folders, files, photographs and books covering a lifetime following the form. I was at first a little daunted by the scale and complexity of the task we were about to embark on, but in the face of Roy's encyclopaedic knowledge, his quiet assurance and our instant rapport, the making of this book became not a task but a mission, and a very enjoyable one at that.

In the quest to make *From Epsom to Tralee* accurate, informative, entertaining and visually appealing, I am indebted to a great many people – besides Roy himself – most notably:

John Slusar and Doug Sutton, experts both, for taking an interest at a very early editorial stage. Their meticulous fact-checking, proofreading and helpful suggestions have improved the book immeasurably;

John Pinfold, Aintree's official historian, who gave unstintingly of his time and knowledge not only of the Grand National, but of the history of racing in general;

Jane Clarke, also a fount of knowledge about Aintree, for her eagle eye;

Martin Rickerd for doing a great job on the first edit back in 2012.

The author and publisher are delighted and honoured that Frankie Dettori consented to write the Foreword, and equally indebted to Sir Peter O'Sullevan, Lady Cecil and Bob Champion for reading the book before press and generously offering their comments.

I am also extremely grateful to all those helpful people at the racecourses who replied to my approaches regarding the accuracy of their entries and my requests for photographs. And without being able to draw on the archives of Racing Post and Associated Press, the book would have been much the poorer.

That it has taken more than two years for this book to reach the bookstands shows the devotion to accuracy of the author and the experts mentioned above. With its breadth and depth, we hope there is something in it for everyone – Turf aficionados, horse lovers, all those with an interest in the history of racing and of the British Isles, and trivia buffs around the world. If readers spot an error, or have further useful information, we would be delighted to hear from them.

Kitty Carruthers
London 2014

AUTHOR'S ACKNOWLEDGEMENTS

The author wishes to add his thanks to the following for their help in the making of this book:

Toby Balding, Michael Bloom, Joyce Brown, Ted Burpham, Vera Challoner, Peter Corbett, John Dillon, Barrie Doddington, Julie Drewitt, David Eustace, Mel Fordham, Michelle Forsyth, Richie Galway, Norman Gundill, Eddie Harty, Francis Hyland, Eric Joy, Holly Kite, Richard Landale, Nickyj Lander, Christian Leech, Pierce Molony, Riona Molony, Sam Morshead, Steward Nash, Graham Orange, Bernard Parkin, Charlotte Pawsey, Wendy Pawsey, Tom Pierce, Martin Pipe, Chris Pitt, Chloe Price, John Randall, Peter Robinson, Teddy Robinson, Gary Sears, Albert Siggins, Jackie Taylor, Colin Turner, Joe Walsh, Malcolm Whitehead, David Williams, Hugh Williams.

PREFACE

You could say that racing is in my blood. My father Reg was a milkman (horse-drawn cart, of course) but in his spare time he was an illegal bookmaker. Our local racecourse was Epsom, where licenses were frequently overlooked, and he often worked on the Hill. Although racing was part of family life, I didn't attend a meeting until my father took me to the Epsom Spring Meeting in 1955. I was instantly hooked and it marked the beginning of a passion that has lasted to the present day.

After boarding school and a brief spell in the Royal Navy, I embarked on a career in bookmaking, learning the ropes courtesy of the London School of Turf Accountancy in Tottenham Court Road. During my spare time I began my mission to visit every racecourse in England, and eventually the whole of the British Isles.

The journey that began at Epsom ended at Tralee in the west of Ireland in 1992, and has taken in meetings under both codes, Flat and National Hunt. I also returned to Wolverhampton and Limerick – courses which had moved from their original locations.

Meanwhile, Folkestone, Hereford and Tralee have closed but, with a fair amount of optimism that one day they will all re-open, they have remained in the book. I visited the new course at Great Leighs when it opened in 2008 (it closed the following year but will re-open as Chelmsford City Racecourse in 2015) and the new course at Ffos Las in Wales (opened in 2009): both were in their infancy at the time I began writing so are not

included. In the next edition of the book they surely will be!

Around the mid-1970s, I started collecting the odd memento and bits of memorabilia from race meetings, and by 1997 had assembled quite a scrapbook of photos, racecards, newpaper cuttings and the like. I began to write a few words on each course – more for my own amusement than with a view to publication. But my notes grew and I began to delve into the background of racing and racecourses, until one day a friend said, 'You should write a book about it!' So I did, and to my delight found a welcome at Medina Publishing. Kitty Carruthers encouraged me from the start and, as an aficionado of the Arabian horse, has added the Arabian racing dimension to the book.

One of the inherent difficulties of a book like this is keeping it up to date: it seems almost every day another record is broken, sponsors change (who remembers the Andy Capp Handicap?), or something extraordinary happens. I have done my best to keep pace, but one must draw a line somewhere and I hope readers will be forgiving if Frankie goes one better and rides all eight winners at a meeting, or if they find Shergar tomorrow.

I have loved every minute of my journey and have written more than 100,000 words in longhand – that's one reason why it's taken so long! I hope you enjoy reading it as much as I have enjoyed writing it.

Roy Gill

Key to racecourse icons

 *Flat*    *National Hunt*    *Arabian Horseracing*

Aintree is a suburb of Liverpool where, at the beginning of April every year, the greatest steeplechase in the world takes place. The Grand National is run over four-and-a-half miles (two circuits) and 30 daunting fences.

During the rest of the year the course is used for only four other races, over just one circuit of those famous fences. The remainder of National Hunt racing is run over the Mildmay course, constructed in 1952 and named in memory of amateur steeplechase jockey Lord Mildmay. This oval-shaped course is much smaller at one-mile-three-furlongs, and far less testing. The Mildmay course was opened on 2 December 1953 by the Earl of Sefton who cut a blue and white ribbon that stretched the width of the last jump. The colours were those of Lord Mildmay. Bryan Marshall would have remembered the day fondly, as he rode the first three winners – Panto, River Trout and Irish Lizard.

Aintree was, until 1976, also a prominent flat course with races such as the Liverpool Spring Cup and a well-regarded classic trial called the Union Jack Stakes. Although never as popular as Haydock Park or Manchester (until it closed), the Lancashire course has provided its

share of racing history. It was known in those days simply as Liverpool racecourse and up to and including the last flat meeting on 1 April 1976 most fixtures were mixed.

Red Rum, the triple Grand National hero of the 1970s, made his flat debut at Liverpool on 7 April 1967 as a two-year-old running in the Thursby Selling Plate over five furlongs. Starting at 5/1 and ridden by Paul Cook, he dead-heated for first place, having made rapid headway two furlongs out. He was bought in for 300 guineas. Who could have imagined what lay ahead?

In those days he was trained at Melton Mowbray by Tim Molony, who was also responsible for another piece of history when, on 30 March 1968, he engaged a young Irish apprentice by the name of Pat Eddery to ride his horse Dido's Dowry in the Hylton Stakes Handicap. It was Eddery's first ride in England. Starting at 20/1, his mount finished sixth to Alpine, trained by Atty Corbett. The race preceded the Grand National (which was won by Red Alligator) so the huge crowd were unknowingly witness to a future champion.

Gordon Richards was another champion to make history at Liverpool when on 8 November 1933 he rode Golden King, the 4/11 favourite, to victory in the Wavertree Selling Plate to record his 247th win of the season, passing Fred Archer's record of 246 which had stood since 1885. Within minutes he received a telegram of congratulations from King George V. Golden King was the 1,400th winner of his career. That afternoon he went on to win the Liverpool St Leger on Attwood for Joe Lawson, and finished the season on 259.

On a mixed card, the last flat meeting took place on 1 April 1976. The final race was the Knowsley Stakes, won by Brian Taylor riding Royal Fanfare for Ryan Price – beating another rising star, Willie Carson, in a photo finish.

The Grand National was first run in 1839. This new race had been eagerly awaited and attracted visitors from far and wide. Because of the huge crowd and several false starts, the race went off two hours late.

The first winner was Lottery, who was owned by John Elmore, a horse dealer from north London who had acquired the horse for £120. He was trained at Mickleham near Epsom by George Dockeray, whose claim to fame was to ride the winner of the 1826 Derby, Lap-Dog. Ridden by top jockey Jem Mason in all his races, Lottery won the inaugural race easily beating 16 opponents. (They were all level weights – the race did not become a handicap until 1843.)

Lottery proved to be the most outstanding horse of his era and later won races at Cheltenham, Stratford, Maidstone and Dunchurch. When he retired, Dockeray used him as a hack but, sadly, he finished his days pulling a cart in Neasden.

The Grand National is always run at breathtaking and stamina-sapping speed. Bryan Marshall, who rode Early Mist (1953) and Royal Tan (1954) to victory, compared the race to 'driving down the Great West Road surrounded by lunatics'. This is particularly true of the 'charge' to the first fence, where there are usually a number of fallers.

Red Rum pictured on the front of the 1978 race card. Having completed the historic hat-trick of Grand National wins in 1977, he was forced to pull out only days before. The race was won by Lucius, ridden by Bob Davies and trained by Gordon Richards.

The sixth obstacle is the formidable Becher's Brook, named after Captain Martin Becher who sheltered in the brook after being thrown by Conrad in the first Grand National of 1839. Incidentally, Captain Becher had ridden the winner of the first ever steeplechase at Aintree – The Duke in 1836. After Becher's there is a bend before the

AINTREE

Foinavon Fence and Canal Turn, followed by a sharp left-hand turn towards Valentine's Brook – an obstacle which regularly proves difficult because horses are often off balance after the sharp turn. Many jockeys consider the Chair, in front of the stands, the most difficult fence of the whole course because of its height and spread. It has a fearsome appearance because it is three inches wider than any other fence. Add to all this heavy going, and the Grand National is the supreme test of horse and rider, incomparable with any other race in the world.

The Grand National fences are by far the most demanding in the country but were once even more severe

Arthur Yates, trainer of 2,950 winners including the great Cloister, winner of the 1893 Grand National.

and a number of fatalities caused many protests. In 1954, four horses were killed and the race became the subject of an angry debate in the House of Lords. Following modifications, the casualty rate has been reduced and the race is not such a test of survival as it might have been in years gone by. It provides more excitement, with more horses finishing – although there is always the chance of a complete pile-up, as happened with 100/1 shot Foinavon's victory in 1967 when all but the winner were brought to a halt at the 23rd fence. Foinavon plodding along at the rear passed the rest of the field to win unchallenged. The fence has since been named the Foinavon fence.

Aintree's fortunes have fluctuated considerably since the days of natural stone walls, ploughed fields and Captain Becher. Racing began at Aintree on 7 July 1829

and ten years later 17 lined up for the first Grand National, known in those days as the Grand Liverpool Steeplechase. In 1838 a journalist for Bell's Life of London (early supporters of the race) coined the phrase 'The Grand National and, in 1847, the managment of Aintree officially adopted the name.

Edward William Topham of Chester became lessee of Aintree in 1848 and eight years later the fixture became a two-day meeting. By the 1860s the Grand National had become a national sporting occasion attracting huge crowds and the best chasers, and the Grand National circuit began to take on its present appearance. The stretches of ploughed fields gave way to turf and the course was railed in. Aintree's heyday was between the two World Wars, when the race reached its height of popularity. With the fences frighteningly severe, it was not unusual to get 4/1 or more against a horse finishing at all. From 1920 to 1922, for example, only 14 horses from 91 runners completed the course.

After the Second World War other racecourses, such as Cheltenham, began to rival Aintree. For the first time horses could pick up good prize money elsewhere and Aintree went into a slow decline.

Mrs Mirabel Topham followed other Tophams in charge of Aintree's 270 acres. A formidable and colourful

woman, she had heated arguments with the Betting Levy Board, the Tote, bookmakers and the BBC – all accused in turn of not giving Aintree its due. An eight-year debate prefaced the agreement allowing the BBC to televise the 1960 Grand National.

Even the opening of a motor racing circuit in the 1950s failed to halt Aintree's declining fortunes. For the first big meeting, the British Grand Prix of 1955, more than 100,000 spectators saw Stirling Moss beat Juan Manuel Fangio and, in 1957, the European Grand Prix was staged, with Stirling Moss again victorious. However, the cost of providing the high standards demanded by international motor racing was prohibitive and the last Grand Prix at Aintree was held in 1962.

The future of the Grand National was put in doubt in 1964 when Mirabel Topham announced that she planned to sell Aintree racecourse. A syndicate reputedly offered Mrs Topham £1 million with a plan to save the racecourse while building houses on the adjoining land. Mrs Topham rejected this bid then tried to sell privately, prompting a public outcry. National Hunt enthusiasts protested vigorously. Eventually she sold the course to property developer Bill Davies's Walton Group in 1973 for £3 million. After years of uncertainty, the Jockey Club bought the course from the

The start of the 1929 Grand National, showing a record number of starters. Gregalach, with Robert Everett up, won at 100/1.

The pile-up at the 23rd fence of the 1967 Grand National, which left Foinavon to win unchallenged.

Walton Group for £3.4 million in 1983 and, to everyone's relief, the Grand National was saved. It is now owned by a Jockey Club subsidiary, Racecourse Holdings Trust.

Of the many Grand National stories none was more dramatic than that of Devon Loch (1956). Owned by the Queen Mother and ridden by Dick Francis, he was clear on the run in, only to collapse 50 yards from the winning post, handing victory to ESB ridden by Dave Dick. The cause of the collapse still remains a mystery, but the Queen Mother was gracious in defeat, commenting, 'Oh well, that's racing'.

Two more unlucky losers were Limerick (1917) at Gatwick, when he slipped and unseated his rider at the final fence, and – even more tragic – Davy Jones (1936) who, starting at 100/1, was some distance clear when the reins broke and he ran out at the final fence, leaving Reynoldstown to record his second win.

As mentioned earlier, Foinavon (1967) was a lucky winner but so was Tipperary Tim (1928). Starting at 100/1 he was one of only two finishers benefiting from a pile-up at the Canal Turn on the first circuit. Indeed, he nearly became the only horse to finish, when Billy Barton came to grief at the last when upsides, before being remounted to finish second. Tipperary Tim was ridden by Bill Dutton, an amateur whose day job was as a solicitor. He later became a very successful trainer on the Flat thanks to two fine sprinters, Pappa Fourway and Right Boy.

It is hard to define the greatest winner, as there have been so many brave and gallant horses. Red Rum's three wins (1973, 1974 and 1977) will probably never be equalled. Golden Miller, who won a total of five Cheltenham Gold Cups, is the only horse ever to achieve the Gold Cup/ Grand National double in the same year (1934) but, though for many people he was 'the horse of the century,' he failed at Aintree in four other attempts. He was fully expected to win in 1935, starting a ridiculous 2/1 favourite, but unseated his rider on the first circuit.

Easter Hero (1929) was another Cheltenham Gold Cup winner to fail at Aintree but he nearly achieved the impossible when, carrying 12st 7lb, he finished second to the 100/1 shot Gregalach. Sixty-six runners lined up that day, a world record, which makes Easter Hero probably the best horse never to win the race. It seems astonishing that he beat 64 rivals and still did not win. He gave 17lb to the winner that day, who was later twice handicapped above Golden Miller in the National weights, so he was attempting the impossible. How, I wonder, did they get 66 horses in the paddock?

Four other horses carried 12st 7lb to victory and all must be classed as great: Cloister (1893) won by 40 lengths after finishing second the two previous years. He was the first horse to carry over 12st to victory since the race became a handicap in 1843. Not only was he the first to carry the maximum weight and win by the biggest distance, but he also recorded the fastest time – which would not be surpassed for 40 years. While his sire was Ascetic, the outstanding jumping stallion of his era, his dam was Grace II, a mare considered so unexceptional

The crowd goes wild with joy as Red Rum, ridden by Tommy Stack, romps home to make history by winning the Grand National for the third time in 1977.

that the village postman rode her on his delivery round. Cloister was hailed a wonder horse after his victory, but his career ended under a cloud when he was mysteriously withdrawn from the next two Nationals just days before the race and the bookmaking fraternity somehow knew in advance – a regrettable end to a brilliant horse.

Cloister's trainer was the remarkable Arthur Yates, who also trained the Grand National winner Roquefort (1885). His many achievements included saddling nine winners from ten runners at a two-day meeting at Torquay in 1905. He trained mostly jumpers during the late Victorian and Edwardian era, a time when there were fewer meetings than today. He was the first trainer to train 2000 winners; by the time he retired in 1913 he had chalked up an astonishing total of 2,950. It was not until 1992 that his record was passed by Arthur Stephenson.

Manifesto (1897, 1899) carried 12st 7lb for his second win. He competed in the race a record eight times. He was placed third three times and fourth once. His third in 1900 was more notable even than his two wins as he was

Jerry M, winner of the 1912 Grand National.

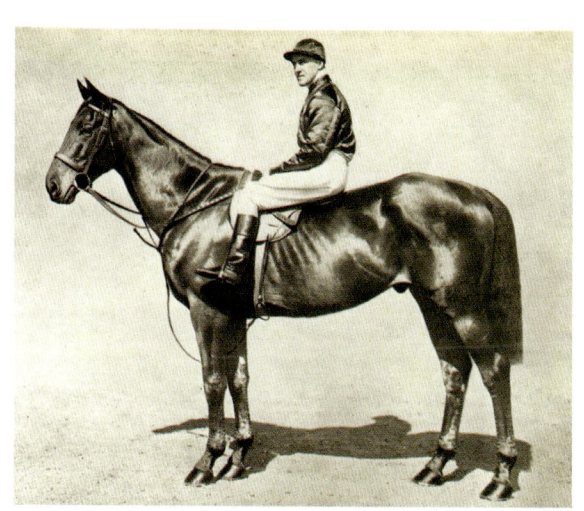

set to carry an astounding 12st 13lb (Jenny Pitman would have winced). He was beaten by the Prince of Wales's horse Ambush II. Manifesto led over the last and, with the concession of 24lb to the Royal horse, he failed by four lengths – and also lost second place through sheer exhaustion on the line to Barsac. It was indeed the race of the century.

Jerry M (1912) was another to shoulder this welterweight. In addition to winning by six lengths, his victory was all the more remarkable because at the Canal Turn he had to jump a horse lying across the fence and his jockey, Ernie Piggott, claimed he didn't even touch him.

Poethlyn (1919) was the last horse to carry 12st 7lb to victory. He had won the previous year at Gatwick, but it must be said that the course there bore no resemblance to Aintree. He started the 11/4 favourite and became the shortest prize winner in the race's history. He was also ridden by Ernie Piggott and won easily to record his ninth consecutive victory. He fell at the first the following year. These feats can never be repeated, as the top weight has been reduced to 11st 12lb under current rules, and there is also a limit on the maximum number of runners (40) for safety reasons.

Probably the classiest winner of the race was L'Escargot (1975). Even at 12 years old he had the distinction of beating Red Rum by 15 lengths and, in his prime, he had won two Cheltenham Gold Cups (1970, 1971).

The roll of honour of Grand National winners would not be complete without the inclusion of Troytown (1920). His victory when only a seven-year-old was nothing short of sensational and some would say he was the greatest winner of all time. He ran in the race only once because, later that year, he had to be put down following a fall in France. He was bred in Ireland, where he was trained by Algy Anthony, who had previously ridden and trained the winner Ambush (1900) for the Prince of Wales. He was ridden in all his races by top amateur Jack Anthony (no

relation), who had already partnered two Grand National winners in Glenside (1911) and Ally Sloper (1915), and who achieved even greater fame later as a trainer with dual Cheltenham Gold Cup superstar Easter Hero.

Troytown was a very strong, powerful horse who had already taken Ireland by storm. (He was bred in County Meath near Navan, where today the Troytown Chase is still run in his honour). He came over to Liverpool in 1919 and would have won the Stanley Steeplechase but for his jockey taking the wrong course. Two days later he won the Champion Chase and, later that summer, won the Grand Steeplechase de Paris at Auteuil in impressive style.

The 1920 Grand National was run in atrocious conditions of driving rain and high winds and, as usual, Troytown set out to make all the running, forcing his opponents into submission one by one. At the fourth-last in the rain-softened ground, he slipped taking off and completely demolished the fence, surrendering the lead briefly – but it made no difference, as he powered into the lead again by the next obstacle. He eventually won by 12 lengths, giving the runner-up over two stone. He was possibly the greatest-ever winner of the race and his jockey likened riding him to riding a steam engine. He said afterwards that the only problem was that Troytown wanted to do another circuit, so the jockey had an awful job pulling him up.

On the weather front, several Grand Nationals have taken place in snowstorms and in 1901 the race was run in a blizzard, with the fences turned into mounds of snow. When the jockeys' request for a postponement was turned down just what happened next is uncertain. Eight reputedly finished but neither spectators nor jockeys could get any

Forty runners and riders line up for the start of the 2013 Grand National. The race was won by 66/1 shot Auroras Encore, ridden by Ryan Mania and trained by Sue Smith.

Troytown and Jack Anthony, winners of the 1920 Grand National. Having won by 12 lengths over boggy, strength-sapping ground, the horse had to be disuaded from setting off on another circuit.

half the jockeys failed to see the recall flag, and some completed the course in vain as the race was declared void. Four years later the race was postponed until the following Monday because of a bomb scare. The winner, Lord Gyllene, entered the history books as the first Monday winner of the Grand National.

The race had always been run on a Friday until 1947, when Prime Minister Clement Attlee requested it be moved to a Saturday as he feared industry could not cope with so many workers taking the day off. The Aintree executive reverted to a Friday in 1957, when Sundew won, but the crowd was so small that the experiment was not repeated.

details of the race. The winner, Grudon, owed his victory to Bernard Bletsoe, his owner-trainer, who had the brilliant idea of packing his feet with butter to prevent snow collecting in them. Ridden by Arthur Nightingall, he skated home.

1993 is a year the Aintree executive would prefer to forget, with two false starts caused by horses getting entangled with the starting tapes. On the second occasion

Finally, let us spare a thought for all the gamblers among us who may have backed any of the following:

Crisp (1973), who surrendered a 30-length lead on the run-in to Red Rum; Devon Loch (1956), who collapsed just yards from the line; Davy Jones (1936), who ran out at the last when a distance clear; and Easter Hero (1929), the 9/1 favourite who beat 64 rivals but still did not win.

Perhaps we should all take a lesson from Captain Tim Forster, who won the Grand National three times. When about to give the leg up to amateur Charlie Fenwick on 1980 winner Ben Nevis, the rider asked him for any last-minute instructions. Captain Forster simply replied, 'Keep remounting'.

Ascot is the only racecourse to belong to the Crown, having been founded by Queen Anne in 1711. Driving out to Windsor in the early summer of that year, she came upon Ascott Common (as it was then known) and decided it would be a fine place for a race meeting. A few months later the *London Gazette* announced that a race – 'Her Majesty's Plate of 100 Guineas' – would be run at Ascot Heath on 11 August. Although the Queen had for many years nurtured a passion for horses and racing, she was by now 46 years old and her enthusiasm had been somewhat dampened by enduring 17 pregnancies – thanks to her drunkard playboy of a husband, Prince George of Denmark. To compound her misery, only six children were born and none of those survived infancy. The Prince of Denmark's death in 1708

gave her the opportunity to pursue her hobby but sadly she died six years later, having had so little time to enjoy the foundations of Ascot that she had proudly laid down.

Her successor, George I, and his son had no interest in racing, and it was not until the reign of George III that royalty visited Ascot again. In 1791, the King and his son, the Prince of Wales, revived interest by bringing a Royal party to see the Oatlands Stakes, the first handicap ever to be run on English turf and won by the Prince of Wales's horse Baronet.

In 1807, George III's wife, Queen Charlotte, instituted the Ascot Gold Cup, which later became the centrepiece of Royal Ascot. The Royal meeting was introduced in 1828 by George IV, whose idea it was to begin with the Royal procession – as is still the custom today. From

Windsor Castle, the King and Queen's carriage, drawn by four Windsor Greys and two scarlet outriders, led the procession of other members of the Royal party. Since then, the only absentee has been Queen Victoria after the death of her husband, Prince Albert.

Until the outbreak of the Second World War, Royal Ascot was the only fixture held on the course, lasting from a Tuesday until Friday in June. It became – and still is – the most prestigious meeting of the year. It is also a huge social event; in the Royal Enclosure morning dress is obligatory for men, and women are expected to wear 'modest length' dresses and hats – fascinators are banned but unorthodoxy in headgear appears to be encouraged. Only recently have women been allowed to wear trouser suits.

The Ascot Gold Cup is now run over a distance of two-and-a-half miles. There was a time when it was expected that the Derby winner of the previous year would stay in training at four, with the Gold Cup as his objective. Regrettably, since 1899 only four horses have won both races and only Ocean Swell (1944) won at Ascot. The three-year-olds Gay Crusader and Gainsborough both won substitute Gold Cups at Newmarket during the First World War, as did Owen Tudor as a four-year-old during the Second World War. The last Derby winner to run in the Gold Cup was Blakeney (1970) as a four-year-old, who finished second to Precipice Wood (the first Gold Cup winner to be trained by a woman, Rosemary Lomax).

19th century winners include West Australian (1854) and Gladiateur (1866), both winners of the Triple Crown. The latter won the Gold Cup by 40 lengths. Isonomy (1879, 1880), who had won the Cambridgeshire on his only start as a three-year-old, was the first horse to win the Stayers' Triple Crown in 1879, winning the Gold Cup, the Goodwood Cup and the Doncaster Cup. He also triumphed in the Ebor Handicap by eight lengths under 9st 8lb. As a five-year-old in 1880 he defied the seemingly-

impossible burden of 9st 12lb in the Manchester Cup and then won the Gold Cup again. The 1884 winner, St Simon, who became the greatest sire of his time, also had two of his offspring triumph, the filly La Fleche (1894) and the colt Persimmon (1897), who was the last horse to win the Derby at Epsom and the Gold Cup at Ascot.

The first half of the 20th century also produced some fine winners, the best of which was Bayardo (1910). He was unbeaten as a two-year-old from seven starts, looking every inch a champion sprinter. He suffered his only two defeats as a three-year-old behind Minoru in the 2,000 Guineas and the Derby. His trainer, Alec Taylor, blamed the hard ground and the fact he was unable to get him fit enough. As a four-year-old he demolished his opponents in all the staying events including the Gold Cup, beating a high-class field by four lengths. He was an outstanding horse and could probably have been a champion over any distance.

During the inter-War period the most exciting race for the Gold Cup was the 1936 duel between the filly Quashed and the American champion Omaha, trained in England by Captain Cecil Boyd-Rochfort. Winner of the Oaks the previous year, Quashed just out-stayed Omaha in a thrilling finish. Boyd-Rochfort compensated by winning the next two Gold Cups with Precipitation and Flares.

After the war, Alycidon (1949) was another outstanding winner, beating his St Leger conqueror of the previous year, Black Tarquin, by five lengths. He went on to win the Goodwood Cup and the Doncaster Cup to become the first horse for 70 years to win the Stayers' Triple Crown. Sagaro was the first horse to win the Gold Cup three times (1975, 1976, 1977). Trained by Francois Boutin in France, he won them all comfortably and was particularly impressive in beating Buckskin (1977) by five lengths. Le Moss (1979, 1980), trained by Henry Cecil, is the only horse to win the Stayers' Triple Crown twice. He also beat his stable companion Buckskin (1979) and in 1980 beat Ardross in each of the Stayers Cup races in tight finishes, leading all the way, as was his custom. After travelling a total of seven miles and three furlongs, his aggregate winning distance was just over a length. Ardross, with Le Moss retired, won it twice (1981, 1982), following which the Gold Cup may have lost some of its prestige, but Yeats (2006, 2007, 2008, 2009) restored it in magnificent style by breaking Sagaro's record in winning four consecutive Gold Cups.

With greater prize money and stud fees now available in middle distance races, the King George VI and Queen Elizabeth Stakes, introduced in 1951, has gradually taken over as the centrepiece of Ascot's year and is regarded as one of Britain's most prestigious flat races. Run in July, it is open to three-year-olds and upwards and is run over a mile-and-a-half.

Royal Ascot is by no means just about the Gold Cup. It includes other Group 1 races, including the Queen Anne Stakes named after the course's founder, which opens the meeting on the Tuesday. The Prince of Wales Stakes, run over a mile and a quarter, is for older horses, while the St James's Palace Stakes and the Coronation Stakes for three-year-old colts and fillies respectively are run over the old mile and are often contested by Guineas winners. For sprinters there are the King Stand Stakes over five furlongs, and the Diamond Jubilee Stakes over six furlongs (formerly known as the Cork and Orrery Stakes from 1926 and the Golden Jubilee Stakes from 2002).

Among the Group 2 races is the Hardwicke Stakes, once the most valuable race of the meeting. One of the many great horses to triumph was Ormonde (1886). Having already won the Derby that year, he won the St James's Palace Stakes and the Hardwicke Stakes, in which he beat the previous year's Derby winner Melton. However, three-year-olds are no longer allowed to run in the race. Two-year-old races are well represented in by

the Coventry Stakes, Queen Mary Stakes, Norfolk Stakes and Windsor Castle Stakes, but recently their winners have not played a leading role in the following year's classics. The two big handicaps are the Royal Hunt Cup, first run in 1843 over a straight mile, and the six-furlong Wokingham Stakes, first run in 1813 and the meeting's second-oldest race.

The final race of the meeting is the Queen Alexandra Stakes which, at over two-and-three-quarter miles, is the longest race of the flat season. It will always be associated with Steve Donoghue and Brown Jack, who together won it six years in succession from 1929 to 1934. (He also won the Ascot Stakes in 1928 to record seven consecutive Royal Ascot victories.) The achievement of Brown Jack, who could arguably have been regarded as the most popular horse of the 20th century, caused scenes of jubilation in the crowd, which had never been seen before or are likely to be seen again. Grown men had tears in their eyes as they welcomed Brown Jack into the unsaddling ring. Owned by the aristocrat Harold Wernher, he was nevertheless regarded as the people's horse. and was held in such high esteem that his skeleton was for many years displayed at the Natural History Museum.

The 1934 Royal Ascot meeting was certainly one to remember, as Newmarket trainer Frank Butters trained nine winners – which remains a record. His winners were Spend a Penny (Queen Anne Stakes), Hairan (Coventry Stakes), Achtenan (Prince of Wales's Stakes), Felicitation (Churchill Stakes and Gold Cup), Shahali (Chesham Stakes), Alishah (Rous Memorial Stakes), Badruddin (Waterford Stakes) and Theft (Windsor Castle Stakes). All except Spend a Penny and Achtenan were owned by his principal patron, the Aga Khan.

Felicitation, his dual winner, wore blinkers for the first time when winning the two-mile Churchill Stakes by ten lengths on the Wednesday and scored an eight-length victory in the Gold Cup under Gordon Richards the very

The bond is unmistakable between Brown Jack and his veteran jockey Steve Donoghue. The nation's favourite with seven consecutive Royal Ascot wins between 1928 and 1934, the horse had a public house named after him in Wroughton, near Swindon, where he was trained.

next day. (Success in the Gold Cup had been regarded as a formality for Hyperion, the 1933 Derby and St Leger winner, but he shocked his admirers by finishing only third).

The nine winners were completed on the Friday with Theft winning the Windsor Castle Stakes at 20/1 ridden by Dick Perryman. This tremendous record was nevertheless somewhat overshadowed by Brown Jack and it was this lovable horse that made all the headlines.

Ascot's only meeting until the Second World War was the four-day Royal meeting, and not until 1946 were other meetings introduced in July and August. In 1950 the Royal meeting was extended to the Saturday and known as Ascot Heath, allowing the general public access to the Royal Enclosures. This popular day continued for more

than 50 years, but in 2002 the Saturday became the fifth day of the Royal meeting to celebrate Queen Elizabeth II's Golden Jubilee and it has now become a permanent fixture, so the Ascot Heath day has, sadly, been lost.

In 1951 Ascot's July meeting featured the first running of the King George VI and Queen Elizabeth Stakes. It was sponsored in 1972 by de Beers, and again in 1975 when they inserted 'diamond' into the title, and it now carries at least as much status and competitiveness as the Prix de l'Arc de Triomphe and the Breeders' Cup Turf. It is also run at a more fitting time of the year for a true championship race, bringing together classic winners of different generations. The inaugural running was won by Mrs Vera Lilley's colt Supreme Court, ridden by Charlie Elliott, and in the following years by Derby winners Tulyar and Pinza. A precedent had been set and King George VI and Queen Elizabeth winners of the highest calibre came thick and fast. The greatest winner was the Italian horse Ribot (1956)

and, although his jockey Enrico Camici described his performance as below par, he still managed to win by five lengths. He was never beaten in 16 races, including two scintillating victories in the Prix de L'Arc de Triomphe.

Derby winners who also won the King George in the same year were Nijinsky, Mill Reef, Grundy (whose victory over Bustino in 1975 was described as the race of the century), The Minstrel, Troy, Shergar, Reference Point, Nashwan, Generous, Lammtarra and Galileo. The only two Derby champions to win the race as a four-year-old, were Royal Palace and Teenoso. Among many other brilliant winners to add to this roll of honour are the magnificent Brigadier Gerard, the French filly Dahlia

King George VI and Queen Elizabeth lead the royal procession in an open landau in 1947.

(twice), Ballymoss, Alcide, Dancing Brave, Swain (twice), Montjeu and Dylan Thomas.

Examples such as these merely confirm that the King George, as an all-aged contest, has changed the face of racing in Britain. The September 'Festival of British Racing', as it was known from 1994 until 2010, was also a meeting of the highest order. The Queen Elizabeth II Stakes was the Group 1 highlight, run over a mile, supported by the Group 1 Fillies Mile for two-year-olds and the Group 2 Royal Lodge Stakes for two-year-old colts. The Fillies Mile, first run in 1973, has been a marvellous race for Newmarket trainer Henry Cecil. Four of his six winners – Oh So Sharp, Diminuendo, Bosra Sham and Reams of Verse – went on to classic glory the following year.

From 2011, there were some major changes in the fixture list. The September Festival was discontinued and a new date in October was devised to include the transfer of the Champion Stakes from Newmarket along with the Jockey Club Cup (renamed British Champions Long Distance Cup) while, in exchange, the Fillies Mile and the Royal Lodge Stakes for two-year-olds were transferred to Newmarket. The new date at Ascot has become known as Champions Day.

While the September meeting continued the trend of racing at Ascot as being of the highest level, the most memorable moment occurred on 28 September 1996 when jockey Frankie Dettori went through the seven-race card. This unique achievement had been approached only twice before, once by Gordon Richards at Chepstow (1933) and once by Alec Russell at Bogside (1957), both six-race cards. Frankie Dettori's record is unlikely to be equalled, let alone beaten, and his winners – heralded in the newspapers the next day as the 'Magnificent Seven' – were Wall Street (2/1), Diffident (12/1), Mark of Esteem (100/30) (QE II), Decorated Hero (7/1), Fatefully (7/4), Lochangel (5/4) and Fujiyama Crest (2/1). The last winner, who won the Gordon Carter Handicap, was

reputed to have cost the bookmaking industry over £40 million. (Richard Hughes came close to Dettori's record when he rode seven non-consecutive winners from eight rides at Windsor on 15 October 2012.)

The course at Ascot has undergone several changes over the years. The current course was reconstructed in 1947, including the re-alignment of the one-mile straight Royal Hunt Cup course, which was practically out of sight from the stands, but the new turf took a long time to settle and the new straight course was not used until 1955. The huge operation was completed by the construction of a new grandstand, opened in 1961. The biggest change came in 1965, when a National Hunt course was built inside the round course. Despite protests from the Queen's then representative, the Duke of Norfolk, that jumping would come to Ascot over his dead body, he was there to see it happen on 30 April 1965. The track had been laid using the turf from Hurst Park, which had closed in 1962.

With National Hunt racing underway some jumping enthusiasts felt that the track was too remote from the stands for the excitement to reach the spectators, but the fact remains that jumping has been a great success there and, on 14 December 1966, the mighty Arkle gained the last of his 27 victories by winning the SGB Chase by 15 lengths. It was his penultimate start as, in finishing second in the King George VI Chase at Kempton Park two weeks later, he fractured a bone in his hoof and never raced again. More recently the likes of One Man, Wayward Lad, Killiney, Lanzarote, Little Owl, Ten Up, Gaye Brief and Desert Orchid have thrilled the Ascot crowds. Desert Orchid's win in the inaugural Victor Chandler Chase on 14 January 1989, during a magic year for the nation's adorable grey, was particularly worth remembering. Having already won the King George VI Chase on Boxing Day, he reverted to the two-mile Victor Chandler at Ascot, conceding 22lb to Panto Prince, who was beating him by a neck after a terrible blunder at the last fence, but he regained the lead on the run-in, demonstrating all his usual determination. His finest hour came two months later when he won the 1989 Cheltenham Gold Cup. I doubt if many King George VI Chase and Gold Cup winners could win a high-class two-mile handicap chase in between – Desert Orchid was the exception.

In contrast to the emotional scenes surrounding Brown Jack and the amazing feat of Frankie Dettori, Ascot has also provided its share of shocks, with the likes of Hyperion (1934) beaten in the Gold Cup, and odds-on failures Petite Etoile (1960) and Santa Claus (1964) in the King George VI and Queen Elizabeth Stakes. Santa Claus was 2/13 favourite and failed by two lengths to peg back Nasram, but he was not the shortest-price horse to be beaten at Ascot. That dubious distinction belonged to Royal Forest (1945) who, having won the Coventry Stakes at the Royal meeting, contested the Clarence House Stakes in September. Ridden by Gordon Richards, he started at odds of 1/25 and was beaten half-a-length by Burpham. Happily, he got his revenge on his opponent by winning the Dewhurst Stakes later in the year and went on to finish fourth in the Derby the following year. He was adjudged to be the shortest-price favourite to be beaten in a British race where SPs were returned.

Another shock result was the the 1974 Queen Anne Stakes, which opened that year's Royal meeting. The finishing order was Confusion (10/1), Gloss (7/1) and Royal Prerogative (6/4f) but, after an objection by the second to the first and by the fourth to the second and third, the first three were all disqualified and the race awarded to the original fourth, Brook (12/1), trained in Italy and ridden by Brian Taylor – who had finished six lengths behind the third horse. There certainly was confusion.

Highs and lows also affected jockeys. Lester Piggott's outstanding record at Ascot included 11 Gold Cup winners and seven King George winners, while on the National Hunt scene, the champion Peter Scudamore rode Sweet

Duke to victory in the final ride of his career on 7 April 1993 in the Alpine Meadow Handicap Hurdle to record his 1,678th win to a huge ovation. These were two jockeys at the very top of their profession who had fond memories of Ascot.

The lows of race riding cannot be better illustrated by the death of Manny Mercer on 26 September 1959. Riding his horse Priddy Fair down to the start, his mount whipped round, unseated him and kicked him in the face as he lay on the ground. He died instantly. He was just 30 years old, doing a job he loved, and had been tipped to become one of the greats. Racing was abandoned for the day – it was a very sad occasion for the whole racing world.

On a brighter note, two trainers for whom Ascot holds a special place are Jack Jarvis and George Todd. Jack Jarvis trained Golden Myth to win the Ascot Gold Cup in 1922, but his season had begun winning the Queen's Prize at Kempton, carrying only 7st 6lb. Jack Jarvis improved him so much he brought him to Royal Ascot to land the Gold Vase (now Queen's Vase) and two days later the Ascot Gold Cup, beating a high-class field. To make it even more remarkable, he went on the following month to win the Eclipse Stakes at Sandown, ridden by Charlie Elliott, beating the favourite and Derby second Tamar. Jack Jarvis went on to be champion trainer three times and win nine Classics, but this remained his finest achievement.

George Todd was responsible for that fine stayer Trelawny, who won the Ascot Stakes–Queen Alexandra Stakes double twice, in 1962 and 1963. In the former race, a handicap, the six-year-old defied the burden of 9st 8lb and 10st. In 1964 Trelawny was second under 10st in the Ascot Stakes, conceding 40lb to the winner, and was due to walk-over in the Queen Alexandra Stakes but was denied the prize when the race was abandoned due to a waterlogged course.

It was not unheard of for days to be lost at Royal Ascot because of bad weather – in spite of being run in 'Flaming June'. The worst year was 1930: Wednesday's Royal

The dramatic headlines from The Daily Herald of 19th June 1930.

GREAT STORM FLOODS OUT ASCOT

BOOKMAKER
KILLED
BY LIGHTNING

FROM GAIETY TO TERROR

TERRIFIED WOMEN IN MAD RUSH

Women Faint in Ruined Ascot Frocks

BRIDGE OF CHAIRS IN PADDOCK

RACES POSTPONED

TORRENT SWEEPS INTO PADDOCK CROWDS

THREE MEN SWEPT TO DEATH

A terrific thunderstorm yesterday flooded Ascot racecourse and caused five of the seven races to be abandoned for the day.

While terror-stricken women were scattering to shelter, with their frocks ruined by the torrential rain, a bookmaker in Tattersalls was killed by lightning.

A man was also killed in Manchester. Three others were drowned in floods.

The dramatic headlines from The Daily Herald of 19th June 1930.

Hunt Cup had just been run in fairly heavy rain when suddenly the heavens opened with an appalling crash of thunder and, without further warning, the rain descended like a huge waterfall. In a matter of seconds people were drenched to the skin and, amid further terrifying claps of thunder and forked lightning, the enclosures were soon awash from the water cascading from the roofs. Some dashed to the tunnel that connected the grandstand to the paddock but this was soon under two feet of water. Panic set in, with women screaming in their efforts to get shelter. A bookmaker in Tattersalls was killed when lightning struck his umbrella. Lakes turned into rivers, one of which went directly across the course. Abandonment was a formality. It was by far the worst storm to hit Ascot, although two days (including the Gold Cup) were lost in 1964 after heavy rain waterlogged the course.

The first day of the 1960 Royal meeting was run in a less intense thunderstorm but nevertheless very unpleasant conditions. However, some backers could have taken advantage if they managed to follow topical tips. Among the winners that day were Blast, Shatter and Typhoon.

Ayr is today without doubt Scotland's premier racecourse, hosting perhaps the two most prestigious races north of the border – the Scottish Grand National and the Ayr Gold Cup.

Both races contribute considerably to the history of Ayr which began at Belleisle, to the south of the city. The first official meeting in the racing calendar was in 1771, although there is a reference to racing as far back as 1576. The final meeting at Belleisle took place on 21 September 1906 when Mr J M Bell's Turbine won the Ayrshire Handicap, Mr T H Walker's Cyrus won the Ayr Gold Cup and in the final race, the Carrick Plate, there was a walkover. The course was just over a mile round with a straight run in of a quarter of a mile. It was crammed with very sharp bad turns and there was no room to extend the paddock and enclosure accommodation to meet modern requirements. So, after two centuries or more, it became a golf course and racing moved to its present site in time for its opening fixture on 18 September 1907.

Whereas Belleisle had only one meeting a year, the new course was quick to establish four, with one in April, one in July, one in August and the old-established Western Meeting in September. The Western Meeting had derived from Belleisle when, in 1824, the Western Meeting Club had been formed to further the interests of sport on the Ayr course. The same year the September fixture was first referred to as the Western Meeting. This private members club soon became established and it was on the land of the Club members that the present course stands today. The club now owns the freehold of the racecourse and buildings.

The new course at Ayr was described as oval, one mile five furlongs round with a six-furlong straight course 100 feet wide, and was beyond comparison with the old course. Ayr could now take on added status and importance. The first race at the opening meeting in 1907, the Inauguration Cup, a six furlong handicap, was won by Mr J Musker's Simon Melton (100/8) ridden by Frank

Bullock, who received a gold-mounted whip. Later at the meeting Wise Mason (7/1) won the Ayrshire Handicap and Charis (100/30) won the Ayr Gold Cup.

It was not until 1948 that the Western Club decided to have steeplechasing at Ayr and proceeded to lay out what proved to be one of the finest National Hunt courses in the land. The new open-top stand near the final fence provided perfect viewing for jumping at Ayr and it became an instant success. The first fixture was on 10 October 1950, when the opening race, the Inauguration Cup, was won by Major Ian Straker's Prince of Goldwell, ridden by his son Clive.

The Scottish Grand National had originally been run at Bogside (some 14 miles north of Ayr) since 1867 but, when Bogside sadly closed in 1965, Ayr became host to this historic steeplechase. The first running of the Scottish Grand National at Ayr in 1966 was won by that top-class chaser African Patrol, trained by Bobby Fairbairn and ridden by John Leech. Ayr kept on the practice of Bogside of making Scottish Grand National day a mixture of flat and jumps but later this was changed to an all-jumping card. A successful sequence of Scottish Grand Nationals followed and was crowned by the immortal Red Rum (1974), when he won at Ayr exactly three weeks after his brilliant and easy win at Aintree. No other horse in the history of the race has won both Grand Nationals in the same year. Red Rum's bronze statue overlooking the paddock commemorates his glorious win.

The race was first known as the West of Scotland Grand National but the name was changed to its present form in 1871, and the distance was increased from three miles to three miles seven furlongs. Since the race has been transferred to Ayr, the distance has increased again to four miles 120 yards.

A few other horses have managed to win both Nationals, but in different years – Music Hall (Bogside 1920/Aintree 1922), Sergeant Murphy (Bogside 1922/Aintree 1923), Kellsboro Jack (Bogside 1935/Aintree 1933), Merryman II (Bogside 1959/Aintree 1960), Little Polvier (Ayr 1987/Aintree 1989) and Earth Summit (Ayr 1994/Aintree 1998). But perhaps the greatest horse to win the Scottish Grand National was Southern Hero, who was the first horse to win the race three times (1934, 1936 and 1939 – at the age of 14). He was second in 1937 and 1938.

In complete contrast, Ayr's other showpiece is the six furlong handicap run in September, the Ayr Gold Cup. It always attracts a large field of top sprinters and has become one of the biggest betting races of the year. It was first run in 1804 at Belleisle, amazingly over two miles for horses only bred and trained in Scotland. Another curious condition was that the sire and dam should never have produced a winner, but this did not last. The first running attracted only three runners and was won by Chancellor, owned by the Earl of Cassilis (later the 1st Marquess of Ailsa). It wasn't until 1855 that the race became a handicap and, coincidentally, this was also the occasion of the first disqualification. Lerrywheut, ridden by Thomas Aldcroft, was first past the post but was disqualified because the jockey dismounted before reaching the unsaddling enclosure; the race was awarded to John Dory; today that might cause a few angry scenes! Another interesting year was 1872 when the winner was Alaric, owned by J H Houldsworth, and ridden by a 15-year-old apprentice jockey making his first visit to the course – Fred Archer.

The year after the present course opened, the Ayr Gold Cup changed to its current distance of six furlongs and became one of the great sprint handicaps of the season. The 1967 race produced the largest field of 33 and was won by Peter O'Sullevan's brilliant sprinter Be Friendly, who went on to win Europe's richest sprint, the Prix de L'Abbaye. The most memorable race was in 1975, when the giant Roman Warrior, trained locally by Nigel Angus, won carrying 10 stone and beating the Steward's Cup winner Import in a photo finish. Separated by the width of the track it was a

fantastic finish and the judge took 15 minutes to make his decision – Roman Warrior by a short head.

Besides the two races already mentioned, in July Ayr used to stage the Scottish Classic, a Group 3 contest first run in 1988 and previously known as the Scottish Derby. Up until then it was the closest thing to a classic that Scottish racegoers saw, but in 1989 a piece of racing history was made at Ayr. The English St Leger was transferred from Doncaster because of a drainage problem on the Yorkshire course – the only time an English classic has been run in Scotland. It was won by Michelozzo, owned by Charles St George, trained by Henry Cecil and ridden by Steve Cauthen.

Another race worthy of mention is the Scottish Champion Hurdle, usually run on Scottish Grand National. Many Champion Hurdle winners from

Al Co and Jamie Moore winning the 2014 Scottish Grand National at 40/1.

Cheltenham have gone on to complete the double, but perhaps the most notable race was the 1978 running. The field of seven included the Champion Hurdle winners and stablemates Night Nurse and Sea Pigeon and a six-year-old Deep Run gelding called Golden Cygnet, trained in Ireland by Edward O'Grady. Running in his first season over hurdles, Golden Cygnet was unbeaten, having won six times, including the Supreme Novice's Hurdle at Cheltenham by an astounding 15 lengths.

Now he was to take on Sea Pigeon and Night Nurse, but tragedy struck when, in front at the last flight, he fell heavily. Sadly, he had to be put down three days later. Sea Pigeon went on to win the race but the memory was of Golden Cygnet, who might have gone on to be the greatest hurdler of all time.

Many great jockeys have shown their skills at Ayr over the years, from Fred Archer to Steve Cauthen on the flat and, over the jumps, Brian Fletcher aboard Red Rum beating Lord John Oaksey riding Proud Tarquin in that epic 1974 Scottish Grand National. But none of these could have had a broader smile than Mrs Muriel Naughton. Riding her own horse Ballycasey in the Spittal Hill Amateur Riders Handicap Chase on 30 January 1976, she became the first woman to ride under National Hunt rules. In a field of eight she finished a well-beaten sixth, but history had nevertheless been made. Ballycasey, a 33/1 chance, had been prominent in the early stages and was disputing the lead at halfway before making a few odd mistakes. In two minds whether to pull up or not, she decided to press on and was eventually beaten by 40 lengths.

Mrs Naughton, 28 years old and a mother of a five-year-old daughter, returned to the unsaddling enclosure to a warm round of applause. Not only had she successfully taken part in the race but she had also driven the horsebox to the course, saddled the horse and then changed in the ambulance room before weighing out. Quite a day!

BALLINROBE

Ballinrobe, the largest town in Co Mayo, lies 28 miles to the north of Galway and has a long tradition of horse racing. Although the present course dates from only 1923, flat racing has taken place in the area since 1773 and steeplechasing, under the auspices of the South Mayo Hunt, made its first appearance in 1834. The original course was at a place known locally as "Shoe Corner" – so named because it was the point on the edge of the town where the country people put on their shoes before entering the town. They removed them at the same place on their way home, presumably to make them last longer. Later, the meeting was held on land owned by Thomas Tighe, who provided it free of charge, and on a course adjacent to the ruined Cloona Castle. After the 1919 meeting, the Committee sought to buy a new, permanent site for the racecourse and in 1921 purchased a picturesque site in the shadow of the Partry Mountains. Although Ballinrobe was allotted fixtures in 1922, it was unable to fulfil them and was not ready for opening until 5 September 1923, details that are commemorated by a plaque at the entrance.

The first race on the course was won by the odds-on-favourite Borora, ridden by Jack Moloney and trained on The Curragh by the leading trainer of the time, Michael Dawson. It is a remarkable coincidence that Borora and Jack Moloney went on to win the first ever race run on the present Naas racecourse in June 1924. A feature of the opening day at Ballinrobe was a double by the Welsh jockey F B 'Dick' Rees, on his way to his third Jockey's Championship in England, on horse's trained by Harry Ussher. A gifted horseman with a keen tactical brain, Rees was acclaimed the best jump jockey of his time and had won the Grand National on Shaun Spadah (1921) and went on to win the Cheltenham Gold Cup on Red Splash (1924), Patron Saint (1928) and Easter Hero (1929). The latter, one of the all-time great chasers, actually won a race at Ballinrobe in 1926, when the property of Frank Barbour.

Steeplechasing Rules (180(i)) once allowed the substitution of riders if a horse fell, provided the substitute could draw the weight at the scales. The last incident of an Irish race being run with a substitute rider was at Ballinrobe on 31 March 1960 in the Western Hunters' Steeplechase, when a rider named Mr H Kerrigan managed to fall off two different horses in the same race. His original mount, Bridge Echo, fell and raced off riderless but Mr Kerrigan remounted Glenmore Girl, who fell at the same fence. With only two other runners left in the race, Mr Kerrigan looked likely to claim the third prize until coming down at the last fence.

Always a minor venue, Ballinrobe was one of the courses identified for closure by the Racing Board in 1968, when an attempt was made to rationalise racing following its acquisition of Leopardstown. The Ballinrobe Race Company fought tooth and nail to keep its fixtures and the Racing Board never carried out its threat. Nowadays, Ballinrobe races over both codes and has proved itself a popular and progressive racecourse. The amenities have been completely redeveloped and land has been purchased to accommodate an extension to the circuit, currently just over a mile, and is expected be ready to use by the time we go to press.

Above: the official opening of the new presentation stand in May 2012.

Below: the old stands in 1991.

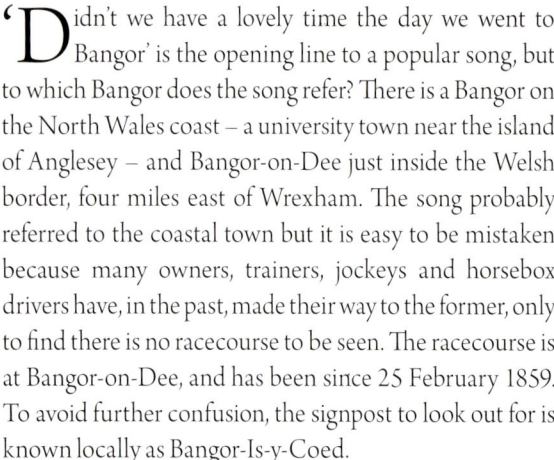

'Didn't we have a lovely time the day we went to Bangor' is the opening line to a popular song, but to which Bangor does the song refer? There is a Bangor on the North Wales coast – a university town near the island of Anglesey – and Bangor-on-Dee just inside the Welsh border, four miles east of Wrexham. The song probably referred to the coastal town but it is easy to be mistaken because many owners, trainers, jockeys and horsebox drivers have, in the past, made their way to the former, only to find there is no racecourse to be seen. The racecourse is at Bangor-on-Dee, and has been since 25 February 1859. To avoid further confusion, the signpost to look out for is known locally as Bangor-Is-y-Coed.

As a result of the large crowds who had been drawn to a cross-country match between two members of his Hunt in 1858, the opening meeting was organised by Sir Watkin Williams-Wynn on an estate called Bryn-y-Pys. One of its main features is that there is no grandstand – viewing is from a steep grass slope resembling a point-to-point meeting. It is an ideal racecourse for picnickers, although it is difficult to judge the winner of a close finish as the finishing straight is head-on.

One young lad, just 12 years old, who did manage to find his way there in 1869 was Fred Archer. An apprentice under the wing of Mathew Dawson, a trainer based at Heath House, Newmarket, he rode his very first winner here aboard Maid of Trent for owner Mrs 'Croppy' Willan (must have had a short haircut!) in the Galloway Steeplechase, weighing just 4st 11lb. Lester Piggott also rode his first winner at the age of 12, but Fred Archer's win was more remarkable since he was very young to be riding in a chase – let alone winning it. Archer went on to ride a total of 8,084 races, winning 2,748.

Bangor is a popular course in a very relaxed atmosphere. The principal race, the Great Bangor Handicap Chase, carried prize money of £240, far greater than most other

The judges box at Bangor-on-Dee.

courses at the time. Grand National winners Gamecock (1887) and Cloister (1893) both won at Bangor before winning at Aintree. Cloister was one of the greatest Grand National winners of all time, carrying 12st 7lb to victory by 40 lengths.

Gamecock ran in seven consecutive Grand Nationals (1885–1891) and in 1886, the year before he won the race, he finished third behind Old Joe and Too Good. There were only eight finishers in what was reported to be a very rough race, but among the also-rans that day was a mount ridden by amateur jockey Frank Cotton.

Ten years later Frank Cotton was appointed Clerk of the Course at Bangor, following in the footsteps of his father; he held the position until 1921. He was succeeded by *his* son Gilbert Cotton, who maintained the family tradition by riding very successfully as an amateur. Apart from riding many winners at Bangor, his biggest success was to win the National Hunt Chase at Cheltenham (1912), on The Rejected IV. Riding the same horse the following year in the Grand National, he was one of many fallers, which led Cotton in later years to become an inspector of courses around the country.

Only three horses finished the Grand National that year, and one of those had remounted. For many years afterwards the number of finishers was in single figures. There were only two finishers in the 1928 Grand National when Easter Hero got stuck in the ditch at the Canal Turn, causing such mayhem that Gilbert Cotton put modifications into place. The ditch was filled in, making the Canal Turn a plain fence as it is today, and all the other fences were sloped to make them less demanding.

Gilbert Cotton served as Clerk of the Course at Bangor and Inspector of Courses for 50 years with great credit; the Gilbert Cotton Memorial Hunters Steeplechase is run every April in his honour. In 1970 he was succeeded by John Moon, who introduced a North Wales Holiday meeting each August. While the axe was coming down on several small courses around this time, this charming course was saved from closure with a great deal of influence from a senior member of the committee – Lord Leverhulme.

Dick Francis, jockey turned thriller writer, had his first proper taste of racing at Bangor and later described the course as his favourite 'because of the flatness and absence of sharp bends'.

So you can still have a lovely time the day you go to Bangor.

Bath races have been held at Lansdown since 1811 when a Mrs Blathwayt, who owned the land, gave permission for a course to be laid out on her property. Earlier records of Bath races were at Claverton Down in 1728 where an annual race week was held until it closed in 1796.

The course lies two miles north of the beautiful spa town of Bath, famous since Roman times for its natural mineral springs. It is the most complete and best-preserved Georgian city in Britain, renowned for Pulteney Bridge spanning the River Avon and fine Georgian streets such as the Royal Crescent. The racecourse is the highest flat course in the country at 780 feet above sea level. The climb to the course is severe and is not recommended by foot. Once upon a time, horse-drawn carriages were available from the town, but even for them carrying four portly bookmakers would have been quite a strain. I hope they were not required to race as well.

The course is shaped like a kidney bean with the last four furlongs on a continual curve, but trainers like using Bath for the excellent downland turf, reputed to be undisturbed since the days of Ethelred the Unready. Because of the shape of the course, certain jockeys could ride Bath far better than others. Those with the best records were Gordon Richards, Scobie Breasley, Joe Mercer and Pat Eddery, all of whom had the art of getting a good position and saving ground. Pat Eddery will have special memories of Bath as it was here he rode his 3,000th winner on 22 July 1991. He was only the fifth jockey to reach this milestone, but which horse should be in the history books is not certain. For good measure Pat rode a treble that day with My Shoushou (Barry Hills), Morocco (Roger Charlton) and Sure Victory (Peter Walwyn) and it is generally accepted that it was Morocco who should receive the credit. To erase any doubts at all, Pat went to Windsor's evening meeting that day to ride one more winner, Green Medina (Henry Cecil).

Bath once attracted high-class horses with their best race, a listed event, the Somerset Stakes. The race used to be run in early April over seven furlongs and provided a prep race for possible 2,000 Guineas runners. Among its winners in the 1940s were two sons of Owen Tudor –

Tudor Minstrel and Abernant. Tudor Minstrel made his racecourse debut at Bath as a two-year-old on 25 April 1946 in the five furlong Lansdown Stakes. He was trained by Fred Darling at Beckhampton and was widely tipped by his jockey Gordon Richards as being the best two-year-old he had ever sat on. Consequently, he started a red hot favourite at 2/5 and, with the race run in the worst weather seen at Bath for many years with strong winds and driving rain, Tudor Minstrel won by five lengths. He remained unbeaten in four races that year, including the Coventry Stakes at Royal Ascot. The following year Fred Darling ran him in the Somerset Stakes on 16 April 1947 and he won in a canter at odds of 6/100. He went on to win the 2,000 Guineas by eight lengths before his shock defeat in the Derby. His trainer had run him twice at Bath with the idea of him getting used to going left-handed. In both cases his theory was not properly tested and, at Epsom on the descent to Tattenham Corner, Gordon Richards reported that, as well as not staying, he was always leading on the wrong leg and was all at sea.

Two years later the Somerset Stakes attracted Abernant, trained by Noel Murless, who took over at Beckhampton following the retirement of Fred Darling. With only two opponents Abernant won also in a canter at odds of 1/25 but unfortunately he was beaten a short head by Nimbus in the 2,000 Guineas.

In complete contrast one race that Bath will always be remembered for is the Spa Selling Plate for two-year-olds. A race that normally would take place without anybody really noticing, on 16 July 1953 it made the headlines for all the wrong reasons. It was the opening

Santa Amaro and Francasal – both French horses with identical markings – were involved in the race horse switch of the century in England in 1953.

race at 2.00pm and was won by a horse called Francasal at 10/1, ridden by William Gilchrist and trained at Epsom by Percy Bailey. The race became the subject of a Jockey Club investigation that was to last over seven months, as a result of which four men were prosecuted and sent to prison for up to three years for attempting to defraud Bath racecourse. The race was eventually declared void.

Francasal and another two-year-old Santa Amoro, who was almost identical, had been purchased in France by a professional gambler, Maurice Williams, and on 11 July both horses arrived in England. Francasal had poor form in France, being placed once in six outings, while Santa Amoro was unraced but clearly the better horse. Francasal was sent to a small yard at Sonning Common near Reading under the care of a horse transporter called Sigmund Webster. Santa Amoro was sent to Percy Bailey at Epsom, but they believed him to be Francasal. Both horses were entered in the Spa Selling Plate at Bath and a similar event at Newmarket on the same day. On the morning of 16 July, the two horses set off for the races, but who went where? It was in fact Santa Amoro

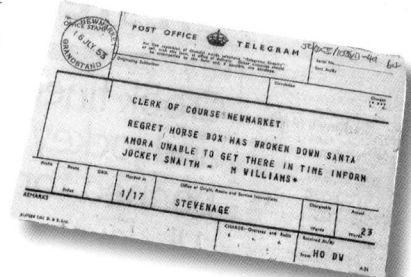

who went to Bath while Francasal headed for Newmarket via Stevenage. It was at Stevenage Post Office that a telegram was sent to the Clerk of the Course at Newmarket stating that the horsebox had broken down and Santa Amoro would be a non-runner, with a request to inform the jockey Willie Snaith. The horsebox then turned round and returned to Sonning Common.

Meanwhile Santa Amoro had arrived at Bath and declared to run as Francasal, so the switch, or ringer, was in place. Although unraced he had a racecourse gallop at Worcester when brought over earlier in the year against another horse Maurice Williams had purchased – Sun Suit, who had won a seller at Nottingham ridden by Lester Piggott. The gallop had proved very informative in that Santa Amoro had more than enough ability to win a seller.

The final part of the coup involved a rag and scrap metal dealer, Leonard Phillips, who, with an accomplice, set out in the early hours from their home in the Rhondda Valley with a small red lorry, eventually arriving about a mile from Bath racecourse. At precisely 1.30 pm they put up an extension ladder against a telegraph pole and, with an oxyacetylene torch, proceeded to cut the telephone wires that connected the course to the outside world. A council worker cutting the grass nearby asked what they were doing only to be told they had a job to do.

Once the wires were cut, Maurice Williams instructed his associates to place over £6,000 on Francasal with up to 20 off-course bookmakers, knowing that none of this money could be laid off to the course. Francasal won comfortably at a healthy 10/1 to land a colossal gamble. The stake would equate to £130,000 today, which at 10/1 would net £1.3 million. On the course just one bet was recorded – £175 to £25.

The winner was bought in for 740 guineas. He did not return to Epsom but joined the real Francasal at Sonning Common. Percy Bailey had been informed that the horse would be returning to France forthwith. The failure of the

telephone system aroused suspicion amongst bookmakers and the Jockey Club became involved immediately, advising all bookmakers to withhold payment pending an investigation. Once it was realised the cables had been cut, and with the evidence of the council worker, the Jockey Club alerted Scotland Yard and both horses were detained and sent to veterinary surgeon George Forbes at Epsom, where they remained throughout the enquiry. Here their identities were discovered; Santa Amoro was still wearing his racing plates.

The police arrested Leonard Phillips. He was charged with causing malicious damage to Post Office property and given a three-month jail sentence. He claimed he did not know who employed him for the job, for which he had been paid £35. At the Crown Court it was never proved that his part in the operation was connected to the plot. Maurice Williams and three other men were eventually sent to trial at the Old Bailey and, on the evidence of over 140 witnesses, were prosecuted and sent to prison.

Since the cutting of the cable was never proved to be part of the plot, the irony of the case is that there was no need for a ringer in the first place. Little was known of either horse and Santa Amoro could have run in his own name. In addition, sending a telegram to Newmarket to inform the course of the non-runner was not necessary in those days. If a horse was not declared to run at least 45 minutes before a race it would automatically be declared a non-runner.

The four men sent to prison – Maurice Williams, Harry Kateley, Gomer Charter and Victor Dill – served out their sentences but Charter, a Cardiff bookmaker, was shot dead on his own doorstep by three men in 1966. His murder was never proved to be connected to the case.

Apart from the punter who won £175 for an inspired lucky guess, nobody received a penny. I doubt if it would be any consolation to the conspirators to know that every June the day is remembered with the running of the Francasal Stakes.

The main problem with Bellewstown is finding it. One racing journalist described it as being 'weird and wonderful and in the middle of nowhere'. Until recently, there was just one meeting in July, lasting three days, but further meetings later in the year have since been added. There are only a few permanent buildings – two old stands (which recently have aquired roofs), one old tote building and one old weigh room. The remainder are marquees erected on the day. Even the stables are temporary buildings. The course is about nine furlongs round but there are no steeplechases – just hurdles and flat races.

Bellewstown racecourse is in County Meath, on the hills of Crockafotha, in a beautiful rural setting with the mountains of Mourne to the north and the Irish Sea to the east. It is not known when racing started but there were records in the *Dublin Gazette* of a meeting in August 1726.

George Tandy, a former mayor of Drogheda, persuaded George III to sponsor a race at Bellewstown in 1780. The race was called His Majesty's Plate and all future monarchs followed the tradition. It was not until 1980 that Queen Elizabeth II discontinued the race and instead sponsored a race at the Curragh known as the Royal Whip, which has continued to the present day.

Bellewstown is most famous for the huge gamble that took place on 25 June 1975, involving Barney Curley. His

wife Maureen owned a five-year-old brown gelding called Yellow Sam, which ran in the Mount Hanover Handicap Hurdle for amateur riders. Trained by Liam Brennan, it had shown very little form in ten races, having never reached a place, and was readily available on the day at 20/1. There was a massive off-course gamble on the horse but the those bookmakers were unable to lay off any money to the course thanks to a very portly gentleman who was occupying the one and only telephone box. He claimed that he needed to be in constant touch with a hospital owing to the condition of a dying relative. As soon as the race was off he disappeared – but it was too late. Yellow Sam had won easily and Barney Curley had won a cool £300,000. (And there was also good news from the hospital – the relative had made a miraculous recovery.)

The infamous Barney Curley, left, and Yellow Sam right, ridden by Mick Furlong.

BEVERLEY

The market town of Beverley was originally part of the East Riding of Yorkshire when the area was also one of the largest training centres in the North of England. Since 1974 there have been several changes. The county boundaries have changed twice, first with the formation of the new county of Humberside and now under the wing of the county of East Yorkshire. The training centre has also disappeared and among the last to train here in the early 1980s were George Toft and Snowy Gray. What has not changed, however, is the picturesque town with its medieval streets dominated by a magnificent Minster. The impressive cathedral-size Gothic church dates from 1220 and must be one of the finest in Europe.

It will come as no surprise that within a large farming area, and where the people of Beverley were often in the habit of matching their horses, it was logical to lay out a racecourse. There was no better place than on an area of

The picturesque Beverley racecourse with the Gothic Minster in the background (above), and opposite the packed stands in May 2014.

common land at Beverley called The Westwood which is still the site of the racecourse today, with the area of land that is raced on known as The Hurn. The first recorded race took place on 22 September 1690.

Meetings were not regular at first but, by 1767, Beverley had grown sufficiently in popularity to erect a grandstand at a cost of £1,000, raised by the issue of 330 'life member' silver badges. By the 19th century the investment was looking so good that even National Hunt racing was held there, courtesy of the Holderness Hunt, but it ceased after only 12 years in 1839. Hull also staged racing at Westwood around this time as it had no permanent track of its own.

It amalgamated with Beverley on several occasions under the name 'Hull and Beverley races' but Hull closed in 1909.

During the 19th century the area surrounding Beverley was becoming more popular for training horses. One trainer, Squire Richard Watt, whose stud and stables were at nearby Bishop Burton, sent out four St Leger winners in the space of 20 years. The first of these, Altisidora (1813), has a pub named after him in the village of Bishop Burton. Another locally-bred horse of this period was the filly Nancy, trained by Job Marson, who won the Ebor and the Goodwood Cup and had the rare distinction of subjecting the great Voltigeur to one of his rare defeats. She also won the 1851 Chester Cup with just 4st 12lb on her back, landing a huge gamble for her many Yorkshire supporters. Sadly, she broke her leg the following season and had to be put down.

The most famous horse of all to be trained locally was the filly Blink Bonny. Trained by William l'Anson, she won the Bishop Burton Stakes as a two-year-old at Beverley and remained unbeaten that season (including the Gimcrack at York) with eight victories. Her finest hours came the following year (1857) when she created history by winning the Derby and the Oaks, and she is still one of only four fillies to achieve this remarkable double. Sadly her jockey John Charlton succumbed to a bribe and he pulled her when odds-on for the St Leger.

This was a golden era for horses from Beverley but classic horses no longer use The Westwood route to Epsom. More recently there have been plenty of very good handicappers seen at Beverley and, in particular, two sprinters who became great favourites with the public. The filly Branston Abbey made her debut at Beverley in April 1991 and went on to win 24 races, which for a mare is a post-war record, and Rapid Lad, who won 12 races at Beverley between 1983 and 1989 and is honoured by the running of the Rapid Lad Handicap. Other notable races include the Hilary Needler Trophy for two-year-old fillies, the Watt Memorial Stakes and the Bishop Burton Stakes, which is now a sprint handicap. Incidentally, the sprint course at Beverley is probably the stiffest in the country, practically all against the collar with a dog-leg three furlongs out which makes it almost impossible to win from a wide draw. (Branston Abbey was drawn one for her debut but still managed to finish third.)

Finally, in the village of Etton, three miles north-east of The Westwood, you will find a signpost indicating the start of the Kiplingcotes Derby. This race has been run since 1519 over a distance of four miles along farm lanes and tracks, starting at an old stone post on the grass verge in the parish of Etton, not far from the old Kiplingcotes railway station, and finishing at Londesborough Wold Farm. It is the oldest flat horserace in England and has been run every year on the third Thursday in March (the 495th race took place on 20 March 2014). It is open to all horses, thoroughbreds or not.

One of the conditions of the race is that should it not take place, for whatever reason, it will never be run again. In the severe winter of 1947 the four-foot snow drifts posed a problem, but local farmer Fred Stephenson and his horse Londesborough Lad walked the whole length of the course to maintain the historic tradition. The race would normally take ten minutes, but their time was just under two hours.

BRIGHTON

It is hard to imagine that the thriving seaside resort that is Brighton today was once a small fishing village, known as Brightelmstone. It was under this title that the racecourse opened on 26 August 1783 on a picturesque part of the Sussex Downs called Whitehawk Hill, 400 feet above sea level overlooking the English Channel.

In the early days Brighton became very popular, thanks

entirely to the patronage of the Prince of Wales, who later became King George IV. His love of Brighton began with the Royal Pavilion which served as his retreat and by 1815 he had the town rebuilt to its present glory with the aid of his close friend, the architect John Nash. He was then able to indulge in his exotic tastes of high living, beautiful women – and, of course, frequent visits to the racecourse.

The course continued to prosper with the addition of a railway link from London, and even the publication of Graham Greene's 1938 novel *Brighton Rock*, with its fictional account of pickpockets and razor gangs overrunning the course, failed to dent attendance, which was rarely below 20,000. During this period there were stands on both sides of the course.

By the 1980s attendances began to drop, partly due to holidaymakers preferring sunnier climes abroad. In 1991 the grandstand in the Silver ring was deemed unsafe, which raised questions about the others. But soon along came the cavalry in the shape of Pratt and Company, Arena Leisure and, in 1998, Sir Stanley Clarke with an endless supply of green and white emulsion.

Because of the hilly nature of the course Brighton fails to attract top-class racing and rarely top-class horses. One exception to this was Isonomy, who in 1879 won the Brighton Cup before going on to complete the Stayers' Triple Crown consisting of the Ascot Gold Cup, Goodwood Cup and Doncaster Cup – an achievement that was not repeated for 70 years. The filly Park Top also won the Brighton Cup in successive years (1967, carrying 8st 2lb, and 1968, carrying 9st 10lb). What a certainty she must have been on the first occasion. Owned by the Duke of Devonshire and trained by Bernard van Cutsem, she had an outstanding career, the highlight of which was winning the King George VI and Queen Elizabeth Stakes in 1969.

With Brighton's similarity to Epsom the other major race was the Brighton Derby Trial, but it failed to produce an Epsom Derby winner and did not continue after 1967. Major L B Holliday's Hethersett won it in 1962, fell in the Derby but did win the St Leger. Sodium won in 1966 but could finish only fourth behind Charlottown at Epsom, although he got his revenge by winning the Irish Derby. In 1967 it was won by Dart Board who finished third at Epsom behind Royal Palace. Cacoethes made a winning debut in a minor race in 1989 before finishing third to the mighty Nashwan at Epsom, but other classic aspirants were few and far between. There were many course specialists at Brighton, none more popular than Operatic Society who from 14 appearances won seven times; a race is now run in his honour.

Lester Piggott takes a tumble after Barbary Pirate's saddle slipped in the final furlong of the Black Rock Handicap at Brighton in August 1960.

Three small but significant pieces of racing history took place at Brighton. Miss Norah Wilmot became the first woman to officially train a winner on the flat when Pat obliged on 3 August 1966. Sheikh Mohammed had his first-ever winner in England on 20 June 1977 when Hatta, trained by John Dunlop and ridden by Ron Hutchinson, won the Bevendean Stakes. Steve Cauthen rode his 1,000th winner in England on 5 August 1987 aboard Picnicing for trainer Henry Cecil.

Many will have fond memories of Brighton, but on a sadder note we must remember Fred Rickaby, who, on 4 August 1914, rode Picton to victory for Lord Derby in the opening race on the day that the First World War broke out, only to be killed while serving with the Royal Tank Corps in France in 1918 . His son, Bill, who was just one year old when his father died, became a very successful jockey himself, winning three classics on Sweet Solera (twice) and Privy Councillor, and had the distinction of winning the largest flat race – the 58 runner Lincoln Handicap of 1948 – on Commissar. (Bill's brother, another Fred, also became an accomplished jockey.)

The last mention, though, must belong to King George IV, who set the ball rolling at Brighton in 1783 and may even have pioneered a downfall that we know so well fast women and slow horses

CARLISLE

Cummersdale Halt may not appear on any present day British Rail map, but soon after Carlisle opened on its present course at Blackhall this small railway station may well have contributed to the saving of Carlisle races.

In the building of a new course in 1904 on what was Blackhall Farm two miles south of the city, the newly-formed committee, led by ex-trainer Sir Loftus Bates, built a lovely new course, with a handsome grandstand (with an open top roof) that still stands today. However, they failed to consider how people would get there, since the only access was a narrow winding lane, which in bad weather turned into a muddy track.

By 1907 the Maryport and Carlisle Railway Company came to the rescue by building Cummersdale Halt Station just minutes away from the enclosures on the west side of the course. This facility attracted thousands for the meeting there on 2 July 1907. For 6d return from Carlisle Citadel Station racegoers did not even have to queue for tickets because they could pay at a turnstile on arrival.

This innovation led the committee to make further improvements, and very soon the narrow lane was widened as the course became more popular. The course was originally a straight mile-and-a-quarter, which made viewing difficult, so over time that was altered and gradually Carlisle began to take shape.

Carlisle first staged racing at Kingsmoor during the 16th century when one of the oldest races, 'The Carlisle Bell', was probably first run. During the mid-18th century Carlisle races moved to a piece of land north of the city known as 'The Swifts', but in the early days it became the scene of violent behaviour and bloody feuding. It attracted many villains, in particular the notorious William Armstrong, known locally as 'Kinmont Willie'. However The Swifts became unsuitable for racing because, being situated on the banks of the River Eden, not only was the course liable to flooding but the final bend into the straight was so tight that many horses plunged into the river. Eventually, due to the decline of

The Swifts the lease was not renewed and Carlisle races moved to its present site.

The opening fixture on 28 June 1904 was poorly attended, largely due to the difficult access previously mentioned but, nevertheless, the first race, a Two Year Old Trial Selling Plate, was won by Friars Wash at 4/1 ridden by J McCall, who received a special whip as a trophy to mark the occasion. The winner was sold for 50 guineas. Later in the afternoon Powder Puff (5/1), trained by McCall's father, won the Cumberland Plate, for which he received a silver cup – a memorable day for the McCall family.

The owner of Powder Puff was George Tod of Edinburgh, who donated the prize money of 500 guineas to the racecourse to ensure the continuity of the meeting. Powder Puff won the Cumberland Plate again in 1906, and again Mr Tod generously donated the prize money. The horse became a favourite with the locals, having also won at The Swifts in their final year.

The Cumberland Plate remains one of Carlisle's major races. First run in 1842, it has always somewhat been overshadowed by its contemporary across the Pennines, the Northumberland Plate run at Newcastle. The latter has always been that little bit more popular and became known as 'The Pitmen's Derby'. The races were usually run about a week apart, with the Northumberland Plate first. Many horses tried to win them both and failed. The best example of this came in 1863, a time when each course did its own handicapping. A great favourite, Caller Ou, winner of 51 races including the 1861 St Leger, won the Northumberland Plate in a canter but finished last of five in the Cumberland Plate the following week.

Other big races at Carlisle were the Kings Guineas from 1763 and its Gold Cup since 1815, but neither survived the changes. One race that has survived however is one of the oldest in the calendar – 'The Carlisle Bell'. The race revived at Blackhall in 1906 but legend has it that it was also run in 1615, when Lady Dacre presented a silver bell to the

The Carlisle Bell, which is inscribed: 'THE SWIFTES HORSE THES BEL TO TAK FOR MI LADE DAKAR SAKE'.

winner. This may not have been the origin of 'The Carlisle Bell', as records show a race run in 1559 during the reign of Queen Elizabeth I. Though an obscure piece of history, it is a fact that the original bell (one of two) is kept to this day in The Tullie House Museum in the city centre.

Another piece of history associated with Carlisle happened on 2 July 1929 when it became one of the first two courses (along with Newmarket) to introduce the Tote. The first day was always going to be interesting in terms of comparison with the bookmaker's odds. Unfortunately for Carlisle, they started 15 minutes later than Newmarket, whose first winner, Huncoat, ridden by Harry Wragg, started at 33/1 with the tote returning an only slightly larger dividend.

Carlisle's first winner was Lemin, who won the Holm Hill Handicap at 15/8, while the Tote paid 5 shillings win and 4s 9d place. For a 2-shilling stake ,this represented odds of 6/4 for a win but 11/8 for a place. There were bound to be some strange dividends in the beginning, none more so than the Cumberland Plate later that afternoon. The winner Pomagne, ridden by Billy Nevett, returned the 6/4 favourite while the Tote paid 9s 9d, odds of nearly 4/1.

Carlisle is a tough course with a steady climb to the post from the three furlong pole, so, with the emphasis on stamina, it has failed to attract top-class horses, except one – Red Rum. Trained not too far down the road at Southport, he managed to win the Windermere Handicap Chase no fewer than three times en route to his Aintree triumphs.

CARTMEL

When the time comes to plan your next holiday, why not consider the Lake District and ,in particular, a tiny village known as Cartmel, which lies just two miles from the small seaside resort of Grange-over-Sands. Not only could you enjoy the delights of Lake Windermere, but, if you happen to be there for a Whitsun or August Bank Holiday, you could also visit Cartmel races.

You could be forgiven for thinking that Cartmel is famous only for its priory, but on seven days a year Cartmel races take place and the transformation is amazing. From a sleepy village Cartmel changes overnight to a wonderful carnival attracting huge crowds, sometimes well in excess of 20,000. All spectators watch the races from the centre of the course – which is unique in itself. It is strongly advised to arrive at least three hours before the first race so that picnics and barbecues can get underway. There is a fairground and side stalls which, combined with the racing, offers a wonderful family day out.

The origins of Cartmel are obscure. There are records of a meeting in 1856 which included hound trailing and foot races. It has also been suggested that the first meeting involved mule races organised by medieval monks from Cartmel Priory. However, by 1875 foot races were abolished and entire National Hunt meetings were taking place. In those days there was only one meeting a year, Whit Bank Holiday Monday. Not until the early 1960s were more fixtures added.

Cartmel will always be remembered for the Gay Future coup in 1974. Gay Future had run on the flat in Ireland, winning an amateurs race at Thurles in April 1974, ridden by ' (customarily listed as 'Mr T A Jones'), the leading amateur in Ireland. He later finished third in a two-mile handicap at Naas, ridden by a young Mick Kinane when an apprentice. He was then trained and schooled for hurdling by Edward O'Grady, but at the last moment transferred to the charge of Tony Collins, a little-known Scottish permit holder. Gay Future ran in the 4.20 at Cartmel, the Ulverston Novices Hurdle, on 26 August 1974. He was in the morning papers to be ridden by an apprentice J McNeil but he switched to another horse owned by Collins, Racionzer, and Gay Future was ridden again by the more experienced amateur, Timmy Jones.

The course takes the runners past Cartmel Priory and through the beautiful countryside surrounding it.

All the fun of the fair at Cartmel in June 2010 as Thunder Hawk and Tristan Davidson challenge Delightful Cliche to win.

As it was a Bank Holiday, there were 12 other meetings around the country and consequently there was no blower or betting shop coverage. There was no on-course money for Gay Future and after opening at 5/1 he drifted out to 10/1. He won easily by 15 lengths. There were thousands of off-course bets for him but coupled in doubles and trebles with two of Collins's other runners, Opera Cloak in the 4.15 at Plumpton and Ankerwyck in the 4.45 at Southwell. Tony Collins travelled down to Plumpton to

report that his horsebox had broken down – when in fact the horse was still at his stables in Scotland. A phone call was then made to the Clerk of the Course at Southwell reporting that the horsebox carrying Ankerwyck had also broken down, but he also was still at home. Now all the money would be running on Gay Future, a clever disguise.

Had a reporter not phoned Tony Collins's stables the coup might never have been discovered. He spoke to the housekeeper, who innocently said when questioned about their runners, 'Well, Opera Cloak and Ankerwyck are still here – I can see them in the field.' It became obvious that Gay Future was the horse involved, but Cartmel was very remote and inaccessible (and before mobile phones were invented) and ,as hard as some bookmakers tried to get to the course in order to reduce the odds, it was too late.

The 'coup' was planned by Tony Murphy, who was aware there was no blower at Cartmel and knew that off-course bookmakers would be unable to return any money to the course. Murphy and Collins were fined £1,000 each, while O'Grady was exonerated. Collins was later warned off for ten years by the Jockey Club. If Cartmel ever needed to be put on the map, Gay Future certainly did it.

Another piece of racing history to attach itself to Cartmel, of a less dramatic nature, occurred on 9 June 1962. It concerned the Furness Selling Handicap Chase over two miles 300 yards. There were only eight runners, the youngest of which was the eventual winner, Waver Lad, a nine-year-old trained by Charlie Bell at Hawick. The race also included two ten-year-olds, one 11-year-old, one 13-year-old, one 15-year-old, one 17-year-old and Creggmore Boy, a 22-year old. He was the oldest horse ever to compete in a race. After finishing fourth at 8/1 he was given a well-earned retirement. His last victory had been in the same race in 1957 and he once finished second as a 21-year-old. He was trained in Lancashire by 75-year-old Horace Cousins – a couple of old codgers together. What wonderful company they must have been for each other.

This North Yorkshire racecourse must be given its proper title and not just plain Catterick, as it is often referred to. The village of Catterick lies one mile south of the racecourse. Catterick Bridge takes its name from a bridge over the River Swale, which flows around the northern edge of the course, where a chapel once stood. A few miles upstream, in the heart of the Yorkshire Dales, is the historic town of Richmond with its cobblestones and market place alongside the ruins of its 11th-century castle, which was itself once a thriving training area.

The course opened on 22 April 1783, three years after the first running of the Epsom Derby, but few classic winners have emerged from this tight, sharp course. One St Leger winner did originate from Catterick Bridge however: Antonio, owned by Tom Ferguson, landlord of the George and Dragon Inn by the bridge. In 1819 Antonio had run in a two-horse race at Catterick in April and finished second, so his chance of winning the Doncaster classic was remote – in fact he was a 100/3 chance. The start was a shambles and five of the field were left at the start, including the first and second favourites. To the delight of his owner, Antonio won, but there were some ugly scenes among the crowd who demanded that the race be re-run; the stewards finally agreed, but Antonio did not take part. Eventually the Jockey Club intervened

Catterick Bridge in 1925.

46

and, two weeks later, allowed the original result to stand. Tom Ferguson could not believe his luck, but his beloved Antonio never won again. Tom was better known for farming and was more interested in his livestock, and was often asked to loan his sheep whenever the racecourse was snowbound, by walking his flock around the circuit to clear the snow.

It was not until 1867 that National Hunt racing began at Catterick but, again, the sharp turns did not suit the long-striding horses, who were never able to get a breather and the chance to settle down. It is to his great credit that the immortal Red Rum managed to win here three times, en route to Aintree. The flat and jump courses intersect each other twice and because of the turns there are no flat distances between seven furlongs and a mile and a half. Until 1906, when the present grandstand was built, there was a mile start beyond where the paddock wall now stands – which nowadays would place it somewhere in the middle of the George and Dragon car park.

It wasn't until 1946, when Major Leslie Petch was appointed Clerk of the Course, that any notable improvements were seen. He realigned the course as

Major Leslie Petch at his home in 1981.

much as was possible and, with the experience of his time at York and Redcar, his innovations were welcomed in improving many facilities for racegoers.

Catterick Bridge will always be known as one of the 'gaff' tracks, but it still has a certain charm. There were a few northern trainers who knew the right horses to bring here – the likes of Denys Smith, Harry Peacock and Charles Elsey. Jockeys who excelled here were Edgar Britt, Joe Sime, Edward Hide and, in particular, Billy Nevett, whose record here earned him the name of 'Cock of the North'. Let us also give a special mention to Val Greaves, who became the first woman to ride against professionals in a hurdle race when partnering Silver Gal in the Brough Novices Hurdle on 14 February 1976.

Sadly, we conclude with the story of another lady rider, Jayne Thompson. On 8 November 1986, riding Hot Betty in a Selling Hurdle at Catterick Bridge, her mount fell at the first flight. Jayne sustained injuries that were so severe that she never regained consciousness and died six days later. She was the first lady rider to lose her life racing. She was just 22 years old, a daughter of Doncaster trainer Ron Thompson, absolutely loved riding and in her short career had already ridden 18 winners.

Poignantly, her own horse Kindred, on whom she had won nine times, pined for her, rapidly lost weight and died two months later – which just shows what utter devotion can exist between horse and rider.

Prestbury Park is the home of Cheltenham, set in the beautiful Cotswolds and in the shadows of Cleeve Hill. The scenery is magnificent and so is the racing, highlighted by the Festival in March. Together they have made Cheltenham the home of National Hunt racing.

The course at Prestbury Park did not become a permanent fixture until 1902, before which many other venues in the area had been used. The earliest recorded racing at Cheltenham was a two-day flat meeting near Bishop's Cleeve in July 1819. Racing came to the village of Prestbury in 1831, followed by Andoversford, Southam, Noverton, Kayte Farm and, one year, even at the back of the cemetery. Mixed meetings were held at Prestbury and it was there, in 1834, that the Grand Annual Steeplechase was first run, won by Fugleman. An early winner of the race was Lottery in 1839, having already triumphed that year in the inaugural running of the Grand National. He returned to

Prestbury in 1840 to win the Grand Annual again, but was not so lucky that year at Liverpool, having been burdened with 13st 7lb and his jockey, Jem Mason, had to pull him up.

Flat racing had ceased by 1855 as National Hunt racing gathered momentum. It was before this time that the prominent racing family of Holman began their long association with Cheltenham and they were instrumental in the future of the racecourse. William Holman (great-grandfather of David Nicholson), who lived at Cleeve Hill, won the Grand Annual Steeplechase as a jockey no fewer than five times. He went on to train three Grand National winners, Freetrader (1856), Little Charley (1858) and Anatis (1860), and was the first trainer to do so. They were ridden by three of the finest jockeys of that era – George Stevens, who also lived locally at Cleeve Hill and who also rode five Grand National winners (which remains a record); William Archer, father of Fred Archer;

and Tommy Pickernel. Of William Holman's five sons, George also rode the winner of the Grand Annual five times, William was manager at Cheltenham and Alfred was involved in laying out the new course at Prestbury – the one that exists today – in 1902.

In 1907 the Cheltenham Steeplechase Company was formed and a two-day festival was introduced in 1911. One of the original races was the four-mile National Hunt Chase, which had been inaugurated at Market Harborough in 1860 and had since had various venues. Since 1911 it has settled at Cheltenham and is still run today as the highlight of the amateur rider's calendar. Of the 12 races run at that historic meeting, three were sellers and only three events still exist – the National Hunt Handicap Chase, the Gloucestershire Hurdle (now Supreme Novices) and the National Hunt Chase, under which title the meeting was run. A huge crowd attended the opening day despite the very wet weather. The first race was the Southam Steeplechase, a seller won by Young Buck II who was subsequently sold for 120 guineas. The second race was the Cotswold Flat Race followed by the main event, the four-mile National Hunt Chase, in which there were 38 runners. The winner was Sir Halbert (33/1), trained by Tom Coulthwaite, who just held on by a neck. On the second day there was a snowstorm and the going was described as 'awful' but it didn't prevent Autocar, in the hands of Bill Payne, strolling home by ten lengths in the National Hunt Handicap Chase (a race that was to become a forerunner of the Cheltenham Gold Cup).

Cheltenham Gold Cup

It was the chairman of the Cheltenham executive, Frederick Cathcart, who changed the face of racing here in 1923. He extended the Festival to three days and in 1924 had the brainwave to introduce a new race, a weight-for-age steeplechase for five-year-olds and over called the Cheltenham Gold Cup, with the original intention of providing a warm-up race for the Grand National. In 1927 he also founded a similar race for hurdlers called the Champion Hurdle. Both were an instant success.

Until then Liverpool had been regarded as the principal meeting, but the pendulum was about to swing. At the time very few non-handicap races existed – the most important being the National Hunt Chase, for amateur riders, and the Champion Chase at Liverpool – so these two additions were more than welcome. The Cheltenham Gold Cup, originally run over three miles three furlongs, became the supreme test of jumping, stamina and courage for staying chasers and the Champion Hurdle became what the name implies. They became the main events of the National Hunt Festival.

The first running of the Cheltenham Gold Cup in 1924 was won by the inexperienced five-year-old Red Splash, who held on in a desperate finish by a head from Conjuror II and Gerald L. Five-year-olds received a 10 lb weight allowance in those days but the trend did not last long as only three five-year-olds have won in the history of the race, and none since 1932.

Easter Hero and Tommy Cullinan in 1930 after winning the Gold Cup for the second time.

Easter Hero was probably the second-best horse ever to win the Gold Cup (behind a certain Irish horse in the 1960s). He was a remarkable horse, winning in 1929 and 1930. After spread-eagling the Gold Cup field by 20 lengths in 1929 he came out a fortnight later to finish second in the Grand National in a field of 66 with the impossible burden of 12st 7lb. The next year Easter Hero won the Gold Cup again by 20 lengths but was unable to run in the Grand National through lameness. In 1931 he was robbed of becoming the first horse to land a hat-trick when the meeting was abandoned because of frost. He retired at the end of that season but the public did not have to wait long for a new hero – Golden Miller.

A five-year-old when he won the Gold Cup for the first time in 1932, Golden Miller proceeded to win the race five years in succession. He might have made it six in a row but bad weather (snow) again caused the race to be abandoned in 1937. In 1932 he won at odds of 13/2 as a virtual novice by a comfortable four lengths after the favourite Grakle had unseated his rider when trying to avoid a fallen rival. Odds-on in 1933, he won by an easy ten lengths and the following year he became the only horse to land the Cheltenham Gold Cup and Grand National in the same year – a remarkable feat that may never be equalled. The races were only 17 days apart and after winning by six lengths at Cheltenham he humped 12st 2 lb to victory at Liverpool in record time. He was owned by the highly eccentric Miss Dorothy Paget, trained by Basil Briscoe and ridden by Gerry Wilson and, although he was to win two more Gold Cups, he was never able to distinguish himself again at Liverpool. In the 1935 Gold Cup he had a titanic battle with Thomond II, winning by three-quarters of a length, but the effort had left its mark as

he fell early in the Grand National, having started at 2/1, the hottest favourite in the history of the race. He had a much easier race to win the 1936 Gold Cup and, with the 1937 race abandoned, he returned to Cheltenham for the final time in 1938, only to be beaten by the younger horse Morse Code.

Easter Hero and Golden Miller had set a high standard and it was not until after the Second World War that the Gold Cup would be won by a comparable chaser. Irish trainer Tom Dreaper sent over Prince Regent to win the 1946 Gold Cup at the age of 11, having been restricted to racing in Ireland for five seasons because of the war. At the time Dreaper hailed Prince Regent as the best horse he had ever trained (see next paragraph for the horse that

Arkle, with Pat Taaffe on board, returning afer his 30-length victory over Dormant in the 1966 Gold Cup. Leading him is his owner, Anne, Duchess of Westminster. Trainer Tom Dreaper follows, wearing a bowler hat and a smile.

changed his mind). Cottage Rake became only the second horse to win the Gold Cup three times (1948, 1949, 1950). Trained by Vincent O'Brien in Ireland and ridden by that fine horseman Aubrey Brabazon, he was not built like a chaser and indeed had the speed to win on the flat, having won the Irish Cesarewitch.

It was in the 1960s that the greatest steeplechaser of all time graced the English and Irish turf. Arkle, owned by Anne, Duchess of Westminster and trained by Tom Dreaper, came to Cheltenham to contest the 1964 Gold Cup with a huge reputation. It was his third appearance at Cheltenham, having won the Honeybourne Chase in 1962 (not at the Festival) and the Broadway Novices Chase in 1963 (now the RSA Chase). He was opposed by the pride of England – Mill House, who had already won the 1963 Cheltenham Gold Cup – and Pas Seul, winner of the 1960 Gold Cup and unlucky not to have won at least two more. Pas Seul was described by Fred Winter as the best horse he had ever ridden. Arkle was up against two experienced opponents but started the 7/4 second favourite and won in breathtaking style. He took up the running after the second-last to beat Mill House by five lengths, with Pas Seul 25 lengths back in third. The English thought Mill House was unbeatable but the Irish crowd knew better.

The reception Arkle received was deafening – it seemed 90 per cent of Ireland had backed him and most of them were there. He went on to win two more Gold Cups – in 1965 he again beat Mill House, this time by 20 lengths, and in 1966 he beat Dormant by an incredible 30 lengths, with the other two finishers trailing. He sustained a bad injury in the King George VI Chase at Kempton in 1966 and was retired, but for which he would probably have won six Gold Cups. As it was, Golden Miller's record was intact, but Arkle, whose own record was 22 wins from 26 starts in chases, could have given Golden Miller over a stone had they ever met.

Arkle would be a hard act to follow, but the 1970s produced six more winners from Ireland. L'Escargot became only the fourth horse to win the Cheltenham Gold Cup twice, in 1970 and 1971, and only the second horse to win the Gold Cup and the Grand National, but unlike Golden Miller they were not in the same year. In his victory at Aintree in 1975 he denied Red Rum a hat-trick.

Glencaraig Lady was one of only four mares to win the race in 1972 for Francis Flood, and Captain Christy won in 1974 when still a novice. He was a very erratic jumper but on a good day he was probably the best since Arkle. One scintillating example came when he beat Bula by 30 lengths in the 1975 King George VI Chase. When he won the 1974 Gold Cup he tried to demolish the last fence but survived to beat the 1973 winner, The Dikler, and Game Spirit by five lengths and 20 lengths.

Arkle's owner, the Duchess of Westminster, also won the Gold Cup in 1975 with Ten Up, trained by Jim Dreaper (son of Tom). In very heavy going he beat Soothsayer, Bula, The Dikler and Captain Christy, and in 1977 Davy Lad won for Mick O'Toole. So the 1970s were a good decade for the Irish and they did not win the Gold Cup again until Dawn Run (1986) and Imperial Call (1996).

The pendulum swung to the English in the 1980s and to the north of England, and in particular to Michael Dickinson. In 1982 from his yard in Harewood, North Yorkshire he trained the first and second in Silver Buck and Bregawn. However this was almost a rehearsal for the following year – in 1983 he achieved the impossible by training the first five horses home. It is incredible enough to have five horses good enough to run, but for all to finish in the first five was unprecedented. The winner was Bregawn (Graham Bradley), followed by Captain John (David Goulding), Wayward Lad (Jonjo O'Neill), Silver Buck (Robert Earnshaw) and Ashley House (Mr Dermot Browne). Surely this was a feat that will never be equalled.

Emotional scenes as Dawn Run and Jonjo O'Neill return victorious after the 1986 Gold Cup.

In 1984 history was made when, for the first time ,the winner of the Cheltenham Gold Cup was trained by a woman – Jenny Pitman. The winner was her beloved Burrough Hill Lad, ridden by Phil Tuck. John Francome had ridden him all season, winning all his four chases including the Welsh Grand National, but he was claimed for Brown Chamberlin, trained by Fred Winter. Burrough Hill Lad beat Brown Chamberlin by three lengths with Bregawn and Wayward Lad unplaced. He was a fine chaser on his day but was plagued by leg injuries and had to be withdrawn from the 1985 Gold Cup just days before. (The race was won by Forgive 'N' Forget.)

The 1986 Gold Cup was a very emotional one, producing jubilant scenes after the race that may never be seen again. The winner was the mare Dawn Run, trained by Paddy Mullins in Ireland and ridden by Jonjo O'Neill. Owned by Charmian Hill (who rode her to victory in a

bumper at Tralee on her debut), she was adored by the public, simply because she was a mare who always ran her heart out. On this occasion the crowd went wild because she was the first horse to win the Champion Hurdle (1984) and the Cheltenham Gold Cup. She jumped the last fence in third place but somehow managed to pass Wayward Lad and Forgive and Forget on the run-in. It was one of those magical moments in racing. (Tears of joy turned to tears of sadness when, three months later, she fell in a race at Auteuil, France and was killed.)

In 1989 it was the turn of England's favourite chaser, the grey, Desert Orchid. By now a ten-year-old, Cheltenham had not been Dessie's favourite course – since 1984 he had run in two Champion Hurdles, an Arkle Chase and two

Queen Mother Champion Chases, and all had resulted in defeat. His finest hours had all been on park and right-handed courses. The ground for the 1989 Gold Cup was heavy, and despite all these factors he showed tremendous courage to outstay outsider Yahoo from the last fence. However his two market rivals, Carvill's Hill and Ten Plus, both fell and the latter took a heavy fatal fall at the third-last when travelling ominously well, which left the old question – would Desert Orchid have won had they not fallen? He ran in the next two Gold Cups, finishing third on both occasions to Norton's Coin (1990) and Garrison Savannah (1991).

Norton's Coin caused the biggest shock in the history of the race by winning at 100/1. It proved to be a fairytale result as he had previously shown little form – beaten last time by 15 lengths in a handicap. His owner/trainer Sirrel Griffiths started the day by milking his herd of cows at his Carmarthenshire farm in Wales, before driving the horsebox himself to Cheltenham. After beating Toby Tobias and Desert Orchid, the trainer was asked by the media the secret behind this fairytale. He explained 'The chickens used to perch on his back in the box. Their company helped to build up his confidence'.

Garrison Savannah (1991) was the second winner for trainer Jenny Pitman, ridden by her son Mark. It wasn't long before Henrietta Knight became the second woman trainer to have a Gold Cup winner, and she did it in style. Best Mate, in the colours of Jim Lewis, was the fourth horse to win the Cheltenham Gold Cup three times (2002, 2003, 2004), joining the illustrious set of Golden Miller, Cottage Rake and Arkle.

Champion Hurdle

The Champion Hurdle, again founded by Frederick Cathcart, was first run in 1927. The race carried the title 'Champion' but up until the Second World War the winners were no more than average. Hurdling was

regarded only as a secondary branch of the sport as most jumpers were bred for steeplechasing. The first winner was Blaris, ridden by George Duller, considered by many as the finest jockey ever over hurdles, who had won over fences on his previous start. The 1928 winner was the ever-popular Brown Jack, but he was not considered to have a hurdling career and reverted to flat racing with resounding success. The first dual winner was Insurance (1932, 1933), owned by Dorothy Paget and trained by Basil Briscoe (both owner and trainer completed doubles with Golden Miller in the Gold Cup). In 1932 Insurance won by 12 lengths, but there were only three runners and one of those was a no-hoper.

The standard of the race improved dramatically after the Second World War with the emergence of National Spirit, Hatton's Grace and Sir Ken. Between them they won eight Champion Hurdles from 1947. Dual winner National Spirit (1947, 1948), trained by Vic Smyth at Epsom, first won at the age of six and was virtually unbeatable for two seasons. He ran in four more Champion Hurdles, being fourth to Hatton's Grace (1949), fourth to the same horse in 1950 after blundering badly at the last, falling at the last when still in the lead in 1951 and being fourth again in 1952. Hatton's Grace (1949, 1950, 1951) was the first horse to win the Champion Hurdle three times. He won a total of ten races over hurdles and was also a good performer on the flat, winning the Irish Lincolnshire and the Irish Cesarewitch twice. Trained by Vincent O'Brien in Ireland, he was a small horse of undernourished appearance who, unlike his predecessor, did not win his first Champion Hurdle until he was nine years old. (His win in 1951 made him the joint-oldest winner, with Sea Pigeon in 1981.) Together with Cottage Rake he lit the torch of the trailblazing career of his illustrious trainer. Immediately Sir Ken (1952, 1953, 1954) became the second triple winner and was regarded at the time as the best hurdler ever seen. Bred in France, where he ran without distinction, he came to England where he was trained by Willie Stephenson in Royston, Hertfordshire. A big raking horse, he was unbeaten during his first three seasons and held the record for a jumper of 17 consecutive wins (16 over hurdles and one on the flat). At the end of his career, he had won a total of 20 over hurdles and four chases, including the Cotswold Chase (now the Arkle Challenge Trophy) and the Mildmay Chase at Liverpool. (His jockey, Tim Molony, holds the record of most wins in the Champion Hurdle, having won on Hatton's Grace (1951) followed by Sir Ken three times).

The standard for hurdling was raised even higher in the late 1960s with the appearance of Persian War, who became the third triple winner (1968, 1969, 1970). Before his first Champion Hurdle victory, Persian War won the 1967 Triumph Hurdle and the following year's Schweppes Gold Trophy carrying 11st 13lb. He went on to win the 1968 Champion Hurdle to complete an amazing season for a five-year-old. Trained throughout his three Champion Hurdle victories by Colin Davies in Chepstow and ridden by Jimmy Uttley, he won the 1969 race with a courageous performance beating Drumikill, ridden by Barry Brogan, after looking beaten coming into the straight. His third title in 1970 was very emotional, following a season plagued with injuries. He was a remarkable horse in the circumstances having had at least half-a-dozen trainers during his career, brought about by his owner Henry Alper interfering with his training programme. Even after his third Champion Hurdle he was moved again to Arthur Pitt for whom he won the Irish Sweeps Hurdle.

From 1968, Persian War had begun a golden era for hurdlers. Up until 1981 it can be said that every winner was a true champion. Persian War ran in the 1971 race finishing second, beaten four lengths by the new kid on the block, Bula. Trained by Fred Winter, it was his twelfth win over hurdles and still unbeaten. He won again in 1972 by eight lengths but was unable to make it a hat-trick in

1973, when he finished fifth behind Comedy of Errors. He tried to get his revenge later in the Welsh Champion Hurdle, but was beaten into second place again by the new champion before turning his attention to chasing. Few horses make the transition with equal success, but he won a total of 13 chases as well as finishing third in the Gold Cup to Ten Up in 1975.

Comedy of Errors (1973, 1975) was the first Champion Hurdle winner to regain his crown. He was beaten by Fred Winter's Lanzarote in between, but his subsequent results suggest he had just had an off day. Trained by Fred Rimell, he proved to be a very good champion, winning 23 hurdle races, including the Fighting Fifth Hurdle at Newcastle three times, the Irish Sweeps Hurdle at Leopardstown twice and the Scottish Champion Hurdle at Ayr. Not only did he get his revenge on Lanzarote in the 1975 Champion Hurdle, but his jockey Ken White rode a brilliant race after being denied a clear run, demolishing his field by eight lengths. Thirty-eight years later Hurricane Fly became only the second horse to win the Champion Hurdle twice and regain his crown with Ruby Walsh in the saddle on both occasions, in 2011 and 2013.

The 1970s were great years for hurdling in Britain and, just when you thought it could not get any better, enter Night Nurse, Monksfield and Sea Pigeon. For six years from 1976, these three heroes of hurdling each won the Champion Hurdle twice in some of the most pulsating races ever seen at Prestbury Park. Night Nurse (1976, 1977) set the ball rolling, winning his first Champion Hurdle when still a five-year-old. It was a brilliant start to his hurdling career, being unbeaten from eight starts, including the Fighting Fifth Hurdle, the Irish Sweeps Hurdle, the English Champion Hurdle, the Scottish Champion Hurdle and the Welsh Champion Hurdle. Trained by M H (Peter) Easterby, he was ridden in all his races by Paddy Broderick. He made all the running at Cheltenham to beat Birds Nest and Flash Imp, with former champions Comedy of Errors and Lanzarote only fourth and fifth. In the autumn of 1976 Night Nurse had extended his winning sequence to ten and then, astonishingly, suffered a 15-length defeat in the Fighting Fifth to Birds Nest. In the Christmas Hurdle at Kempton he got his revenge on Birds Nest, but failed by a neck to beat Dramatist in a three-way photo finish and, consequently, in the 1977 Champion Hurdle he was allowed to start at 15/2. On that occasion he made most of the running to beat Monksfield, Dramatist, Sea Pigeon and Birds Nest. It was the highest-quality Champion Hurdle, as all of these would have been a worthy winner in a normal year.

In the 1978 Champion Hurdle, Night Nurse's crown was challenged and, having lost some of his speed, he finished third to Monksfield and Sea Pigeon; he then went chasing. His conquerors were to share the next four Champion Hurdles with some breathtaking races. The 1979 race was one of the best finishes ever seen at Cheltenham, with Monksfield and Sea Pigeon engaged in an epic duel from the last flight with victory going to Monksfield, ridden by Dessie Hughes amid scenes of wild hysteria. Both horses gave everything to the line and this must go down as one of the greatest races ever seen at the Festival. In the 1980 Champion Hurdle they met again and although Sea Pigeon was now ten years old he managed to turn the tables, ridden by Jonjo O'Neill, by seven lengths from his great rival – a richly deserved win. Sea Pigeon won again in 1981, this time ridden by John Francome, from Pollardstown and Birds Nest, and so shared (with Hatton's Grace, 1951) the honour of being the race's oldest winner. Over the previous six years the unluckiest horse was Birds Nest, trained by Bob Turnell and ridden by his son Andy. He contested every race from 1976, finishing second once, third once and fifth twice. He was unlucky to be foaled in the wrong year and must be regarded as the best horse never to have won the crown.

The popular, tough mare Dawn Run joined a select band by winning the 1984 Champion Hurdle by three parts of a length from Cima. As mentioned earlier, she went on to make history by winning the Cheltenham Gold Cup in 1986, the first horse to win both. She may be thankful, however, that a mare's allowance of 5lb was introduced before the Champion Hurdle – without which, considering the narrow margin of her victories, she might not have won.

See You Then (1985, 1986, 1987) became the fourth horse to win the Champion Hurdle three times. His trainer, Nicky Henderson, deserves the utmost credit as his horse was plagued with injuries throughout his career. Bred for the flat (by Royal Palace), he was very temperamental and a fall on the road damaging a knee when a four-year-old may have been responsible for him being so unsound. He won the 1985 Champion Hurdle when a five-year-old by seven lengths at 16/1, although his victory was overshadowed by the 4/6 favourite Browne's Gazette whipping round at the start. John Francome was due to partner the horse but he was injured in the previous race, so Steve Smith-Eccles picked up a welcome spare ride, a partnership that continued. It was soon afterwards that his training problems began in earnest. His fragile legs were complicated by an inflamed corn and Henderson was able to get only one run out of him before the 1986 Champion Hurdle, which amazingly he won by seven lengths, beating the 1983 winner Gaye Brief. In 1987 matters got worse and, without a race for almost a year, he ran at Haydock just 11 days before Cheltenham, managing to beat moderate opposition, followed by his third victory in the Champion Hurdle. The following year he pulled up lame in the Kingwell Hurdle at Wincanton and never ran again. The achievements of See You Then were little short of a miracle – what heights could he have reached if he had stayed sound?

Another brilliant training performance was that of Martin Pipe with Make A Stand (1997). Pipe bought him for £8,000 out of a Leicester claimer in August 1995 and somehow improved him to win a Champion Hurdle when still a novice. He started his 1996/97 campaign winning a handicap hurdle at Stratford before steadily climbing the ranks. He won four major races, including the Lanzarote Hurdle at Kempton and the Tote Gold Trophy at Newbury, making the running and displaying quick-fire, accurate hurdling. At Cheltenham he adopted the same tactics, spread-eagling the field by halfway. He won by five lengths, giving Tony McCoy his first win in the race and recording the fastest time for good measure. Martin Pipe had transformed Make A Stand from a mark of 114 to a rating of 165 – an improvement of over three stone.

As the end of the 20th century approached, four horses had entered the history books as triple winners – Hatton's Grace, Sir Ken, Persian War and See You Then – but none of them could make it four. Three of them tried; Hatton's Grace finished fifth to Sir Ken (1952), Sir Ken finished fourth behind Clair Soleil (1955) and Persian War finished second to Bula (1971). In 1998 another star emerged in Istabraq. Trained by Aidan O'Brien in Ireland, he had already won the Royal & Sun Alliance Novices' Hurdle the previous year and continued his winning streak by becoming another Champion Hurdle triple winner (1998, 1999, 2000). He also won the Irish Champion Hurdle at Leopardstown. Ridden in all his races by Charlie Swan, he won 18 hurdles from 20 starts. As 2001 approached he was poised to win his fourth Champion Hurdle but was denied by a cruel stroke of luck – racing was abandoned because of a foot and mouth epidemic. He joined the other champions as the fifth triple winner, but at least he had won at four consecutive Festivals.

Other Races at the Cheltenham Festival

Since 2005 the Festival has been run over four days and the format has changed substantially since the first Festival of two days in 1911, extended to three in 1923. Apart from the Handicaps, every race can be regarded as a championship event. By 2009 there were 12 Grade 1 races (more than Royal Ascot can boast) and even the supporting races are of the highest level.

Since 1911 many races have been added to the Festival, some have ceased and many have had their names changed, some more than once. The Grand Annual and the National Hunt Chase are the oldest races, followed by the Gloucestershire Hurdle (which later ran in two divisions) and the National Hunt Handicap Chase. The Foxhunters Chase was first run in 1912. The Broadway Novices Chase started in 1921 and from 1964 became the Totalisator Champion Novices' Chase, sponsored by the Tote and aimed at future Gold Cup aspirants; in 1974 it became the Sun Alliance Novices' Chase, in 1997 the Royal & SunAlliance Chase and finally, in 2009, the RSA Chase. Gold Cup winners to emerge from the race are Ten Up, Master Smudge, Garrison Savannah, Looks Like Trouble and Denman. The novice chase for two-milers is the Arkle Chase, formerly the Cotswold Chase (first run in 1925), and the target for prospective winners would be the championship race for two-milers, the Queen Mother Champion Chase. Those to be successful in both were Remittance Man, Klairon Davis, Flagship Uberalles, Moscow Flyer, Azertyiop and Voy Por Ustedes.

The Queen Mother Champion Chase is now the third most prestigious race of the Festival. First run in 1959 under the title of the National Hunt Two Mile Champion Chase, it replaced, oddly, the National Hunt Juvenile Chase for four-year-olds, which had been won by Grand National winners Grakle and ESB and Cheltenham Gold Cup winners Patron Saint and Medoc. That race was last run in 1958 and since then chases for four-year-olds have been abolished. It was not until 1980 that the Queen Mother graciously consented for her name to be used (to mark her 80th birthday). The race has produced some thrilling finishes, starting with Barnbrook Again (1990) beating Waterloo Boy by half a length. In 1994 Viking Flagship, Travado and Deep Sensation jumped the last together and, in an unforgettable

The Queen Mother meets Edredon Bleu, winner of the Queen Mother Champion Chase in 2000, with trainer Henrietta Knight on her left.

Flyingbolt (centre) is generally rated the second best National Hunt horse of all time after Arkle. Pictured at Cheltenham in 1965, in one of the best performances of his life he and Pat Taaffe went on to win the Massey-Fergusson Gold Cup.

race, Viking Flagship, ridden by Adrian Maguire and trained by David Nicholson, prevailed by a neck; he returned a year later to defend his title successfully. The popular Edredon Bleu (2000) was another thrilling winner when beating Direct Route by a short head, with both horses breaking the track record. One Man (1998) lifted the Cheltenham roof when at last breaking his course hoodoo, having failed miserably at the Festival three times, including two Gold Cups. Only one horse has won the Queen Mother Champion Chase three times – Badsworth Boy (1983, 1984, 1985) – while a host of horses have won it twice; but since it became the Queen Mother Chase the list contains just Pearlyman (1987, 1988), Barnbrook Again (1989, 1990), Viking Flagship (1994, 1995) Moscow Flyer (2003, 2005) and Master Minded (2008, 2009). The race is always run at a blistering pace and is many people's highlight of the Festival and, while those already mentioned were supreme champions, the greatest ever to win the race was Flyingbolt in 1966, who took it by 15 lengths pulling up (at the shortest price in the history of the race: 1/5). He also came close to winning the Champion Hurdle the next day, finishing third.

The Gloucestershire Hurdle (1911), known since 1975 as the Supreme Novices Hurdle, is the oldest hurdle race still run, and traditionally opens the Festival on the Tuesday.

One of the finest achievements was that of Vincent O'Brien, who won the race ten times in eight years (when there were two divisions) between 1952 and 1959. In three years he won both divisions and his 1954 winner Stroller went on to win the Champion Hurdle. Probably the greatest winner was the ill-fated Golden Cygnet (1978), who may well have won the Champion Hurdle for several seasons. Trained by Edward O'Grady in Ireland, he arrived that year at the Festival unbeaten in four outings over hurdles and started a warm 4/5 favourite. He demolished his rivals, winning by 15 lengths, in what must be regarded as the best-ever display of hurdling at speed by a novice. He followed up by winning again at Fairyhouse before taking on Night Nurse and Sea Pigeon in the Scottish Champion Hurdle at Ayr. He took up the running before the last with the race at his mercy, but fell heavily at the last flight leaving Sea Pigeon to claim victory. He injured his neck so badly he had to be put down three days later. Had he survived, Sea Pigeon may not have won two Champion Hurdles.

The other novice hurdles are the Neptune Investment Management Novices' Hurdle (known as the Ballymore Properties Novices' Hurdle from 2007 to 2009 and the Sun Alliance Hurdle from 1974 to 2006; it was originally the Aldsworth Hurdle), run over two miles, five furlongs; and the Triumph Hurdle for four-year-olds only, which usually opens the card on Gold Cup day. It has been run at Cheltenham only since 1968, having been inherited from Hurst Park (where it was first run in 1939) when that course closed. The Triumph Hurdle will always be a favourite race for champion trainer Martin Pipe, as, in 1981, Baron Blakeney romped home at 66/1 to record his first Festival winner.

Since 2005 the championship race for three-mile hurdlers has been the World Hurdle, formerly the Stayers Hurdle from 1972 and before that the Spa Hurdle, which was transferred from the New Year meeting in 1946. The Queen Mother's only win at the Festival was when her horse Antiar won the Spa Hurdle in 1965.

Two horses have dominated the World Hurdle in recent times – Inglis Drever (2005, 2007, 2008), trained by Howard Johnson, and Big Bucks (2009, 2010, 2011, 2012), trained by Paul Nicholls. (His fourth consecutive World Hurdle equalled Sir Ken's record in 1953 of winning 16 consecutive hurdle races). Both might have struggled to beat Baracouda (2002, 2003) when in his prime. Trained in France by Francois Doumen, he was denied a hat-trick in 2004 by Iris's Gift, trained by Jonjo O'Neill, in a tremendous battle up the Cheltenham hill. He raised the

quality of long-distance hurdlers with a record of 18 wins from 24 starts. Until his defeat by Iris's Gift he had won 14 of his previous 15 races.

The Champion Bumper (originally the Festival Bumper) was first run in 1992. Bumpers, or National Hunt Flat races as they are officially known, were very common in Ireland, but until recently only seen occasionally in Britain. So it came as no surprise that Ireland won eight of the first ten runnings. The first winner was Montelado, trained by Patrick Flynn in Ireland and ridden by Richard Dunwoody, and the best horse to emerge from the race was the 1997 winner Florida Pearl, also from Ireland. The 1999 winner Monsignor not only caused a surprise by winning at 50/1 but created an unusual piece of history. By winning the Supreme Novices Hurdle in 2000 he is the only horse to win two consecutive races at the Festival. (The Bumper was the last race on the final day in 1999 and the Supreme was the opening race of the 2000 Festival).

As mentioned earlier, the format of the races at the Festival has undergone many changes. Since the extension of the meeting to four days new races have appeared in the shape of a Cross Country Chase (modelled on a similar course at Punchestown), the David Nicholson Mares Hurdle, the Racing Post Plate (formerly the Mildmay of Flete Handicap Chase) and the Ryanair Chase, which became a championship race over two miles five furlongs and sadly replaced the Cathcart Cup. Other races that are now defunct include the National Hunt Juvenile Chase (1911–1958), replaced by the Champion Chase; the Coventry Cup Chase (1928–1936), of which the first three winners were the remarkable Dudley, Rathcoole and Blaris, who had already won the first Champion Hurdle; and the Newent Chase (1923–1942), a seller for most of the time which was won in 1937 by Ferrans, a 15-year-old who holds the joint record for the oldest horse to win at the Festival. The Birdlip Selling Hurdle was run only four times (1952–1955) and was the last surviving seller to be run at

the Festival. (It was also the only Festival race to be won by Lester Piggott, when he scored on Mull Sack in 1954 for his father Keith.) The United Hunts Chase (1923–1973) has since been transferred to the Hunter Chase meeting in April. The winner on four occasions was that fine hunter-chaser Baulking Green (1963, 1964, 1965, 1967), but the race was more historically famous for the 1966 winner Snowdra Queen, trained by Jackie Brutton who became the first woman to officially train a winner in Britain. The Birdlip George Duller Hurdle (1958–1973), a three-mile handicap hurdle, was also transferred to the April meeting.

The Irish

The Cheltenham Festival is without question the finest four days of National Hunt racing in the world but one important aspect that makes it really special is the presence of a large proportion of the Irish population. Thousands will make their annual pilgrimage across the Irish Sea to the Cotswolds, bringing with them that passion and enthusiasm to take on the best of the English in their own backyard. It creates a tremendous atmosphere and friendly rivalry that would be sorely missed without them. Over the years they have been known to land a gamble or two and never

A few of the vast contingent of Irish who turn out for the Cheltenham Festival.

a year goes by without them having two or three so-called bankers at the meeting, and most of them oblige. The roar of the crowd as one of these bankers takes up the running between the last two jumps is sometimes deafening. Arkle would have been a good example when winning the first of his three Gold Cups in 1964 at odds of 7/4, and Flyingbolt when winning a division of the Gloucester Hurdle in the same year. Golden Cygnet's win in the Supreme Novices Hurdle in 1978 gave the bookmakers a mighty headache, as did Istabraq in all of his four wins at the Festival and many more too numerous to mention.

Perhaps the two biggest gambles pulled off by the Irish were Staplestown in the 1981 County Handicap Hurdle and Destriero in the 1991 Supreme Novices Hurdle. Staplestown was trained by Edward O'Grady, already one of the most successful Irish trainers at the Festival and responsible for Golden Cygnet. Having won once and placed once in his last 12 outings, he was readily available at 33/1 but so much money piled in for him that he started 11/2 favourite. He somehow showed a remarkable improvement. Destriero was owned by Elizabeth Furlong, whose husband Noel had recently paid £500,000 to Customs and Excise over an alleged VAT fraud. In doing so he had avoided arrest and was allowed into Britain; he attended the Festival with the object of quickly recouping his money with the help of Destriero. The horse had run only twice in the last two years, winning a bumper and a maiden hurdle in pretty moderate company. Destriero won by four lengths at 6/1, beating a future Champion Hurdle winner Granville Again, and Furlong is reputed to have taken £1 million out of the ring. He had also placed huge doubles with the stable's The Illiad in the Champion Hurdle but he was unplaced. The Illiad's price dropped from 12/1 to 11/2 second favourite and had the double come off he would have netted an estimated £10 million.

Cheltenham stages 16 days' racing every year, including the newly-named Open meeting in November.

It was at this meeting that the Mackeson Gold Cup (steeplechase) was first run in 1960 and Massey-Ferguson also sponsored a valuable chase at the December meeting. In 1964 the management of the course was taken over by Racecourse Holdings Trust, one of whose innovations was to build a new course running almost parallel to the existing one. The idea was to use the two courses equally throughout the season to preserve the ground. At the Festival the old course is used for the first two days and the new course for the last two. The Trust instigated many other course changes, one of which was moving the starting position of the Cheltenham Gold Cup, which until 1977 had been behind the grandstand.

Only a very select band of horses have won at four or more Festivals – Golden Miller (five), Sir Ken (four), Arkle (four), Istabraq (four), Big Bucks (four) and Quevega (six) – all of them supreme champions. Let us not forget one more – Willie Wumpkins. He won the Aldsworth Hurdle in 1973 while trained in Ireland by Jeremy Maxwell before moving to Britain where he was bought by Jane Pilkington, a permit-holder from Stow-on-the-Wold. He won the Coral Golden Handicap Hurdle (Final) three times. Ridden by the amateur Mr A J Wilson on each occasion, he won in 1979 by five lengths, beating future Gold Cup winner Little Owl. In 1980 he won by four lengths and in 1981, at the age of 13, he won by 12 lengths. Each victory was achieved in heavy ground and was his only win during each season. His starting prices were 25/1, 10/1 and 13/2 respectively, and following his last success he retired gracefully – a hugely popular horse and a fine training performance, fully entitled to join that illustrious quintet.

Finally, a story from 21 March 1942. Raymond Glendenning was giving a radio commentary from Cheltenham, but the course was covered in a thick fog. To avoid giving weather information to the enemy he decided not to mention it at all and made up his own commentary. That was the best winner of all.

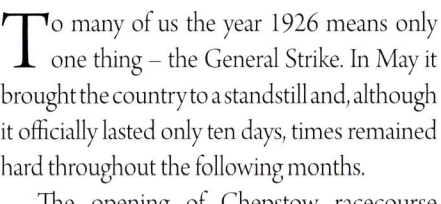

Chepstow has always drawn big crowds: above in 1980 and below in 1926.

To many of us the year 1926 means only one thing – the General Strike. In May it brought the country to a standstill and, although it officially lasted only ten days, times remained hard throughout the following months.

The opening of Chepstow racecourse on 6 August 1926 was, therefore, somewhat overshadowed by national events. The racecourse was built during the preceding year in lovely Piercefield Park and for the opening flat meeting a crowd of over 20,000 attended, most of them unemployed. Many of the population were experiencing financial problems but the opening meeting still managed to attract racegoers from London with the help of the Great Western Railway, which offered a tempting return fare of 13s 6d from Paddington.

National Hunt racing began at Chepstow on 2 March 1927, although this also had a shaky start when the second day's racing had to be abandoned because of bad weather. There had also been a local colliery disaster the previous day, so, altogether, it had been an untimely start. There had been plenty of National Hunt racing in the area from 1839 but all the venues eventually closed. The earliest meeting had been at Cophill Farm, where an Easter Monday Steeplechase was run. This annual fixture continued at a different venue each year, the last to survive being at nearby St Arvans in 1914.

A huge boost to the prosperity of Chepstow proved to be the closure of the Ely course at Cardiff in 1939. Cardiff held centre stage in National Hunt racing in Wales because they had hosted the Welsh Grand National since

1895, but run over two-and-a-half miles. However, a new venue was now needed and after Newport played host for one year in 1948 (before they were declared bankrupt) the Welsh Grand National finally moved to Chepstow in 1949, putting the course firmly on the map.

The race distance was increased to three miles five furlongs and it was first run at the Easter meeting. It was won by Fighting Line, ridden by Dick Francis, who was to win again in 1956 on board the remarkable Crudwell. In order that horses could have the opportunity of running in both the Welsh and Aintree Grand Nationals, in 1976 the race was brought forward to February and after two abandoned races brought forward again in 1979 to the end of December, where it has remained.

The first horse to achieve the Welsh Grand National/Aintree Grand National double was Rag Trade (1976). Others were Corbiere (1982 Welsh, 1983 Aintree, but same season), Earth Summit (1997 Welsh, 1998 Aintree, same season), Bindaree (2003 Welsh, 2002 Aintree) and Silver Birch (2004 Welsh, 2007 Aintree). Three horses have won the Welsh Grand National and the Cheltenham Gold Cup – Cool Ground (1990 Welsh, 1992 Gold Cup), Master Oats (1994, run at Newbury, 1995 Gold Cup) and Burrough Hill Lad (1983, 1984, same season).

Only two horses have won the race twice – Limonali (1959, 1961), ridden on both occasions by David Nicholson, and Bonanza Boy (1988, 1989) who carried 10st 1lb on his first victory but an additional 24lb a year later. His trainer, Martin Pipe, also won in spectacular fashion in 1991 with Carvill's Hill carrying 11st 12lb in heavy ground, beating Party Politics by 20 lengths, but 1992 saw his finest achievement when he saddled the first four home (Run for Free, Riverside Boy, Miinnehoma and Bonanza Boy).

There have been several notable achievements by jockeys on the flat at Chepstow, but none as remarkable as Gordon Richards. Having won on his last mount at Nottingham the previous day, he went to Chepstow on 4

Runners in the 1926 Welsh Grand National.

October 1933 and rode all six winners. The following day he rode the first five winners at Chepstow, making a total of 12 consecutive winners. Astonishingly he failed on his last mount, a hot 1/3 favourite. Frankie Dettori, by riding Line of Thunder to victory at Chepstow on 27 August 1990, became the first teenager to ride one hundred winners in a season since Lester Piggott in 1955. Lester himself returned to the saddle after an absence of five years to ride his wife Susan's horse Nicholas to victory at Chepstow on 16 October 1990. Pat Eddery will also have fond memories of Chepstow as, on 23 October 1990, riding Miranda Jay, he became the first jockey since Gordon Richards in 1952 to complete two hundred winners in a season.

Chepstow received another boost in 1966 with the opening of the Severn Bridge. Already becoming one of the leading racecourses, it was now more accessible – including to the 2003 Welsh Grand National winner Bindaree. Just hours prior to the big race there was a massive traffic jam across the bridge and the surrounding areas, and it was raining heavily. Nigel Twiston-Davies's horsebox transporting Bindaree was stuck on the bridge with the traffic at a standstill. Bindaree was unloaded and led the remaining two miles amid the traffic to the racecourse stables. He still had to run three-and-three-quarter miles and jump 22 fences in bottomless ground, yet he still won. That was some performance, but at least they gave him a lift home.

Chester is the oldest racecourse in the country, opening in 1540 during the reign of Henry VIII and, although there are records of racing elsewhere in the country at the time, Chester is the oldest still held in its original location.

No racecourse in the world has a more historic setting than Chester, known as the 'Roodee'. In Roman times the River Dee washed up to the ancient walls where racegoers stand today, but, as time went by, the Dee steadily silted up, leaving what we see today – a water meadow of 85 acres trapped between the city walls and the river. Chester opened on Shrove Tuesday 1540; a Silver Bell was presented and remained an annual prize for over 50 years. The course, which is just over a mile in circumference, was founded by Henry Gee, the Mayor of Chester until his death in 1545. (It is from Henry Gee that the term 'going to the gee gees' originates.)

Racing moved to St George's Day in 1609 but by the 1640s Chester was embroiled in the Civil War and the 'Roodee' was used as a mustering ground for citizens defending their city, which eventually fell to the Roundheads in 1646. Racing was prohibited until after the Restoration in 1660.

It was not until 1758 that the date of the meeting moved again and this time it became a five-day festival in May. The feature race in those days was the three-mile Chester City Plate and the first horse to capture the hearts of the locals was Statesman, who won the race in three consecutive years from 1765.

The festival has remained in May to this day, but has been reduced to three days' racing of the highest quality. It comprises three classic trials – the Chester Vase over the full Derby distance and first run in 1907, the Cheshire Oaks run over a furlong shorter, and the Dee Stakes over ten and a half furlongs, dating back to 1813. The Chester Vase has been the most successful as a trial, producing Epsom Derby winners Papyrus, Hyperion, Windsor Lad, Henbit and Shergar as well as other classic winners Law

Society and Old Vic. Derby winner Quest for Fame was also a gallant second to Belmez in 1990.

Two other top-class races at the May meeting are the Ormonde Stakes and the Chester Cup. The former is run in honour of the great 1886 Derby winner owned by the Duke of Westminster, and although he never ran at Chester he was bred locally at the Eaton Stud. It was originally a two-year-old race over five furlongs but in 1936 it was open to older horses over one mile five furlongs. 1952 Derby winner Tulyar was successful here en route to Epsom glory.

The most popular race at Chester is the Chester Cup, first run in 1824 although it was called the Tradesmen's Cup until 1893. It is run over two and a quarter miles, which requires the field to pass the winning post three times. The first Cup was won by Doge of Venice, a six-year-old who beat just six opponents in the hands of T Nicholson. In 1829 the race went to Halston, owned by fearless gambler Jack Mytton, who took thousands out of the ring, but five years later his luck ran out when he was found dead in a debtor's prison. The popularity of the race grew and soon the Cup was a heavier betting race than the Derby and was attracting runners from all over the country, inspiring a huge ante-post market.

Alice Hawthorn, a superb racemare who won 52 races in seven seasons, landed a huge gamble when winning the Cup in 1842 carrying only 6st. However in 1844 she was unable to concede 5st 8lb to Red Deer, the first three-year-old to win the Cup. The owner of Red Deer, Lord George Bentinck, is said to have won £100,000. Despite several false starts, the result was never in doubt when he beat Alice Hawthorn by 'about fifty lengths'.

Twenty-eight runners lined up for the Cup in 1853 and it was a controversial one. The 3/1 favourite Trifle, ridden by John Wells for the Wantage gambling trainer Tom Parr, would probably have won but for constant interference during the final circuit. The race went to rank

outsider Goldfinger (who was not unbacked), owned by Dr William Palmer who not only netted £3,000 in stakes but also took £12,000 out of the ring. The validity of the gamble came into question when it was discovered that Dr Palmer was found to have administered illegal medication to his horses, as well as to some of his patients. For example, two years later his filly Nettle, who was purchased with the insurance payment obtained by the murder of his wife, went berserk during the 1855 Oaks and in doing so broke the leg of her jockey Marlow. No one was quite sure who had been got at – the horse or the jockey. Justice seems

Forest Edge ridden by John Egan wins The Stellar Group Handicap Stakes, watched by Manchester United players during the first day of the Boodles May Festival at Chester in 2013.

It would not have seemed right if the nation's most popular horse of the 20th century, Brown Jack, had not appeared on the Chester Cup winners board, and he duly obliged in 1931 (a warm-up for Royal Ascot. no doubt). Another popular horse was Trelawny, who won the Cup in 1960 when trained by Syd Mercer. He was the most lovable, versatile horse and excelled over long distances. Later in his career he won the Ascot Stakes (twice), the Queen Alexandra Stakes (twice), the Goodwood Cup and the Spa Hurdle at Cheltenham. Throughout his distinguished career he was in the care of three other great trainers – Jack Colling, Fred Rimell and George Todd.

The most versatile winner of the Chester Cup was the 'Pride of Yorkshire', Sea Pigeon (1977, 1978). Having started his career with Jeremy Tree, he won his only race as a two-year-old at Ascot and at three was thought good enough to contest the 1973 Derby, finishing seventh behind Morston. He then embarked on a hurdling career, initially with Gordon Richards but from 1976 to the end of his career with Peter Easterby in North Yorkshire. Already a winner of the Scottish Champion Hurdle, he returned to the flat after an absence of three years to win consecutive Cups in the hands of Mark Birch, the latter with the steadier of 9st 7lb. He must be the most versatile horse of the century, for even after Chester he managed to win the Ebor Handicap carrying 10st and, in the twilight of his career, two Champion Hurdles (1980, 1981). A true champion.

Before the 1977 Chester Cup his jockey Mark Birch was so confident that he told all and sundry that if Sea Pigeon was beaten he would show his bare backside in front of Malton Town Hall. Happily for all concerned, it wasn't necessary.

to have been done, however, when Palmer was hanged at Stafford the following year for poisoning a close friend, John Parsons-Cook. (Well, maybe not that close.)

Crowds continued to flock to Chester, and more than 100,000 are estimated to have witnessed the 1886 Cup, won by five-year-old Eastern Emperor, and in 1893 Chester had their first 'gate' meeting, with 84,166 each paying a minimum of one shilling. It was the first year the race was run as the Chester Cup and they saw Dare Devil winning for the second successive year, having won the final running of the Tradesmen's Cup the previous year.

Clonmel lies in South Tipperary at the foot of the Comeragh Mountains in the valley of the beautiful River Suir. Racing was open and free to spectators for over a hundred years at Clonmel but was enclosed in 1913 by Villiers Martin Jackson and became commercially-run Powerstown Park, named after part of the town. The name of the racecourse changed to Clonmel in the late 1970s but today locals still prefer to give its original title.

Powerstown Park was the first racecourse in Ireland to have overnight declared runners, in March 1930. Courses were required to make this change with the installation of the Tote in the country.

The right-handed course undulates through the scenic woodland and has a stiff uphill finish. The most important races here are the Captain Christy Novices Chase, the Seamus Mulvaney Chase and the Tipperary Cup. One of the best-attended winter races is the Clonmel Oil Chase: a notable four-times winner (1997-2000) of this Grade 2 race was the popular Dorans Pride, trained by Michael Hourigan and a favourite with Irish racegoers.

Clonmel racecourse is also used for hare coursing and has been the venue for the Irish National Coursing Championships since 1925.

Hare coursing is a popular sport at Clonmel. Here Smart Ali, the winner of the 88th Irish National Coursing Championship at Clonmel in 2013, turns the hare.

Cork racecourse was formerly Mallow, where it is located, in the County of Cork but some 20 miles from the city. The last meeting under the name of Mallow took place on 5 October 1994, after which a massive redevelopment began, including the building of a new grandstand. The rebuilding took over two-and-a-half years and was opened by the Irish Minister of Agriculture on 17 May 1997 Since then, a new pavilion has been built, and the grandstand has been further revamped.

The origins of steeplechasing are only a few miles north of Mallow at Buttevant where, in 1752, the first steeplechase took place. It all began when Edmund Blake challenged his neighbour Cornelius O'Callaghan to a cross-country race from St John's Church in Buttevant to St Mary's Church in Doneraile, some four-and-a-half miles away, jumping stone walls, ditches and hedges and keeping the steeple of the church in sight (hence steeplechasing) so both riders could see their finishing point.

By 1777, six consecutive days of racing were on offer in the Mallow area. The present course at Mallow opened in 1924 following the demise of Cork Park in 1917, and was formed and instigated under the control of Lieutenant-Colonel F MacCabe, who saw the need for a new racecourse in Ireland's largest county.

Now under its new title of Cork and with all its new facilities it has become one of Ireland's most delightful racecourses. The huge sugar refinery that used to belch out smoke beyond the back straight has been demolished, making the vista even more beautiful.

The Cork Grand National steeplechase of 1869 at Cork Park where the ground was said to be 'wet and sloppy'. From the Illustrated London News Vol LIV.

The Curragh, from the Gaelic 'Cuireach' meaning 'racecourse', has a history stretching back to the 3rd century, when the vast plain on which the racecourse now stands was the site of chariot races. By the 17th century, the Curragh had become the venue for organised horse racing and later the headquarters of the Turf Club, the governing body of Irish racing that had originally been founded in a coffee house in nearby Kildare.

The Turf Club have been organising racing at the Curragh since 1784. Before that, a continuous record of racing there is extant from 1751 and a Royal Plate has been run on the course since at least 1673, when Charles II donated two plates.

The oldest race in the modern Irish Racing Calendar is The Royal Whip, first presented by King George IV in October 1821. Run over four miles, Sligo's four-year-old Langar beat Roller, three years his senior; Roller had his revenge in 1822 when carrying 12st 4lbs, only to see

Langar recover it the following year when they were aged six and nine respectively.

In addition, the Anglesey Stakes, founded in 1829 and run over six furlongs and 63 yards, for two-year-olds, is the oldest race in Ireland run over its original distance.

The Curragh is similar to Newmarket in England, being the headquarters of Irish racing and also a major training centre. Unlike Newmarket, however, it is the home of all five classics and a total of ten Group 1 races – the five classics plus the Tattersalls Gold Cup, the Moyglare Stud Stakes, the National Stakes, the Pretty Polly Stakes and the Phoenix Stakes. (There are only two other Group 1 races in Ireland – both at Leopardstown.) In 2014 it also hosted the President of the UAE Cup, an Arabian Racing Organisation race for purebred Arabian horses.

The Irish Derby was first run in 1866, originally over one-and-three-quarter miles – it was reduced to one-and-a-half miles by 1872. The first running attracted only

A damp day as the runners parade before the 1963 Irish Sweeps Derby.

An exhibition of Vincent O'Brien's career was held at the Curragh in 2009.

three runners and the largest field numbered only 15 until the first running of the Irish Sweeps Derby in 1962. Prize money increased dramatically, attracting runners from Europe, and 24 went to the post that year. Vincent O'Brien's Larkspur tried to become the first horse since Orby (1907) to land the English/Irish Derby double but could finish only fourth behind the French-trained Tambourine.

Since 1962, just 16 horses have completed the English and Irish Derby double – Santa Claus (1964), Nijinsky (1970), Grundy (1975), The Minstrel (1977), Shirley Heights (1978), Troy (1979), Shergar (1981), Shahrastani (1986), Kahyasi (1988), Generous (1991), Commander in Chief (1993), Sinndar (2000), Galileo (2001), High Chaparral (2002), Camelot (2012) and Australia (2014).

The most successful trainer of Irish Derby winners is currently Aidan O'Brien with 11, followed by Vincent O'Brien (no relation) with six and Michael Dawson, Paddy Prendergast and Frank Butters with four each.

Aidan O'Brien's achievement is the most remarkable as his 11 winners – Desert King (1997), Galileo, High Chaparral, Dylan Thomas (2006), Soldier of Fortune

(2007), Frozen Fire (2008), Fame And Glory (2009), Cape Blanco (2010), Treasure Beach (2011), Camelot (2012) and Australia (2014) spanned just 17 years. For good measure, he has also saddled the first three on five occasions and has won Ireland's premier classic in seven consecutive years (2006–2012). In 2008 he became only the second trainer in the history of Irish racing to win all five classics in one season. His winners were Henrythenavigator (2,000 Guineas), Halfway to Heaven (1,000 Guineas), Frozen Fire (Derby), Moonstone (Oaks) and Septimus (St Leger). He followed Jack Rogers, who in 1935 achieved the same record with just two horses – Museum (2,000 Guineas, Derby, St Leger) and the filly Smokeless (1,000 Guineas, Oaks).

Jack Rogers won 11 classics and was champion trainer three times. He had an astonishing year in 1935, starting his clean sweep by saddling the first three in the 2,000 Guineas – Museum, Parisian and Chirgwin – with the first two both starting at 100/1. He followed that with Smokeless in the 1,000 Guineas. In the Derby he had four of the eight runners – 5/4 favourite Smokeless, African Lily, Museum and Parisian. Museum, owned by Sir Victor

Sassoon and ridden by Steve Donoghue, won at 100/8 with Smokeless third. Smokeless then took the Oaks and Museum went on to win the St Leger, easily beating stablemate African Lily, before which he won the Ebor Handicap at York carrying 7st 13lb. Museum was the first horse to win the Irish Triple Crown. Unbeaten Windsor Slipper became the second in 1942 – it is unlikely there will ever be a third, as the St Leger is now open to older horses. Jack Rogers died in 1940. His grandson, Mick Rogers, trained Epsom Derby winners Hard Ridden and Santa Claus.

Legendary trainer Vincent O'Brien's six Irish Derby winners came courtesy of Chamier (1953), Ballymoss (1957), Nijinsky (1970), The Minstrel (1977), El Gran Senor (1984) and Law Society (1985), but one of his finest achievements was in his first season as a public trainer, in 1944. He brought off the Irish Autumn double with two 20/1 shots. Drybob dead-heated in the Irish Cambridgeshire at the Curragh, with stable companion Good Days unplaced. In the Irish Cesarewitch at Phoenix Park a month later, Good Days won by a neck with Drybob fourth to complete a remarkable double for an inexperienced trainer.

There must be something about the name: Aidan O'Brien's son Joseph and daughter Sarah are both successful jockeys, and Gillian O'Brien, niece of Vincent, won both the 1982 and 1983 Irish Cesarewitch with Five Nations – another remarkable double, as Five Nations was off the course for a whole year in between due to an injury.

Right: thirty runners in the 2013 Tote Super Trifecta Irish Cesarewitch head down the back alongside the M7 motorway. In the background is the bell tower of the Curragh Camp, built in 1870 and home to the Irish Defence Forces Training Centre.

DONCASTER

The present course is on Town Moor, which was vested to Doncaster Corporation by King Henry VIII. The first recorded meeting was on 22 July 1728 but it is safe to assume that there were earlier, if not continuous, meetings. This would also apply to Cantley Common, which was adjacent to Town Moor. Possibly the earliest course was at Wheatley Moor, a few miles away, which was shown on a map dated 1595.

Doncaster is steeped in flat racing history and the oldest and final classic of the season, the St Leger in mid–September, is the centrepiece. Founded by Anthony St Leger, the race was first run in 1776. St Leger devised a sweepstake for three-year-olds which, for the first two years, was run at Cantley Common – the race was not

The stands at Doncaster (below) stood for centuries until being demolished in 1968. The 1969 changes were followed in 2007 by a £35m refurbishment which transformed the course, as seen above.

given a name until 1778 when it moved to Town Moor. In those days it was run over two miles and six unnamed fillies contested the inaugural running. The winner was named after the race as Allabaculia and was ridden by J Singleton. It was not until 1813 that the distance was reduced to a mile and three-quarters as it is today.

The St Leger is the final leg of the Triple Crown, following the 2,000 Guineas and the Derby. Only 15 horses have completed the treble, and only 12 at Doncaster since Pommern (1915), Gay Crusader (1917) and Gainsborough (1918) ran their St Legers at Newmarket during the First World War. Of the remainder, West Australian (1853) was the first trained by John Scott, who, during his career, trained the winners of a staggering 16 St Legers and a total of 40 classics, a feat that may never be beaten. West Australian went on to win the Ascot Gold Cup the following year. Other notable Triple Crown winners were the French horse Gladiateur (1865), who went on to win the Ascot Gold Cup by 40 lengths, and Isinglass (1893), who won 11 races from 12 starts which included the following year's Eclipse when he beat the 1894 Derby winner Ladas. Bahram (1935), trained by Frank Butters, retired after winning the St Leger to remain unbeaten in nine starts, while Nijinsky (1970), trained by Vincent O'Brien, was the last horse to win the Triple Crown.

However, the finest horse to win the Triple Crown was Ormonde (1886), who remained unbeaten in 16 races. Trained by John Porter at Kingsclere, he was described as the perfect racehorse and was never extended in any of his races in what was a vintage year. His opponents included The Bard, who had won all of *his* 16 races as a two-year-old, Saraband and Minting, whose trainer Mathew Dawson proclaimed him as the best horse he had ever trained (at the time he had already trained five St Leger winners).

Only nine fillies have won their own Triple Crown (1,000 Guineas, Oaks and St Leger), of which Sceptre (1902) was outstanding, also winning the 2,000 Guineas,

and La Fleche (1892), also trained by John Porter, who only narrowly failed to win the Derby. The best filly to win the Triple Crown was, undoubtedly, Pretty Polly (1904), who won 22 of her 24 races; many people agreed that, had she run in all the classics, she would have won the lot. Meld (1955) and Oh So Sharp (1985) were the most recent winners of the fillies' Triple Crown.

Of those horses that completed only Derby/St Leger doubles, the finest were The Flying Dutchman (1849), Voltigeur (1850), Persimmon (1896) and Diamond Jubilee (1900) – the last two owned by the Prince of Wales, later to become King Edward VII – Coronach (1926), Hyperion (1933), Windsor Lad (1934), Tulyar (1952) and Reference Point (1987). Dunfermline (1977) completed the Oaks/St Leger double by beating hot favourite Alleged, who went on to win the Prix de l'Arc de Triomphe twice. Suffering his only defeat in the St Leger was one of the biggest shocks in the history of the race but in 1981 there was even a bigger one when Shergar – 4/11 favourite, winner of the Derby, Irish Derby and King George VI and Queen Elizabeth Stakes – could finish only fourth behind Cut Above. Some said his defeat was down to a hard season; but over a hundred years ago many horses would run on consecutive days.

A good example of this was in 1795 when Hambletonian won the St Leger and the next day won the Doncaster Cup, which in those days was run over four miles. In 1850 Voltigeur dead-heated in the St Leger with Russborough and, as was the custom, there was a rerun two hours later, won by Voltigeur. Three days later Voltigeur won the Doncaster Cup, beating his great rival The Flying Dutchman. This would be unheard of today.

As mentioned, John Scott's record of training 16 St Leger winners may never be beaten but another trainer who holds a record almost as astonishing is James Croft. From his stables in Middleham, Yorkshire he saddled the first four in the 1822 St Leger. The winner was Theodore,

Pretty Polly, winner of 15 consecutive races including the St Leger, painted by G Paice in 1906.

who started at 200/1, followed by Violet, Professor and Corinthian. What made it more remarkable was that there were 23 runners.

Frank Butters almost equalled this feat in 1932 when saddling the first, second, fourth and fifth. The winner was Firdaussi (20/1) and all four were owned by the Aga Khan.

The Doncaster Cup (first run in 1766) is the oldest race on Town Moor and is run at the St Leger meeting, along with the Park Hill Stakes for fillies (first contested in 1839 and run over the St Leger distance), the May Hill Stakes for two-year-old fillies and the historic Champagne Stakes for two-year-old colts. The Champagne Stakes dates from 1823, when the winning owner had to present six dozen bottles of champagne to the Doncaster Race Club. Nowadays the winning owner *receives* the champagne – for many years from Laurent Perrier, whose sponsorship did so much to maintain the prestige of this famous race. There is a long roll of illustrious winners who went on to classic success such as The Flying Dutchman, La Fleche, Rock Sand, Pretty Polly, Fairway, Mahmoud, Big Game, Grundy, Wollow and Warning, but the most outstanding and remarkable winner was The Tetrarch (1913).

Known as the 'Spotted Wonder' because his grey coat was sprinkled with white blotches , he was unbeaten

that year, winning at Newmarket, Epsom, Royal Ascot, Sandown Park, Goodwood, Derby and finally Doncaster. The Tetrarch never ran again due to a leg injury sustained in training the following spring . Trained by Atty Persse, he reputedly gave 61 lbs to an older horse in a trial and beat him in a canter. The older horse was a seven-year-old called Captain Symons who had won at the Chester May meeting. The Tetrarch was probably the fastest horse ever to race in Britain. Before his first race Atty Persse managed to keep very quiet about his 'wonder horse' and he started at a generous 9/2. (He must have been the bet of the century).

Another prestigious race for two-year-olds is the Racing Post Trophy, run over a mile in late October. It was first run in 1961 under the title of the Timeform Gold Cup, a brainchild of Timeform's founder Phil Bull. In 1965 it became the Observer Gold Cup and in 1976 the William Hill Futurity Stakes. It has been run under its present title since 1989 and throughout its history has been won by some outstanding horses. It has produced Prix de l'Arc de Triomphe winner Vaguely Noble and Derby winners Reference Point, High Chaparral, Motivator, Authorized (run at Newbury) and Camelot. The outstanding Derby winner Shergar was only runner-up to Beldale Flutter in his second race. The inaugural race in 1961 was won by Miralgo. Two horses to finish unplaced that day were Larkspur and Hethersett, who won the following year's Derby and St Leger respectively. The second running was won by the outstanding Irish filly Noblesse, who was the most impressive ten-length winner of the Oaks the following year.

Doncaster has traditionally opened the turf flat season since the closure of Lincoln racecourse in 1964 and thereby inherited the Lincoln Handicap, run over the straight mile. The first winner of the race at Doncaster was Old Tom (1965). Doncaster also hosts the November Handicap following the closure of Manchester in 1963, which had traditionally brought down the curtain on the flat season with the Manchester November Handicap. The first winner at the new venue was Osier in 1964. For the first three years the race was known as the Manchester Ovaltine Handicap.

National Hunt racing began at Doncaster on Cantley Common in 1847, but as flat racing prospered it ceased in 1911 and did not become a regular feature again until after the Second World War. It resumed on 6 December 1946 but has remained in the shadows of flat racing. The main feature of the National Hunt season is the Great Yorkshire Chase, run in January.

A double celebration for Frankie Dettori as he wins the 1995 St Leger on Classic Cliche, his 1,000th winner in England.

Doncaster underwent a complete facelift in 1969 with the building of a new grandstand and repositioning of the paddock immediately in front of the stands. An indoor betting ring was introduced but this proved unpopular; while the facilities were first-class for racegoers, problems developed on the course itself and during the St Leger meeting of 1989 a drain collapsed during the running of the Portland Handicap, causing Madraco, ridden by Paul Cook, to fall. The remainder of the meeting was abandoned and the St Leger was transferred to Ayr the following week. In 2007, a massive £35 million refurbishment took place with the building of a new grandstand, exhibition centre, stables and bloodstock sales ring.

History was made at Doncaster on 26 July 1992 when the first Sunday meeting in Britain took place on Town Moor. On-course betting was declared illegal and the local constabulary were in full attendance, ready to arrest anybody seen striking a bet. The meeting passed without incident. It was not until the Newmarket meeting in May 1995 that the law was changed to allow Sunday betting.

Two jockeys made their own piece of history in the St Leger. Frankie Dettori rode his 1,000th winner in England partnering Classic Cliche 1995, while Pat Eddery rode his 4,000th winner on Silver Patriarch in the 1997 race. Doncaster will be special to them both.

Finally, a story from 1835. Queen of Trumps, owned by Edward Mostyn, became the first filly to win the Oaks and the St Leger. In winning the St Leger she beat the Derby winner Mundig, and the 1,000 Guineas winner and Oaks runner-up Preserve. She won very easily and was obviously an outstanding filly. Three days after the St Leger, she ran in the Scarborough Stakes and started the 1/10 favourite to beat two moderate opponents. With about a furlong to go a bulldog ran on to the course and brought her to her knees, leaving outsider Ainderby to win the race and land a substantial bet for her owner. It was rumoured Ainderby's owner Captain Frank Taylor also owned the bulldog.

DOWNPATRICK

Downpatrick, Co Down, the burial place of St Patrick, became the base of the Down Royal Corporation of Horsebreeders, which was incorporated by Royal Charter by James II in December 1685.

From this date an annual six-day fair took place until 1789 after which the Corporation moved its meeting to the Maze racecourse (known now as Down Royal). The original course at Downpatrick was discontinued in 1867, taken over by the Downe Hunt Club and used as a training ground notably by Willie Rooney, a well known point-to-point trainer.

A new course, situated near the original site, opened in 1870 under the title of the County Down Hunt and is the racecourse that exists today, very sharp and undulating with a steep uphill finish. It was not until after the Second World War in 1945 that the course regained its original title of Downpatrick.

Turbulent times lay ahead, however, and the course was again threatened by closure in 1974. During the Northern Ireland troubles the grandstand was blown-up by the IRA and later funding was withdrawn by the Government. Despite this, Downpatrick has not only survived but prospered, gaining a reputation as the friendliest course in Ireland. The revival followed a broadcast by the Ministry of Agriculture with overwhelming local support, led by local trainers Jeremy and Judy Maxwell and manager Iain Duff. The meeting attracted a huge crowd, not seen at Downpatrick since the Queen Mother's visit in 1962.

The rolling countryside of Downpatrick with its undulating racecourse under the summer sun.

Below: the bell which is rung to tell the jockeys to mount.

It was on the 6 April 1962 that the Queen Mother came to Downpatrick during an official visit to Northern Ireland. She came specially to see her horse Laffy win the Ulster Grand National. In the hands of Willie Robinson, the Peter Cazalet trained Laffy received a tremendous reception from the large crowd, the like of which never seen before or since.

Ann Ferris, a daughter of the aforementioned Willie Rooney, became a pioneer for women in steeplechasing by riding the winner of the Ulster Grand National in 1976 on Mourneview, trained by her father. It coincided that year when she broke her father's record of 23 point-to-point winners in a season. Mrs Ferris added the Irish Grand National to her tally in 1984.

Finally, back to the beginning. Legend has it that the Byerly Turk, one of the foundation stallions of the thoroughbred breed, raced at Downpatrick on his way to the Battle of the Boyne in 1690 where his owner, Captain Robert Byerly, was fighting on the Williamite side. While it is accepted that the Byerly Turk was involved in that battle, no record of any race exists. What a shame.

DOWN ROYAL

Down Royal is often referred to as the Maze racecourse, due to its close proximity to the prison.

It is the second racecourse in Northern Ireland and, like Downpatrick, was established by a Royal Charter granted by James II on 22 December 1685 for the improvement in horse breeding in the County of Down.

Down Royal ran into financial difficulties following the establishment of the Irish Free State in 1922. Not being eligible for prize money grants from the Racing Board, for years their prizes were considerably lower than those available in the Republic. In 1965 even an annual Government Grant of £3,000 and sponsorship of the Ulster Derby was not enough to keep pace with rival races. Inadequate funding from betting, no tote facilities, the troubles in Northern Ireland and, finally, the Adirondack affair in July 1981 threatened the very existence of the racecourse.

Adirondack, a second-string and rank outsider, made the running in the Gate Handicap Hurdle, for which

Tilbury, in the same ownership, was the medium of a massive gamble and started the 6/4 favourite. Hard as he tried, Tilbury failed to peg back his stable companion and could finish only second, to the fury of connections as the bookmakers cheered in delight. During the pandemonium that followed, the winning jockey got separated from the Turf Club official, who was leading him to the scales to weigh in (normal procedure in those days) and failed to weigh in. When the Stewards disqualified Adirondack, awarding the race to Tilbury, the bookmakers stood down in protest, refusing to work for the rest of the day. When the bookmakers gave notice that they would not be working on the second day of the meeting either, Down Royal management decided to abandon the following day's fixture. This incident depressed attendances for several years afterwards and by November 1983 the future for Down Royal looked bleak. Two offers to save the racecourse were received, one from bookmaker Alfie McLean and the other from Kelso Stewart, well-known as the owner of French Tan, runner-up in the 1970 Cheltenham Gold Cup. The latter's proposal was the one accepted, Stewart bought the course for £275,000 and leased it back to the Race Company.

The racecourse is as popular as ever, now that it stages the Ulster Derby and Ulster Oaks. National Hunt racing is now served by the valuable JNwine.com Champion

Chase (the James Nicholson Wine Merchant Champion Chase), first run in 1999 and won by Florida Pearl. The following year, Cheltenham Gold Cup winner Looks Like Trouble won, beating Florida Pearl and Dorans Pride. With the race now firmly established, it invariably draws a top-class field.

Right: enthusiastic crowds gather at Down Royal in the 1930s.

Below: Runners approach a fence, with the beautiful County Down countyside in the background.

DUNDALK

Dundalk is in County Louth, close to the border with Northern Ireland. The racecourse is half a mile north of the town at Dowdallshill, at the foot of the Cooley Mountains and beside Carlingford Lough.

History was made at Dundalk in 2007 when it became the first all-weather course to be opened in Ireland. The project, costing €35 million, culminated in a grand opening on Sunday 26 August by the Irish Minister for Foreign Affairs, Dermot Ahern, in front of a sell-out crowd of 7,000. The first race on the new surface was won by Johnny Murtagh, riding Miss Victoria for trainer Mick Halford.

The new Dundalk Stadium, which includes a greyhound track in the centre, replaced the old turf course that had been used for both flat and jumps, which ceased in 2002. Dundalk has now become only the third racecourse in Ireland to stage flat racing only (the others are The Curragh and Laytown).

Racing began in Dundalk at Haggardstown and Blackrock Strand in the early 1800s. The present site at Dowdallshill was used haphazardly and run by

The opening of the new state-of-the-art stadium in 2007, complete with all-weather horseracing and greyhound tracks (above), and the old stands (below).

soldiers on a point-to-point scale but, thanks to 19 local businessmen, each subscribing £25 (around £2,500 today), Dowdallshill was officially opened on 28 May 1889 and run on a businesslike footing, with the building of a new grandstand and all the up-to-date features of a modern racecourse of the time. To ensure the opening meeting attracted only the desired clientele, the charge for admission that day was a staggering ten shillings (£50 today), with an extra five shillings to get into the enclosure.

Incidentally, among the 19 shareholders from the town were Patterson, draper; Tempest, printer; T Callan Macardle, brewer; H F McCann, the original baker; H C Backhouse, town grocer; Thomas Williamson, hardware merchant; and J P Murphy, solicitor. Dundalk owes them all.

The all-weather course means that even heavy snow is no deterrent as Ellusive Ridge and Pat Smullen win the Group Bookings race in December 2010.

UNDER IRISH NATIONAL HUNT STEEPLECHASE RULES AND RULES OF RACING.

Dundalk Steeplechases and Flat Races,

Tuesday, 28th May, 1889,

OVER THE DOWDALLSHILL COURSE, HALF-A-MILE FROM DUNDALK.

Arranged and laid down under the supervision of Mr. R. MᶜK. Waters. All Fly Fences, and entirely under grass.

STEWARDS:

H. C. BACKHOUSE,	VINCENT S. CARROLL	M. C. MOYNAGH,
SAMUEL BRADFORD, J.P.	JAMES CONNOLLY,	JAMES MURPHY, J.P.
R. L. BROWN, J.P.	M. P. LYNCH, J.P.	HENRY O'CONNELL,
THOMAS J. BYRNE,	T. CALLAN MACARDLE,	JOHN D. O'NEILL,
THOMAS CALLAN,	CHARLES MacMAHON,	WM. M. PATTERSON, J.P.
PAUL V. CAROLAN.	H. F. MᶜCANN,	THOMAS WILLIAMSON, Jun.

Hon. Treasurers :
W. M. PATTESON, HENRY O'CONNELL, T. CALLAN MACARDLE, DUNDALK.

Hon. Secretary :
THOMAS J. BYRNE, ROIMANBA, DUNDALK.

Judge, Handicapper and Clerk of the Scales :
MR. T. BRINDLEY, DUBLIN.

Manager, Starter, and Clerk of the Course :
MR. R. MᶜK. WATERS, KILPATRICK, MONASTEREVAN.

CLOSING OF PLATES

All Plates close with Mr. R. MᶜK. WATERS, Kilpatrick, Monasterevan ; or Mr. T. BRINDLEY, 14, Upper Merrion Street, Dublin.
DUNDALK STEEPLECHASE PLATE–1st entry, 1 sov. on SATURDAY, 4th May ; 2nd entry, 2 sovs. on SATURDAY, 18th May.
GREAT NORTHERN HANDICAP, STEWARDS' PLATE, STAND PLATE, DUNDALK MILITARY PLATE, and FARMERS' PLATE, close on SATURDAY, 18th May.

RAILWAY ARRANGEMENTS.

Arrangements have been made with the Great Northern Railway Company to run Special and Ordinary Trains at Reduced Fares.
Horses carried back free at Owner's risk by the Great Northern Railway Company.

EPSOM

Known formally as Epsom Downs Racecourse, Epsom is famous all over the world because of one race – the Epsom Derby, first run in 1780. Racing on the downs at Epsom had begun much earlier, however, with the first recorded meeting on 7 March 1661 attended by King Charles II, a very enthusiastic racing supporter.

The Derby

The Derby was named in rather a bizarre way. Sir Charles Bunbury and the 12th Earl of Derby both felt that a new race should be run for three-year-old colts to accompany the Oaks, a race for three-year-old fillies which had its first running the previous year in 1779. They tossed a coin for the name; Lord Derby won and the greatest flat race in the world was born. The first Derby was run on Thursday 4 May 1780, and there was some consolation for Sir Charles Bunbury as his colt Diomed won – with a prize of 1,125 guineas. It was not until 1787 that Lord Derby himself won the race, with Sir Peter Teazle.

The first four Derbys were run over a mile and started out of sight in a position behind the present grandstand. In 1784 it was run for the first time over a mile-and-a-half but the start was beyond the present one, in the village of Langley Vale. In 1848 a third start was given to the Derby but this time the first few furlongs were too steep, so a fourth start was chosen; this is the existing one and has been used since 1872. Another modification to the Derby course has been the famous Tattenham Corner which leads into the four furlong straight – this used to be much sharper before it was altered in 1915.

The Derby and Oaks grew in popularity, largely because there were no qualifying heats, which had been the pattern for early horse racing. The Derby was nearly always run on a Thursday until 1837, after which Wednesday became the traditional day (apart from wartime substitutes and the 1953 Coronation Derby) until 1994. Since 1995 it has been run on a Saturday, despite the opposition of many ardent racegoers.

Some memorable winners

There have been many brilliant winners of the Derby and comparing different generations is always difficult. Races are run at a faster pace today than in the 18th and 19th centuries, when recorded times would suggest that they only cantered for the first half mile. The following, in chronological order, would be among the best.

John Bull (1792). The first Derby winner ridden by Frank Buckle, who regarded him as the best. Buckle rode 27 classic winners, including five Derbys.

Eleanor (1801). Second winner for owner Sir Charles Bunbury. She was the first filly to win the Derby; her trainer, Cox, died two days before the race but managed to let everyone know 'she's a hell of a mare'. She raced until she was seven and won 26 times in her career, more than any other Derby winner.

Priam (1830). Sired by Derby winner Emilius (1823) and trained at Newmarket by William Chifney, he was undoubtedly the best winner during the first 50 years of the race. (He walked from Newmarket to Epsom, setting off 12 days before the race with four companions. Overnight stops were made at 'The Cock' at Epping and the stables at Sloane Street, London, before arriving at Mickleham Downs, so he had nine clear days to complete his preparation for the race.)

Cotherstone (1843). Third winner trained by John Scott following Mundig (1835) and Attila (1842). He also won the 2,000 Guineas but was beaten in the St Leger by a head, so he was nearly the first Triple Crown winner.

The Flying Dutchman (1849). Won 14 races from 15 starts including the Ascot Gold Cup. His only defeat was by Voltigeur in the Doncaster Cup. He gained revenge on Voltigeur in a match at York in 1851.

Sir Joseph Hawley, though dubbed the 'lucky baronet' was a cold and misanthropic character. He was one of the most successful racehorse owners of the 19th century, winning four Derbys.

Voltigeur (1850). Won his only race as a two-year-old in the Richmond Stakes at Goodwood and did not run again until the Derby. He won the Derby easily at odds of 16/1. He died in 1854 when he was badly kicked by a mare.

Teddington (1851). Owned by Sir Joseph Hawley, who also owned Derby winners Beadsman (1858), Musjid (1859) and Blue Gown (1868). He won the Derby in a canter and later won both the Ascot and Doncaster Cups. At stud, he sired Grand National winners Emblem (1863) and Emblematic (1864).

West Australian (1853). The first winner of the Triple Crown. Beaten only once on his debut as a two-year-old in the Criterion Stakes at Newmarket but turned the tables on his conqueror, Speed the Plough, later in the week. Won the 2,000 Guineas by only half a length, and the Derby by only a neck, although described as 'easy'. His St Leger success was a canter, despite his jockey Frank Butler receiving a bribe to 'stop' him. As a four-year-old he won the Ascot Gold Cup. His trainer John Scott was responsible for five Derby winners and hailed West Australian as the best horse he ever trained.

Thormanby (1860). The first of six winners trained by Mathew Dawson. His dam was Alice Hawthorn, who won

an incredible 52 times. Thormanby won nine times as a two-year-old to keep up the family tradition. In the Derby he beat a tough opponent in The Wizard, trained by John Scott. He also won the Ascot Gold Cup the following year.

Gladiateur (1865). Bred in France and owned by Count Frédéric de Lagrange, whose father was one of Napoleon's generals. He is the only horse to have won the Grand Prix de Paris as well as the English Triple Crown. For this fine achievement he earned the nickname of 'The Avenger of Waterloo' and a full-size statue of him still commands the entrance to Longchamp. He was dogged with lameness, yet still managed to win the Derby very easily. His greatest performance came in the 1866 Ascot Gold Cup. His leg was worse than ever and his jockey Harry Grimshaw was told to nurse him for the first mile. At Swinley Bottom he was 300 yards behind the leader but still won by 40 lengths.

Cremorne (1872. The first Derby to be run on the present course). He gained revenge on Prince Charlie, who had beaten him in the 2,000 Guineas. He won 20 times from 26 starts including nine as a two-year-old. He later won the Grand Prix de Paris and a strong Ascot Gold Cup by eight lengths as a four-year-old.

Galopin (1875). A fast two-year-old, winning at Epsom and at Royal Ascot (twice) and beaten only narrowly in the Middle Park Stakes. He was a very versatile horse because, after he won the Derby, he reverted to sprinting. He was beaten only once from 11 starts. His owner, Prince Batthyány, suffered with a weak heart, so he retired Galopin before he was four as he feared any more excitement could prove fatal. At stud he sired the great St Simon and Derby winner Donovan (1889).

Ormonde (1886). Sired by Derby winner Bend Or (1880), he was owned by the 1st Duke of Westminster and trained by John Porter. He remained unbeaten in 16 races including the Triple Crown in what was a vintage year. He had won the 2,000 Guineas in a canter beating a high-class field including Minting, who his trainer Mathew Dawson had rated unbeatable. In the Derby, Ormonde beat The Bard, who had won all his 16 races as a two-year-old and himself would have won nine Derbys out of ten. Ormonde went to Royal Ascot and won the St James's Palace Stakes and Hardwicke Stakes on successive days. He was regarded as the outstanding horse of the 19th century.

Donovan (1889). An exceptional horse who won 11 times as a two-year-old, including the Brocklesby Stakes at Lincoln in the first week of the season, the July Stakes, the Ham Stakes at Goodwood, and the Middle Park and Dewhurst at Newmarket. He was odds-on for the 2,000 Guineas but jockey Fred Barrett dropped his hands and was beaten a head. He won the Derby comfortably, followed by the St Leger. He broke down when a four-year-old but amassed a career total of 18 wins from 21 starts. Killed in 1905 when he ran into a tree.

Isinglass (1893). Beaten only once in four seasons including the Triple Crown. He won £57,455 in prize money, a colossal amount at the time (2010 equivalent £5 million), which was surpassed only by Tulyar nearly 60 years later. The spring of 1893 was exceptionally dry and the ground, for most of his races, was very hard. Despite hating the ground, Isinglass won, but his action was like a cat on hot bricks! In 1894 the weather relented and he won the Eclipse Stakes in a canter on easier ground, beating that year's Derby winner, Ladas.

Persimmon (1896). The first of the Prince of Wales's three Derby winners and by far the best. Sired by the great St Simon, his trainer Richard Marsh introduced him to the racecourse at Royal Ascot where he duly won the Coventry Stakes. He was so impressive that the future King realised he had a live Derby horse for the following year, which was confirmed when he won the Richmond Stakes. He developed a cough and failed in the Middle Park, and at three he was slow coming to hand. Only weeks before the race did he begin to sparkle

and, amongst jubilant scenes, he won the Derby by a neck beating St Frusquin. As a four-year-old he reached his peak and remains the last Epsom Derby winner to also win the Ascot Gold Cup. He followed that by winning the Eclipse (half the distance) and was once described by the Hon George Lambton as the perfect racehorse. At stud he sired the great filly Sceptre.

Spearmint (1906). Developed a fever as a yearling. He was a moderate two-year-old and ran only in the Derby when his stable companion, Flair, broke down. He worked well with stable companion Pretty Polly and was backed for the Derby from 20/1 to 6/1, winning easily. His jockey Danny Maher rated him second to Bayardo.

Hyperion (1933). Sired by wartime Derby winner Gainsborough (1918) and owned by the 17th Earl of Derby. Very popular winner because of his size (one of the smallest Derby winners standing only 15 hands). He

was beaten four times in his career, but was unbeaten as a three-year-old, winning the Derby and St Leger, both impressively. Trained at Newmarket by the Hon George Lambton, who was too ill to travel to Epsom to see him win, his owner moved him to a new trainer, Colledge Leader, as a four-year-old but he failed to win either of his races, including the Ascot Gold Cup. At stud he became the most influential sire of the century, being champion six times and the sire of 11 classic winners and numerous successful broodmares.

Windsor Lad (1934). Regarded a lucky winner of the Derby, with hot favourite Colombo shut in on the rails, but subsequent results prove otherwise. Only an average two-year-old, he improved physically as a three-year-old and was beaten only once more, earning the reputation of being one of the outstanding middle-distance colts between the wars. Trained by Marcus Marsh, he was

THE 200th DERBY STAKES

EPSOM
WEDNESDAY 6th JUNE 1979
Official Programme 30p

THE DERBY STAKES

Today sees the 200th running of The Derby –
the most famous race in the British Calendar,
hose name is used throughout the world to symbolise
lmost every country's supreme test of the racehorse.

Inaugurated in 1780 and named after
the 12th Earl of Derby,
the race has been run annually without a break.

To choose one horse for today's racecard frontispiece
from the roll of Derby winners is an invidious task.

How does one compare, for instance,
the French champions Gladiateur (1865) and
Sea Bird II (1965) or
the Aga Khan's Bahram (1935; who F. Butters
rated the best horse he ever trained) and
Mahmoud (1936; who still holds the Derby
course record of 2 min 33.8 secs) or
Nijinsky, or ....?

We have selected Hyperion (1933) for three reasons:
he raced in the colours of Lord Derby;
he was subsequently six times leading sire of winners,
and his sons have been champion sire in England,
United States, Australia, New Zealand, South Africa,
Argentina, Belgium and Sweden:
and his portrait was described by Sir Alfred Munnings
as "my one and only good painting of a horse".

Hyperion, winner in 1933, being led in by his owner Lord Derby (below). In 1979 his picture (by Munnings) appears on the official programme.

the first Derby winner for jockey Charlie Smirke (who was making a comeback after a five–year absence for allegedly stopping an odds-on favourite at Gatwick). After the Derby his only defeat was in the Eclipse (when he got shut in) but he then went on to win the St Leger, the Coronation Cup and the Eclipse Stakes in 1935.

Bahram (1935). Bred and owned by HH the Aga Khan III, he was only the second Triple Crown winner to remain unbeaten. Unlike his predecessor, Ormonde, he had only nine starts and never raced at four, retiring after an easy win in the St Leger. Trained at Newmarket by Frank Butters, Bahram made a winning debut in the National Breeders Produce Stakes at Sandown, beating by a neck his stable companion Theft, who was unfortunate to occupy the same position in the 2,000 Guineas as well as fourth in the Derby.

Tulyar (1952). The last of five Derby winners owned by the Aga Khan following Blenheim (1930), Bahram, Mahmoud (1936) and My Love (1948). Showed only moderate form as a two-year-old, winning just two nurseries at Haydock and Birmingham. As a three-year-old he improved beyond all recognition and was never beaten, winning the Henry VIII Stakes at Hurst Park, the Ormonde Stakes at Chester, the Lingfield Derby Trial, the Derby (beating a young Lester Piggott on Gay Time), the Eclipse Stakes, the King George VI and Queen Elizabeth Stakes and the St Leger. He had amassed winnings of over £76,000, thereby beating the record set by Isinglass (see above). He never raced at four and was sold to the Irish National Stud.

Sea Bird II (1965). Probably the finest winner of the 20th century. Trained in France by Etienne Pollet, he suffered his only defeat as a two-year-old behind his stable companion Grey Dawn, after winning his first two races. As a three-year-old he was never extended, winning the Prix Greffulhe and the Prix Lupin before an effortless victory at Epsom, although the opposition that day was not strong. His scintillating win later in the year in the Prix de l'Arc de Triomphe, beating a high-class field by six lengths, stamped him as the best horse of the century. He never achieved those dizzy heights as a stallion – with two exceptions, the filly Allez France who also won 'The Arc' (1974) and the Champion Hurdle winner Sea Pigeon (whose early career included a run in the 1973 Derby, where he finished seventh to Morston).

Sir Ivor (1968). Bred in the USA, he was sent to Ireland to be trained by Vincent O'Brien and became his second Derby winner. Winner of three of his four races as a two-year-old, including the Grand Critérium at Longchamp, he was winter favourite for the Derby. As a three-year-old he won the 2,000 Guineas on his seasonal debut but was not certain to stay the Derby trip. Lester Piggott gave him a masterful ride at Epsom, delaying his challenge until the last moment and showing an electrifying burst of speed to eventually beat Connaught by one and a half lengths. He was beaten in the Eclipse and the Irish Derby before winning the Champion Stakes and, finally, the Washington DC International in his native America.

Nijinsky (1970). He was the last horse to win the Triple Crown and the first since Bahram. He also recorded the fastest time for 34 years. A big, strong colt, he won all of his five starts as a two-year-old, ending with an easy victory in the Dewhurst. At three he landed the 2,000 easily and come Derby day he was still unbeaten. Among his rivals was the French colt Gyr, whose trainer Etienne Pollet had postponed his retirement to train, and who was considered unbeatable. Nijinsky beat him comfortably by two and a half lengths. (Gyr franked the form later by winning the Grand Prix de St Cloud). Nijinsky went on to win the Irish Derby and the King George VI and Queen Elizabeth Stakes, but was far from impressive winning the St Leger. It transpired he had contracted ringworm, which was held responsible for interrupting his unbeaten record in his final two races, the Prix de l'Arc de Triomphe and the Champion Stakes.

Mill Reef (1971). He was the third brilliant winner of the Derby in the space of four years. Owned by Paul Mellon and trained by Ian Balding, he was beaten only once as a two-year-old from six starts (beaten a short head by My Swallow in France). Among his victories was a scintillating performance, winning the Gimcrack Stakes at York in heavy ground by ten lengths. In the 2,000 Guineas he finished second in that unforgettable classic behind Brigadier Gerard with My Swallow third, after which Mill Reef was never beaten again. He won the Derby comfortably but his finest hours followed, with wins in the Eclipse Stakes, where he beat the crack French four-year-old Caro, and the King George VI and Queen Elizabeth Stakes at Ascot, which he won easily by six lengths. He finally won the Prix de l'Arc de Triomphe in a blaze of glory. His career as a stallion looked threatened when he shattered his near fore on the gallops but, by a miracle, veterinary surgeons saved his life and a career at stud. Two of his sons were the beneficiaries of equine science when Shirley Heights (1978) and Reference Point (1987) both won the Epsom Derby.

Walter Swinburn, aged only 19, takes Shergar past the post to win the 1981 Derby by ten lengths – the biggest margin in the history of the race.

Troy (1979). Winner of the 200th running of the Derby. Won twice as a two-year-old but his best performance was finishing second behind Ela-Mana-Mou in the Royal Lodge Stakes at Ascot. At three he improved dramatically, winning his first six races for his trainer Dick Hern and jockey Willie Carson. The season began with a win in the Sandown Classic Trial, followed by the Predominate Stakes at Goodwood and then the Derby where, after looking hopelessly shut in on the rails, he produced an astonishing burst of speed to win, going away by seven lengths. He then won the Irish Derby, the King George VI and Queen Elizabeth Stakes and the Benson and Hedges Gold Cup at York. In his final race he showed signs of a hard season, finishing only third in the Prix de l'Arc de Triomphe.

Shergar (1981). Ran only twice as a two-year-old and, as a late developer, did not make his racecourse debut until September, winning his maiden at Newbury. His trainer, Michael Stoute, took the unusual step of pitching him in the Group 1 William Hill Futurity Stakes next, so he must have held him in high regard. He finished a respectable second to Beldale Flutter. At three, he made exceptional progress and made his seasonal reappearance, winning the Guardian Classic Trial at Sandown by ten lengths, followed ten days later by winning the Chester Vase by 12 lengths. There was a massive gamble on him for the Derby and he went to the post odds-on at 10/11, having been 33/1 in the spring. His winning margin was ten lengths and is the longest in the history of the race. He next won the Irish Sweeps Derby, followed by the King George VI and Queen Elizabeth Stakes, both effortlessly, but he ran disappointingly in the St Leger, finishing only fourth, after which he was retired to stud.

What happened next was more sensational than his whole career. He was mysteriously kidnapped from the Ballymany Stud in County Kildare and was never found again. He had been syndicated at stud for £10 million, but the ransom demands were never met by the syndicate.

His kidnappers (presumed to be the IRA) were left with a stallion that would have inevitably died in their hands.

Lammtarra (1995). The first Saturday Derby since the 'Coronation' Derby (1953) was an astonishing one. Lammtarra was the first Derby winner since Grand Parade (1919) to win on his debut as a three-year-old. It was only his second race in public, having won the Washington Singer Stakes at Newbury as a two-year-old the previous August, when trained by Alex Scott (who was shot dead at his Glebe House Stud at Newmarket two months later). Trained now by Saeed bin Suroor, he followed his Derby by winning the King George VI and Queen Elizabeth Stakes and the Prix de l'Arc de Triomphe. He retired unbeaten in four races.

Sea The Stars (2009). A magnificent Derby winner, superbly bred by Cape Cross out of an Arc winner, Urban Sea. Trained by John Oxx in Ireland, he was beaten only once – on his debut as a two-year-old at the Curragh in 2008. He then won a maiden at Leopardstown, followed by the Beresford Stakes at the Curragh. At three he went straight for the 2,000 Guineas, which he won impressively, then beat the top-class Fame and Glory in the Derby. He went from strength to strength, winning the Eclipse at Sandown, the Juddmonte at York, the Irish Champion Stakes at Leopardstown and finally the Prix de l'Arc de Triomphe. His jockey, Mick Kinane, was due to retire at the end of 2008 but delayed it by a year – you can see why.

Only six fillies have triumphed in the Derby – Eleanor (1801), Blink Bonny (1857), Shotover (1882), Signorinetta (1908), Tagalie (1912) and Fifinella (1916, although her victory was a wartime substitute Derby at Newmarket). It is quite remarkable that four of these also won the Oaks (48 hours later) – Eleanor, Blink Bonny, Signorinetta and Fifinella. It would be unheard of these days for fillies to contest both races and, even with a 5lb allowance, very few fillies now line up for the Derby.

Controversy

In complete contrast, there have been some scandalous Derbys, many of them due to the fact that in the early days jockeys were allowed to bet. The most scandalous of all was St Giles (1832), who had shown only moderate form yet started the race as 3/1 favourite. He was jointly owned by John Gully, who had just served time in prison, and Robert Ridsdale, well known for corrupting various members of the racing fraternity. They both seized upon the opportunity of bribing at least 18 jockeys of the 22 runners to make sure of St Giles's victory. He duly won and it was almost certain he was a four-year-old. It was alleged that they took £100,000 out of the ring, which would equate to about £7.5 million these days.

His jockey (or in this case partner in crime) was William 'Bill' Scott, who was not a stranger to the odd scandal or two himself. He was renowned for being a heavy gambler and would think nothing of having huge sums on himself. In 1840 he backed his mount Launcelot heavily to win the Derby, but found to his dismay that he was losing the battle up the Epsom straight to a young jockey, William MacDonald, riding the eventual winner Little Wonder. He yelled to his fellow jockey, 'A thousand pounds for a pull.' MacDonald replied, 'Too late, Mr Scott, too late!'

Again, in 1846, William Scott should have won a fortune but started celebrating too early. During the morning of the Derby he was so drunk on brandy that he was in no state to sit on a horse, let alone ride it. He was riding Sir Tatton Sykes, already a winner of the 2,000 Guineas which he owned himself. After several rows with the starter he was left 60 yards adrift and was eventually only beaten a neck by Pyrrhus the First after swerving across the course. He managed to keep sober for the St Leger, which he duly won, so Sir Tatton Sykes was another horse that should have won the Triple Crown.

Bloomsbury (1839) was another suspicious Derby winner. He was originally owned by Robert Ridsdale (see above), but he was forced to sell all his horses to pay his debts after a gamble that went astray. The new owner was his brother William Ridsdale, another villain, who also trained the horse. The race was run in a severe snowstorm and Bloomsbury won easily at odds of 25/1. There were objections from the owners of the placed horses on the grounds that there was a discrepancy in the winner's breeding, meaning that Bloomsbury was not who he was declared to be. The objection was overruled but it is fair to say Bloomsbury was probably a four-year-old. The Ridsdales had struck again.

The 3rd Earl of Egremont, one of the most respected gentlemen in racing, was also unwittingly part of a plot. He holds the record for having owned five Derby winners and bred another. He owned Assassin (1782), Hannibal (1804), Cardinal Beaufort (1805), Election (1807) and Lap-Dog (1826) and he bred Spaniel (1831). After Lap-Dog his trainer, R 'Bird' Stephenson, was on his deathbed and had requested Lord Egremont to visit him, upon which he whispered in his ear, 'My Lord, I have to tell you now that at least two of your Derby winners were four-year olds,' but declined to say which ones. It transpired that on Lord Egremont's stud at Petworth some two-year-olds were put in the paddock with the yearlings and not even the staff realised.

The 1844 Derby was another controversial race, when a horse falsely described as Running Rein came in first but was later disqualified, having proved to be a four-year-old called Maccabeus. A six-year-old called Leander also ran in the race, but was ironically brought down by Running Rein and had to be put down.

It was also alleged that jockey Sam Rogers had blatantly stopped his mount Ratan from winning – Ratan happened to be owned by a notorious gambler, William Crockford, who had presumably laid against his own horse to win a tidy sum. The race was awarded to the second horse, Orlando.

There have been just two dead heats in the Derby and, until 1930, the dead heaters would be required to race again in a run-off later in the afternoon. In 1828 The Colonel, 7/2 favourite, and Cadland (4/1) dead-heated and Cadland won the run-off by half a length; but, in 1884, when St Gatien and Harvester dead-heated, the owners agreed to split the stake. There has not been a dead heat since.

The most dramatic Derby was in 1913, when Suffragette Emily Davison threw herself in front of King George V's horse Anmer at Tattenham Corner and later died of her injuries. Early theories suggest it was a suicide attempt to gain recognition for the Suffragette movement and equal rights for women, but more recent research has discovered

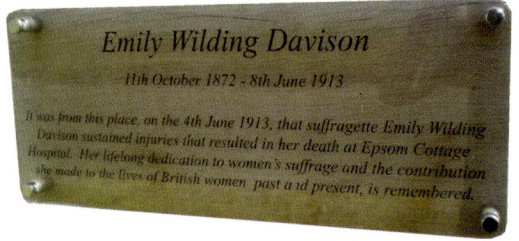

Below left: Suffragette Emily Davison lies on the ground at Tattenham Corner. Whether or not she meant to bring the horse down, the King's jockey Herbert Jones was also injured, though not seriously.

that the poor woman was trying to attach a scarf or a rosette to the bridle of the King's horse. This would have been impossible at racing speed and she was inevitably knocked down. It also transpired that she had a return train ticket to London and was due to attend a Suffragette meeting later that evening, so her suicide – if suicide it was – could not have been premeditated.

However, more drama was to follow when the first horse past the post, the favourite Craganour, was disqualified in what was described as a very rough race and the 100/1 chance Aboyeur awarded the race. Still more controversy was discovered later, when the horse that finished third, Day Comet, was overlooked by the judge and assigned no official place. The placings were never corrected and the original fourth, Louvois, was incorrectly placed second.

Leading Jockeys and Trainers

Lester Piggott has been the most successfully jockey, with nine wins. He rode his first winner at the age of 18 – Never Say Die (1954), his fourth ride in the race. He rode two winners for Noel Murless, Crepello (1957) and St Paddy (1960), four for Vincent O'Brien, Sir Ivor (1968), Nijinsky (1970), Roberto (1972) and The Minstrel (1977), and also the French-trained Empery (1976). His ninth and final winner was Teenoso (1983) for Geoff Wragg. One record Lester could not equal was that of Steve Donoghue,

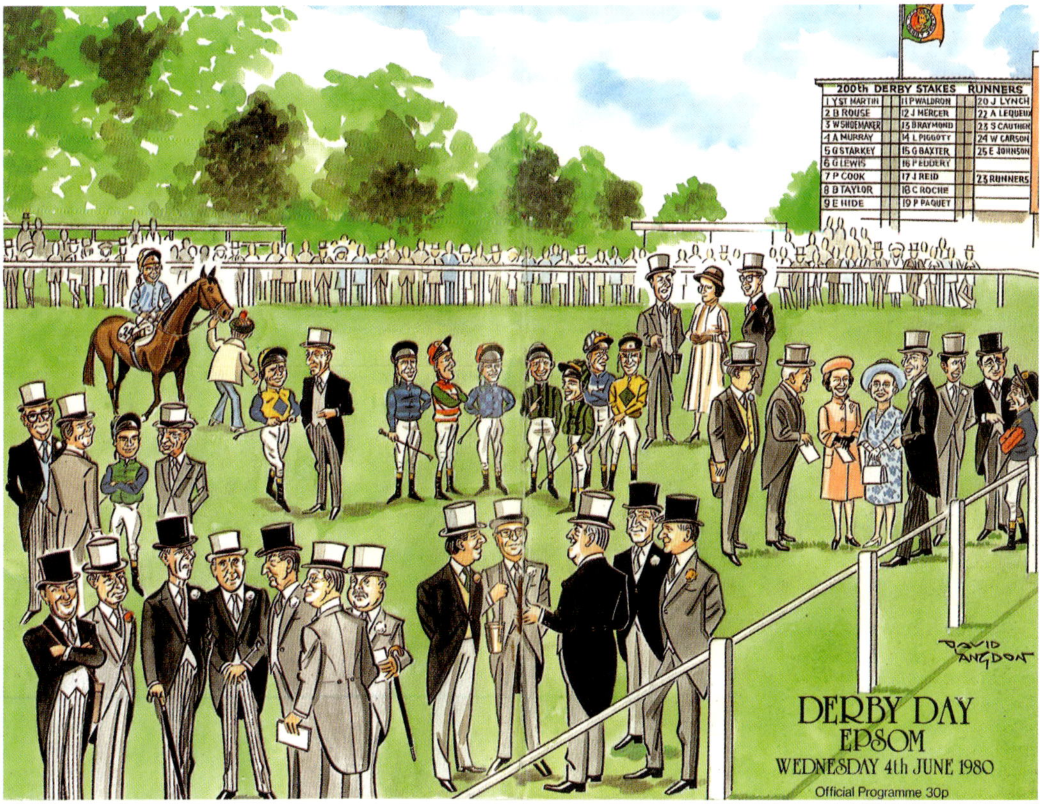
200th DERBY STAKES RUNNERS
1 Y ST MARTIN
2 B ROUSE
3 W SHOEMAKER
4 A MURRAY
5 G STARKEY
6 G LEWIS
7 P COOK
8 B TAYLOR
9 E HIDE
11 P WALDRON
12 J MERCER
13 B RAYMOND
14 L PIGGOTT
15 G BAXTER
16 P EDDERY
17 J REID
18 C ROCHE
19 P PAQUET
20 J LYNCH
22 A LEQUEUX
23 S CAUTHEN
24 W CARSON
25 E JOHNSON
23 RUNNERS
DAVID LANGDON
DERBY DAY
EPSOM
WEDNESDAY 4th JUNE 1980
Official Programme 30p

DERBY DAY
1. W. Carson
2. G. Lewis
3. A. Breasley
4. B. Taylor
5. J. Mercer
6. P. Eddery
7. W. Shoemaker
8. S. Cauthen
9. E. Hide
10. G. Starkey
11. Lord Howard de Walden
12. Lady Derby
13. Lord Derby
14. Sir A. Weinstock
15. Sir M. Sobell
16. H.M. The Queen
17. H.M. The Queen Mother
18. Lord Porchester
19. H.R.H. The Prince of Wales
20. W.R. Hern
21. L. Piggott
22. E.P. Taylor
23. R. Sangster
24. Y. St Martin
25. V. O'Brien
26. G. B. Dawson
27. Gen. Sir J. d'Avigdor-Goldsmid
28. Lord Halifax
29. P.M. Beckwith-Smith
30. J. O. Hambro
31. T.F. Blackwell
32. Maj. Gen. Sir Ranle Feilden
33. T. P. Neligan
34. J. Romanet
35. W. Whitelaw
36. Sir D. Plummer
37. E. de Rothschild

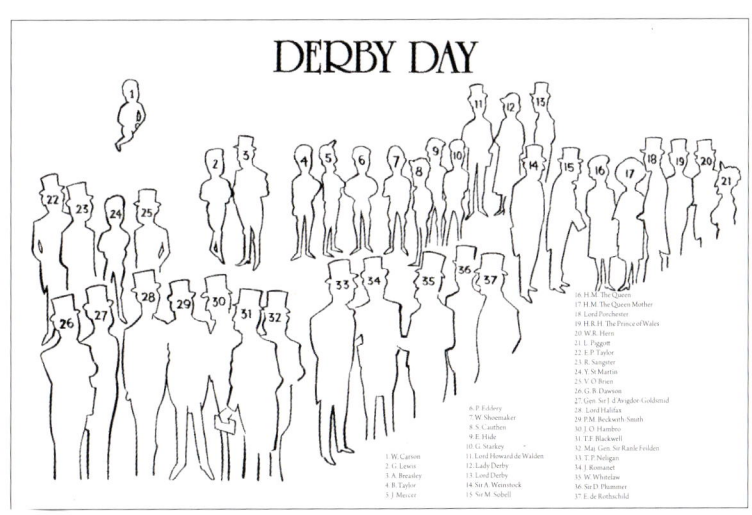

for among the six winners he rode, three were consecutive – Humorist (1921), Captain Cuttle (1922) and Papyrus (1923).

Robert Robson, John Porter and Fred Darling share the record for training the most winners, with seven each. Robert Robson's first winner was Waxy (1793), who sired three of his later winners, Pope (1809), Whalebone (1810) and Whisker (1815). The seven were completed by Tyrant (1802), Azir (1817) and his best horse, Emilius (1823). John Porter was successful over a period of 30 years, starting with Blue Gown (1868), followed by the filly Shotover (1882), St Blaise (1883), Ormonde (1886), Sainfoin (1890), Common (1891) and Flying Fox (1899). As mentioned earlier, Ormonde was probably one of the greatest winners of the 19th century. Fred Darling was one of the greatest trainers of the 20th century and his seven winners commenced with Capain Cuttle (1922) followed by eight-length winner Manna (1925), Coronach (1926), Cameronian (1931), Bois Roussel (1938), Pont l'Eveque (1940), which he owned himself, and Owen Tudor (1941) – although the latter pair won substitute wartime Derbys at Newmarket. Coronach was probably his best winner as he went on to win the Eclipse and the St Leger that year; but his greatest horse was Hurry On, who did not run in the Derby but sired Captain Cuttle and Coronach as well as Call Boy (1927), who won the Derby in the colours of the dying theatrical impresario Frank Curzon.

Two trainers have saddled six winners each – Mathew Dawson and Vincent O'Brien. Mathew Dawson, who trained from Heath House stables at Newmarket, saddled 28 classic winners between 1853 and 1895, a position that currently places him third in the classic winning trainers list. His first Derby winner was Thormanby (1860), who made his seasonal debut in the race, but his greatest horse was St Simon, who surely would have won the 1884 Derby had he been entered by his owner-breeder Prince Batthyány. The matter became academic when the

Prince died suddenly in May 1883, thus rendering all his engagements void according to the contemporary rules. He was unbeaten in nine races, including the Ascot Gold Cup as a three-year-old. Fred Archer summed him up as the only horse he would put slightly better than Ormonde. He was also a huge success at stud and was champion sire nine times. Among his 17 classic successes were Derby winners Persimmon (1896) and Diamond Jubilee (1900).

The legendary Vincent O'Brien also trained six Derby winners, starting with Larkspur (1962) and Sir Ivor (1968), both owned by Raymond Guest. Triple Crown winner Nijinsky (1970), Roberto (1972) – which saw Lester Piggott at his very best denying Rheingold by a short head – The Minstrel (1977) and the unbeaten Golden Fleece (1982) – the final pair both owned by Robert Sangster – completed his tally.

The Less Fortunate Ones

There have been many unlucky losers of the Derby, which means, of course, some lucky winners. Some of the best horses to grace the English turf failed to win the Derby for various reasons and there will always be plenty of hard luck stories. In 1857 Mr Drinkald struck an unusual bet – £10,000 to a suit of clothes – on his colt Black Tommy, a 200/1 chance, who was involved in a close finish with the filly Blink Bonny. Awaiting the judge's decision, the poor bookmaker must have been close to a coronary, but to his relief Black Tommy had lost by a neck.

One of the finest horses not to win the Derby was Robert the Devil (1880), who was beaten a head by Bend Or, ridden by Fred Archer at his brilliant best, to prevail in a very exciting finish. They met each other several times with 'The Devil' proving later to be the better horse, trouncing Bend Or in the St Leger and Champion Stakes.

At the time, the connections of Robert the Devil lodged an objection that Bend Or was not who he claimed to be. It was claimed that as a foal at the Duke

King Edward VII watches the races from the balcony of the grandstand in 1902.

of Westminster's Eaton Stud, Bend Or had been accidentally switched with a foal named Tadcaster, also by Doncaster but out of a different mare. The objection was overruled. It was not until 2011 that modern technology revealed the truth with the aid of DNA tests from the skeleton of Bend Or on display in the Natural History Museum. Their findings proved that Bend Or was Tadcaster and vice versa. Robert the Devil should have been the winner of the 1880 Derby as a result of the winner's false registration.

By finishing only fourth to Ard Patrick, Sceptre (1902) nearly created history that would never be repeated. The filly, owned and trained by gambler Robert Sievier, won every classic except the Derby and spent her career running indiscriminately whenever her owner fancied a bet. Had she been trained by Mathew Dawson or John Porter, she might have swept the classic board.

History *was* made in 1909 when Minoru, carrying the colours of King Edward VII, became the only horse owned by a reigning monarch to win the Derby (he also owned Derby winners Persimmon and Diamond Jubilee when Prince of Wales), but the unlucky horse was the second, Louviers, who was beaten a short head according to the judge. There were no cameras for photo finishes in those days, so did the judge give the race to the King? The best horse in the race, however, was undoubtedly Bayardo, who finished fourth. His trainer, Alec Taylor, admitted that he could not get his horse fit enough for the Derby and later in the year this was proved when he trounced Minoru in the St Leger. He was beaten only once more, winning a total of 22 races from 25 starts, and was regarded as the greatest ever winner of the Ascot Gold Cup in 1910. He was probably one of the best horses not to win the Derby.

In the sensational 1913 Derby, as mentioned, Craganour finished first but was disqualified for bumping and boring. Many thought it was the eventual winner Aboyeur who had caused the most interference and his jockey, Edwin Piper, had no thought of objecting. The objection came from the steward's room and from one steward in particular – Eustace Loder, Epsom's senior steward. The two remaining stewards abstained, leaving Loder to be judge and jury. He had a personal hatred for Craganour's owner, Charles Bowyer Ismay, for conducting an affair with his sister-in-law, thus the writing was on the wall for the disqualification of the 6/4 favourite which defrauded the public of millions of pounds.

Craganour had also finished second in the 2,000 Guineas, when most spectators thought he had won. The judge had made a mistake and, because they raced wide apart, gave the result to the wrong horse. Charles Bowyer Ismay could have won two classics yet didn't win either.

But he did have one piece of luck. In 1912 he sailed on Titanic's maiden voyage and survived. You can't have everything.

Two other unlucky losers were Abbots Trace ridden by Steve Donoghue, who collapsed when disputing the lead one furlong from the winning post in the race won by Spion Kop (1920), and Swift and Sure, who was going well and moving up to the leaders when a dog ran into his path and nearly brought him down; he eventually finished fourth behind Coronach (1926). Hot favourite Fairway, owned by Lord Derby, arrived at the start of the 1928 Derby in a muck sweat, having been mobbed by well-wishers as he left the paddock, and had hairs plucked from his tail; by the time he reached the start he was in such a frightful state that all chance of winning had gone. He finished nearly last behind the easy winner Felstead, a son of Spion Kop, but later in the year won the St Leger.

Baron 'Tommy' Dewar (of whisky fame), who owned Abbots Trace, died in 1930 before he could see his colt Cameronian (1931) win the Derby. As had been the custom, entries for the Derby were void upon the death of their owner, but the rules were changed just in time. He ran in the colours of his nephew, John Arthur Dewar, who had inherited all his horses. The unlucky horse in the race was the third, Sandwich. Owned by former

Prime Minister the 5th Earl of Rosebery and ridden by Harry Wragg, he encountered plenty of traffic problems, weaving his way through the field and finishing fastest of all. Harry was known as 'The Head Waiter', but this time he had waited too long.

Colombo was another horse to be deemed unlucky behind Windsor Lad (1934), mentioned earlier as one of the best winners of the 20th century. Colombo had been unbeaten as a two-year-old from seven starts when ridden by Steve Donoghue, but owner Lord Glanely had been unsatisfied with Steve's riding in one race where he won only narrowly. Lord Glanely appointed Rae Johnstone, who had very little experience of riding at Epsom, to ride Colombo as a three-year-old. Colombo won the Craven Stakes and the 2,000 Guineas (by only one length) and started a hot 11/8 favourite for the Derby. Rae Johnstone allowed Colombo to get shut in on the rails up the home straight and was beaten into third place. There were many arguments afterwards, not helped by Steve Donoghue himself, who claimed that if he had ridden Colombo he would have won on the bit. Was he unlucky, or perhaps he did not stay?

One horse which certainly did not stay was Tudor Minstrel in 1947. Ridden by champion jockey Gordon Richards, he was regarded as unbeatable and started the 4/7 favourite. He did not settle and, early in the straight, he was in trouble and, eventually, could only finish fourth behind the French colt Pearl Diver. Gordon Richards had still not managed to win the classic and had to wait until Pinza (1953) to break his duck after 28 years.

A tragedy occurred in the Derby won by St Paddy (1960). It was the fourth Derby winner owned by Sir Victor Sassoon, but it was marred by the death of the

Larkspur and Neville Sellwood get home ahead of what is left of the 26 starters in the 1962 Derby. In his wake are Arcor, Le Cantilien and a loose horse.

French-trained 2/1 favourite Angers. On the descent to Tattenham Corner his jockey Gerard Thiboeuf, having only his second Derby ride, heard the horse's foreleg snap and he was put down within minutes. Before the race he had been valued at over £100,000.

Vincent O'Brien's first Derby win, with Larkspur (1962), was a particularly dramatic one. The win was overshadowed by the fall of seven horses, again on the descent to Tattenham Corner. One horse clipped the heels of another, resulting in them both falling and bringing down five others. Among the fallers was the 9/2 favourite Hethersett, owned by Major Lionel Holliday, whom Larkspur only just managed to avoid. Remarkably, six horses were unscathed but one of the outsiders, King Canute II, broke a leg and had to be put down. Six jockeys were taken to hospital, including the veteran Harry Carr, who was riding the favourite. The stunned crowd had witnessed a scene more like Aintree than Epsom with loose horses galloping up the straight.

One of the unluckiest horses in the history of the Derby was Dancing Brave (1986). Having already won the 2,000 Guineas, he went to the post a warm 2/1 favourite. Ridden by Greville Starkey, stable jockey for his Sussex trainer Guy Harwood, he came round Tattenham Corner

Above: Walter Nightingall's string at exercise, the old grandstand in the background.

into the straight almost last and, even knowing that his mount had a blistering turn of foot, Starkey gave him too much to do and he failed by half a length to peg back Shahrastani. Subsequent results proved he was the better horse and, ridden now by Pat Eddery, he won the Eclipse Stakes, the King George VI and Queen Elizabeth Stakes (beating Shahrastani), and defeated one of the hottest fields ever in the Prix de l'Arc de Triomphe (again beating Shahrastani). In his final race he could finish only fourth in the Breeders' Cup Turf in America, and he retired to stud having won eight from his ten starts. He remains one of the top three best horses not to win the Derby.

Many of the early Derbys had numerous false starts, with as many as 12 counted in one year, so in 1837 the first flag start took place (the race was won by Phosphorus). Diamond Jubilee (1900) was the first Derby from a starting gate, while Royal Palace (1967) became the first winner from starting stalls. Hannibal's win in 1804 was the first Derby to be reported in *The Times*. Sir Visto (1895) was the first to be recorded on film, Call Boy (1927) the first to be broadcast and April The Fifth (1932) the first to be televised. The first Derby to be decided by a photo finish camera was in 1949, when it showed that Nimbus had beaten Amour Drake a head with Swallow Tail a further head away in third. (Ironically it was also at Epsom on 22 April 1947 that the photo finish was first used when deciding the outcome of the Great Metropolitan Handicap).

Other Epsom Races

The Oaks has always been somewhat overshadowed by the Derby, although it has always been run over a mile and a half. The start of the first five Oaks was located in the parish of Banstead before it moved to the Langley Vale start in 1784. The first winner in 1779 was Bridget, owned by Lord Derby, who had named the race after his hunting lodge.

There have been some brilliant winners of the fillies' classic, the best of which was Pretty Polly (1904), although she had a relatively easy task with only three opponents. She won in a canter at the prohibitive odds of 8/100 and was an extremely talented and versatile filly, winning 22 of her 24 races and beating two Derby winners during her four-year career. Reigning monarchs have been a little luckier in the Oaks than in the Derby. King George VI won in 1942 with Sun Chariot (substitute at Newmarket), while Queen Elizabeth II enjoyed success with Carrozza (1957) and Dunfermline (1977).

Epsom is associated with other well-known races – The Coronation Cup for four-year-olds over the Derby course, the City and Suburban Handicap, first run in 1851, and the Great Metropolitan Handicap, first run in 1846 over Epsom's defunct, perhaps even eccentric, two-and-a-quarter miles across the Downs. It has now dropped in status and, for safety, is run over the shorter distance of one-and-a-half miles.

Another notable feature of Epsom is its five-furlong course. Being all downhill, apart from the last few yards, it is renowned for being the fastest five-furlong course in the world. The fastest time ever recorded was by Indigenous: in 1960 he clocked 53.60 seconds, an average of 41.98 mph.

Princess Anne rode her first race at Epsom in the Farriers Invitation Private Sweepstake over one-and-a-half miles on 23 April 1985. Riding Against The Grain, an 11/1 shot, she finished fourth to No U Turn ridden by Elaine Mellor, who created a small piece of history herself. Apart from beating Princess Anne, she became the first woman ever to ride into the Winner's Enclosure at Epsom.

Finally, two stories concerning two horses that ran in the Derby during the 19th century, one a winner and the other an also-ran – but what happened next?

Do not adjust your sets: below left is the finish of the Shetland Derby in 2012. The race, for riders aged 9 to 14 and run over three furlongs, was won by Kate Thompson and Ulverscroft Hunter. Below right is the finish of the 2013 Investec Derby, which was won by Ruler of the World with Ryan Moore on board.

The unbeaten Ormonde (1886) retired in July the following year, which coincided with Queen Victoria's Golden Jubilee. It was suggested that his owner, the Duke of Westminster, should ride him in the Royal Procession but instead the Duke invited Ormonde to a garden party at his London residence, Grosvenor House. Here he could parade his pride and joy among many distinguished guests, including the Prince and Princess of Wales, four Kings, and two Queens. Ormonde journeyed to London by train, arriving at Waterloo station and walking over Westminster Bridge and through Green Park (for which he needed special permission). Once at the garden party he was admired by everyone – except Queen Marie-Henriette of the Belgians, who could not prevent Ormonde eating her bouquet of red carnations.

Voluptuary finished unplaced in the 1881 Derby after leading the field round Tattenham Corner. Retirement – not yet! His next race was the 1884 Grand National, his very first chase, which he won. When he eventually retired he was bought by a well-known actor, Leonard Boyne, who launched him into a new career on the stage. Appearing in a play called *The Prodigal Daughter* nightly at Drury Lane Theatre, Voluptuary was required to jump an artificial water jump, depositing his jockey in the water.

Now that's what you call versatility, but it was a great shame really – most horses expect to retire to the paddocks.

Pour Moi and Michael Barzalona celebrate victory in the 2011 Investec Derby, beating Treasure Beach by a head and Carlton House, the favourite, by three-quarters of a length.

Lady Carla being led in after winning the 1996 Oaks. On the left is the owner, Wafic Said. The horse was trained by Henry Cecil and ridden in all her races by Pat Eddery.

EXETER

Five miles south of the city of Exeter lies an area of common land known as Haldon Hill, where Exeter races have taken place since 1738. Indeed, there are grounds for believing that it began during the reign of Charles II (1660–1685), which would make it one of the oldest racecourses in the country.

Originally called Haldon Racecourse, in its long history the course was to have two name changes. In 1823, the land was purchased by Sir Lawrence Palk, later Lord Haldon. Sir Lawrence improved the quality of racing which up until then had been on the flat. He had a stand built in 1829 and changed the course name to Devon and Exeter. The third change in name – to Exeter – occurred in August 1992.

Flat racing died out in 1876 and racing was not revived at Devon and Exeter for 22 years, but it came alive again with the first National Hunt meeting on 21 September 1898. Although it attracted only 25 runners for that opening day, it marked the beginning of one of the finest jump courses in the country. The first race was

the Powderham Hurdle Race, worth £23 and won by J Woodman riding Hill Green, and later in the afternoon the first steeplechase was won by Rosemallow. The second day's racing consisted of five races, all won by horses which had been in action the previous day.

At 850 feet above sea level, the course is the highest in the country and also very stiff. The circuit of two miles covers the largest acreage of any racecourse and the back straight is particularly demanding, with lots of undulations followed by an uphill climb for the final mile. The steeplechase course provides an excellent test for any promising young horse. There could be no finer example of this than when the magnificent grey Desert Orchid made his steeplechase debut here, winning a two-mile novice chase by 25 lengths when ridden by Colin Brown on 1 November 1985. He jumped impeccably, and was soon to become one of the nation's favourites.

Other horses who were later to become top-class chasers to run here as novices were the Grand National winners Well to Do, Mr Frisk, Seagram and Bindaree, triple Cheltenham Gold Cup winner Best Mate, as well as Diamond Edge, Topsham Bay and Whats Up Boys. The 1972 Grand National winner Well to Do won his first and last chase at Devon and Exeter and has since had a race here named after him.

Exeter's season is dominated by one race – the Haldon Gold Cup, first run in 1982. Run over an extended two miles, it has produced a galaxy of stars and a dramatic race that will never be forgotten. The most notable winners were Very Promising (1987), Barnbrook Again (1988), Sabin du Loir (1990, 1991), Waterloo Boy (1992), Viking Flagship (1997), Flagship Uberalles (1999), Best Mate (2001) and Edredon Bleu (2002, 2003). In the 1990 race, Sabin du Lour beat Desert Orchid by six lengths with Waterloo Boy unseating his rider at the third-last – quite a star-studded field.

But the most dramatic race was in 2005, with an equally eye-catching line up. The field of eleven included triple Gold Cup winner Best Mate, champion two-mile novice Ashley Brook, a future champion Kauto Star (still

only a five-year-old), Monkerhostin and Contraband, who had beaten Kauto Star at Cheltenham in the Arkle Chase. The race went to Monkerhostin, ridden by Richard Johnson, beating Kauto Star and Ashley Brook. Sadly, it will be remembered mainly for the death of Best Mate. Just two months short of his eleventh birthday, he was pulled up before the third-last and on walking back to be unsaddled he had a heart attack and collapsed in front of the stands. Not since the days of Arkle had a horse so captured the hearts of the public, leaving the whole of the National Hunt world in mourning.

On a brighter note, two National Hunt champion jockeys both rode their first winners at Exeter. Since the 1984/85, season only three jockeys have been crowned champion and it is a remarkable coincidence that two of them should get off the mark here. On 31 August 1978 Peter Scudamore rode his first winner, Rolyat, for trainer Toby Balding in the Amateurs Handicap Hurdle. He won in grand style by 25 lengths to start off a career lasting 15 years, during which he was champion eight times.

The second jockey to take the route was A P McCoy, who on 7 September 1994 won on Chickabiddy, a mare trained by permit holder Gordon Edwards from his small stable near Minehead. It was the start, as they say, of something big, as McCoy has become the greatest National Hunt jockey of all time – having passed the 3,000 winners mark in February 2009 and the 4,000 mark in November 2013.

Another who will remember Exeter just as passionately is Lorna Vincent, who became the first lady professional jockey to win under Jockey Club rules. On 17 August 1998, riding Pretty Cute, a 25/1 outsider, for Somerset trainer Les Kennard, she beat five male professional jockeys to win the Whitstone Opportunity Handicap Hurdle.

These three all had a lot to remember about their special day at Exeter. I wonder who had the biggest smile.

Racing began at Fairyhouse, less than ten miles from central Dublin, in 1848 as a point-to-point meeting staged by the local West Union Hunt. Three years later it became the first racecourse in Ireland to be enclosed and quickly established itself as one of Ireland's premier courses.

Fairyhouse is the home of the Irish Grand National, the most prestigious race in Ireland's National Hunt calendar. It was first run in 1870 and won by Mr L Dunne's Sir Robert Peel. Run each year on Easter Monday, the Irish Grand National is the centrepiece of a three-day festival.

Many of the greatest horses in National Hunt history have run in the race, including some of the best from England. One trainer who has carved his name on the history of the race is Tom Dreaper, whose claim to fame goes beyond being the trainer of the immortal Arkle.

He won the race ten times, starting with Prince Regent (1942) and followed by Shagreen (1949) and Royal Approach (1954), before winning the race in seven consecutive seasons from 1960 to 1966 with seven different horses. The mare Olympia won in 1960, followed by Fortria the following year carrying 12st. He was recording his seventh win of the season, including

the Champion Chase at Cheltenham for the second time. Fortria finished an unplaced favourite in 1962 but Dreaper still won with the mare Kerforo, and Last Link made it four in 1963 under Paddy Woods.

Tom Dreaper, trainer of ten Irish Grand National winners.

Nina Carberry and Organisedconfusion cross the line to win the 2011 Irish Grand National, helped by the loose horse Sarteano, and becoming the fourth Carberry to win the race in four decades.

Arkle won in 1964, having three weeks earlier demolished Mill House in the Cheltenham Gold Cup. In 1965 Splash gave Paddy Woods his second Irish National in three years and Dreaper made it seven in 1966 with Flyingbolt, who was rated only 2lb. inferior to Arkle. Flyingbolt's victory was quite exceptional as he had run twice at Cheltenham, winning the Champion Chase and the next day finishing third in the Champion Hurdle. In the Irish National he carried 12st 7lb in heavy ground, conceding 40lb to the runner–up, Height O'Fashion.

This seven-timer was a family effort, as Betty Dreaper took the reins when her husband was sidelined with illness, and the tradition continued when son Jim Dreaper took over. He won the Irish National four times in five years – Colebridge (1974, beating L'Escargot) and Brown Lad three times (1975, 1976, 1978), both owned by Mrs P Burrell.

Only four horses have won the Irish Grand National and the Aintree Grand National but none in the same year – Ascetic's Silver (1904 Irish, 1906 Aintree), Rhyme N'Reason (1985 and 1988), Bobbyjo (1998 and 1999) and Numbersixvalverde (2005 and 2006). Indeed, only a few English horses have lifted the prize, but Desert Orchid crowned a magnificent career with victory under Richard Dunwoody in 1990 despite trying to unseat him at the last.

History was made in 1984 when Ann Ferris became the only lady jockey to win the Irish Grand National on Bentom Boy. But the most astonishing story goes back to the 1929 Irish Grand National, won by the six-year-old mare Alike. She was owned and ridden by Frank Wise, who rode not only with three fingers missing but also rode with a wooden leg.

Racing began at Fakenham on 14 April 1905. In those days it was known as the West Norfolk Hunt, which had held their meetings at East Winch near King's Lynn since 1839. They moved to Fakenham, a charming small Norfolk town, and although meetings were run under National Hunt rules a certain point-to-point atmosphere has remained. The course itself is very small, with a circumference of only seven furlongs and ninety-five yards, making it possibly the smallest in Britain.

The first race was the Fakenham Town Plate, won by the 2/1 chance Uncle Fred, owned and ridden by Mr George Poole, whose later claim to fame was to train the 1921 Grand National winner Shaun Spadah. Later in the afternoon the Prince of Wales Cup was won by Ivanhoe, owned by A L North and ridden by Mr A Buxton, followed by the King's Cup, won by the favourite Merry Monk III ridden by his owner Mr E Lawson-Johnston. The Prince of Wales Cup is still run today, while the King's Cup has naturally been replaced by the Queen's Cup. Both are Hunter Chases

ridden by amateur riders and are the highlight of Fakenham's season, usually run at Easter and Whitsun.

It was not until the meeting on 30 March 1964 that the West Norfolk Hunt officially changed its name to Fakenham. The first race under its new title was the Litcham Handicap Hurdle, won by Four Elms, trained locally by Jack Bloom and ridden by his son, Michael, a top amateur. On this special day the Prince of Wales Cup and the Queen's Cup were both run, won by Prilliard and Essandem respectively. The latter, a fine chaser trained by Eldred Wilson, has since had a hunter chase at Fakenham named after him.

It was at this time that Pat Firth took up his post as Clerk of the Course and among the changes he made was to move the paddock to the front of the stands and to acquire the Tote buildings from Lincoln (which had recently closed) and the Tote Investors office from Ascot. With Fakenham so close to Sandringham, he invited the Queen to be patron. She graciously accepted and the course grew in popularity, prize money increased and the calendar gradually expanded to four meetings a year.

Before the 1980s, Fakenham's meetings were dominated by permit holders and amateur riders. Two of the most successful amateurs for nearly 30 years from the 1950s were David Turner and Michael Bloom, both of whom hailed from strong racing families. David Turner rode mainly for his father, Joe, who trained at Bury St Edmunds. Among many winners at Fakenham, this

Michael Bloom and Josephine Turner with their trophies for being leading riders of 1969.

combination's greatest achievement was to win the Prince of Wales Cup four years in succession from 1974–1977 with Even Harmony. David Turner also rode 343 point-to-point winners and Fakenham still run the J M Turner Novice Hunter Chase in honour of his father.

Michael Bloom was equally successful at Fakenham, riding for his father and later his mother. His first winner was Starlight VIII in March 1951 (then West Norfolk Hunt). He was leading amateur in 1973–74 and rode 145 point-to-point winners, becoming champion in 1969. Two prolific winners for him were Chambertin and Prince Carlton. When Michael Bloom retired from riding he took over the family stables at Wymondham and provided many winners for his son Nigel, who in 1994 also became champion point-to-point rider. Quite a family!

Another leading amateur rider at Fakenham in the 1980s was Simon Sherwood, who later rode Desert Orchid to many of his famous victories. These days more professionals ride at Fakenham so those glorious days for the amateurs are now just a memory.

For the Blooms and the Turners, Fakenham became a way of life, but to Grand National and Cheltenham Gold Cup trainer Jenny Pitman, Fakenham *changed* her life. In the early days, Jenny ran a few hunters at point-to-point meetings and the odd hunter chaser under rules. On 26 May 1975 she decided to run Biretta, a well-bred eight-year-old gelding, in the J M Turner Novices Hunter Chase. Ridden by Bryan Smart, Biretta finished second, beaten two lengths by Urlanmore, but the winner had crossed Biretta badly at the last fence. A stewards enquiry was announced and the winner was disqualified. It was Jenny Pitman's first win under National Hunt rules and she was absolutely elated. The owner, Tony Stratton-Smith (who was allowed to deputise as trainer on this occasion), persuaded Jenny a few weeks later to apply for a professional licence.

This meant appearing before the stewards of the Jockey Club at Portman Square, who were not renowned for granting licences to women trainers. Even with references from Fred Winter and Lord Cadogan she feared the worst. However, after a long hearing and a barrage of questions her application was successful. A life-changing moment – the rest, as they say, is history.

Jenny Pitman, the legendary trainer whose first National Hunt win came at Fakenham in 1975

Racing at Folkestone was suspended in late 2012 and its last meeting was held on Tuesday 18 December. The course owners, Arena Racing Company, said that this was a temporary suspension following Shepway District Council's withdrawal of support for Arena's proposals to redevelop the course. Folkestone's fixtures were to be transferred to other ARC-owned courses. At the time of going to press, the situation is unresolved.

Folkestone is a coastal town, but from the racecourse you would be unable to detect the slightest smell of a sea breeze because the course lies eight country miles inland, in the village of Westenhanger. You could perhaps argue that it should be renamed, just as Edinburgh became Musselburgh in 1996 due to a similar geographical situation.

The first meeting at Westenhanger (or, rather, Folkestone) was a two-day National Hunt fixture on 30 March 1898. The opening race was a Maiden National Hunt Flat race over two miles; it attracted only two runners and was won by the 8/11 favourite Summer Light, ridden and trained by Guy Marsh. The feature race on the opening day, worth 170 guineas, was the Folkestone Handicap Hurdle, won by E J Rose's chestnut gelding Fossicker, ridden by Arthur Nightingall, a member of the famous racing family from Epsom and the rider of three Grand National winners. The following day the Great Kent Handicap Chase was won by Mr W H Lambton's Ebor carrying 12st 7lb, which was not uncommon in those days.

Racing had flourished in Kent during the 19th century but few courses survived. Nearby Dover's closure at the end of the century led to their fixtures being transferred to Folkestone, but the early years were difficult. They had obtained a licence from the Jockey Club with an optimistic view of attracting racegoers from France but this did not happen and in 1900 went into liquidation before being rescued by their administrators, Pratt and Company. With the close proximity of the River Stour there were also problems with the ground, and horses sank so deep that there were many fallers. On one day, of the 22 horses in three chases, only five finished, of which four had remounted; in 1905 a chase was declared void when all six runners fell.

Folkestone began to attract racegoers from London, thanks to the opening of Westenhanger Station, adjacent to the course. From Charing Cross first class passengers could purchase a day return for ten shillings, while lesser mortals paid only five shillings but were required to alight at a halt further away so as not to mingle with the members.

Folkestone staged Flat racing as well as National hunt, but it is National Hunt racing that provided two special moments. History was almost made on 29 September 1948 when trainer Fulke Walwyn, owner Dorothy Paget and jockey Bryan Marshall won the first five races but were beaten into second place in the final race. The winners were Langis Son 10/11, Loyal King w/o, Endless 7/4, Jack Tatters 11/10 and Legal Joy (evens), but in the final race (the Lydd Handicap Chase) Loyal Monarch 3/1 was beaten five lengths by Civvy Street, trained by Major Edward Champneys. Dorothy Paget collected a total of £776 in prize money on that momentous day.

It was at Folkestone on 20 October 1964 that the Queen Mother greeted her 100th winner – Gay Record in the Sevenoaks Handicap Chase. It had been an agonising wait for the Queen Mother as she had been on the ninety-nine mark since Makaldar had won at Haydock in March. Gay Record, the 1/3 favourite, was recording his seventh victory, and was ridden by Bobby Beasley – deputising for Gene Kelly, his normal jockey, who was sidelined with a broken collar bone and had partnered Gay Record in five of his seven wins. Gay Record was trained by Jack O'Donoghue (who sent out Nickel Coin to win the 1951 Grand National) from his small Reigate stables in Surrey; O'Donoghue had acquired Gay Record

Peter Cazalet, trainer of over 1,000 winners.

from Peter Cazalet's yard because the horse had a nervous temperament. Jack's tender handling did the trick and it was a very proud moment for him to be associated with Her Majesty's 100th winner. Ironically the Queen Mother had two runners later that afternoon, Silver Dome and Mel – both trained by Peter Cazalet – but both were beaten.

Peter Cazalet was among the most successful trainers at Folkestone. He trained at the magnificent Fairlawne stables near Tonbridge, 30 miles from the course. He was champion trainer three times and trained over a thousand winners, of which a quarter were for the Queen Mother. He never won any of the big three races but came close in the Grand National with Davy Jones (1936), Cromwell (1948) and the Queen Mother's Devon Loch (1956). His best chaser was the flying Dunkirk, a champion two–miler, but he tragically died taking on Arkle in the 1965 King George VI Chase. Peter Cazalet died in 1973.

Wye racecourse near Ashford closed in 1974, leaving Folkestone as the only course in Kent, but attendances remained low, and there was still no sight of any French visitors, even though a tunnel was dug for them.

The last race was held on 18 December 2012, and the course closed for redevelopment. To Folkestone's many supporters, the day 'felt like a funeral.'

Now and then: below, the old buildings which were replaced in 2010 by the new grandstand, which includes conference and exhibition facilities.

Fontwell Park would not exist if it were not for racehorse trainer Alfred Day. Born in 1858 in Dorset, where his father William was a successful trainer, he moved to Sussex in 1887 and bought a house five miles west of Arundel called The Hermitage, with stabling for over 30 horses. From there he took up training, but not before buying up odd bits of adjacent land to serve as training grounds. (At the time there were few other houses around and no such place as Fontwell). In addition to training he had a small farm and created his own special garden.

He had limited success as a trainer but had several winners at his local course, Goodwood. Highlights of his career were winning the Goodwood Cup with Barmecide (1893), the Stewards Cup with Romney (1907) and the Goodwood Stakes with Ignition (1911). He also won the Lincolnshire Handicap in 1890 with The Rejected (records show that Alfred Day had the licences in the names of his head grooms, Chandler and Hoyle; until the First World War this was not uncommon).

Alfred Day's nephew was the sports journalist Meyrick Good, in whom he would often confide. One evening after the First World War, while walking through his beautiful gardens, he intimated that as he was well into his sixties he was thinking of retiring and wondered what was to become of his land. Together they came up with the idea of transforming the training grounds into a racecourse.

They knew it would not be accepted for flat racing as the Jockey Club insisted on every course having a straight mile, but it would be ideal for National Hunt racing, being similar in size to nearby Plumpton; so an application was made to the National Hunt Committee in 1921.

The initial application was rejected as a licence had already been granted to open a new course at Bournemouth, even though this was 70 miles away. On these grounds a second application was soon submitted, stating that the application was not for a new course but to replace the racecourse at Portsmouth Park which had been closed by the War Office during the First World War for use as an ammunition dump (and, incidentally, has remained closed ever since). The likelihood of racing returning to Portsmouth Park was remote and, to help matters, the new figure-of-eight course planned for Bournemouth (modelled on the Parisian course at Auteuil) was very slow to materialise as new turf had still not been laid.

Eventually, helped by a recommendation from the Duke of Richmond, owner of Goodwood, a licence was granted in August 1923 to open a new course at Fontwell Park. (By now the village of Fontwell had appeared in an Ordnance Survey map of 1910). A new limited company was formed to purchase the land from Alfred Day and to pay building the course (a figure-of-eight course for the steeplechasers and an oval one for the hurdlers) and the erection of the stands – a cost of almost £7000. An opening two-day meeting was held on 21–22 May 1924. (In the meantime Bournemouth still had not opened; it did so the following year, but closed in 1928 due to financial difficulties.)

An estimated crowd of 12,000 flocked to Fontwell for the opening day by road and rail, taking advantage of the second class return fare of 7s 11d from London Victoria to Barnham Junction, two miles from the course, where they were met by trams and buses and ferried to the course. The opening race was the Walberton Steeplechase (named after the neighbouring village, which predated Fontwell) over three miles. It was won by champion jockey Fred Rees (known as Dick), on Gem, beating Len Lefebvre on Pride of Manister by a length and a half. Dick Rees was presented with a handsome silver cup on which was inscribed 'Presented to rider of first winner on figure-of-eight course at Fontwell Park at the inaugural meeting'. The winning trainer was Gilbert Bennett at Epsom, who had two other winners that day. Dick Rees finished the 1924 season as champion again with 108 winners and a record that stood for 28 years. He was probably the best National Hunt jockey between the two World Wars, and was a great favourite at Fontwell. He was champion jockey five times, won the Grand National on Shaun Spadah (1921) and rode the winner of the Cheltenham Gold Cup three times – Red Splash (1924), Patron Saint (1928) and the great Easter Hero (1929).

A momentous occasion at Fontwell occurred on 10 October 1949 when Monaveen won the Chichester Handicap Chase. He was owned jointly by Queen Elizabeth (wife of King George VI) and her daughter Princess Elizabeth (our present Queen). It was the first time a Queen of England had won a horse race in Britain since Queen Anne in 1714, and the first of 449 winners for Queen Elizabeth (later as the Queen Mother).

Monaveen had been purchased by Lord Mildmay of Flete on behalf of the Queen but ran in the colours of Princess Elizabeth. Lord Mildmay was himself a very distinguished amateur rider and Monaveen was sent to Peter Cazalet's stable at Tonbridge, where Lord Mildmay rode regularly. It was professional Tony Grantham, however, who rode Monaveen on that historic day, Lord

Princess Elizabeth (as she was then) inspects Monaveen after Tony Grantham had ridden him to vicotry in the Chichester Handicap Chase in 1949.

Runners clear the first flight at Fontwell Park, when racing was given the go-ahead after three inspection in February 2004.

Mildmay having explained he would be 'too nervous'. Monaveen went on to win the inaugural Queen Elizabeth Handicap Chase at Hurst Park later that year and the following spring was a creditable fifth to Freebooter in the 1950 Grand National. Sadly he was killed in a fall at Hurst Park in December.

Tragedy struck the same year when Lord Mildmay disappeared. Taking a swim before breakfast one morning off a beach in Devon, he was never seen again and was presumed drowned. He had injured his neck badly when riding Cromwell for Peter Cazalet in the 1948 Grand National. He finished third and it was a miracle that he finished at all. He was only 41 when he disappeared, and the muscle spasms in his neck may have contributed to his untimely death.

He left all his horses to Cazalet, among them the French-bred Manicou, who became the Queen's second National Hunt winner, this time owned by her outright. He made his debut for her in the Petworth Hurdle at Fontwell in November 1950 and then ran in chases for the rest of the season, winning the King George VI Chase at Kempton as a five-year-old.

One of the best horses to be seen at Fontwell was

National Spirit and he was a huge favourite with the public. He did not race until he was five but still managed to win 32 times (13 Flat and 19 Hurdles). He ran in six consecutive Champion Hurdles, winning the first two in 1947 and 1948, then running with great distinction behind Hatton's Grace (three times) and finally behind Sir Ken. He was trained by Vic Smyth at Epsom and owned by Leonard Abelson, who didn't like his original name of Avago and changed it. (He liked to give his horses optimistic names). Between the Spring of 1946 and January 1949 National Spirit was practically unbeatable, winning five times at Fontwell Park, including three Rank Challenge Cups. He ran in a total of 85 races and lived until 1970, dying at the ripe old age of 29.

The National Spirit Hurdle has, since 1965, been run in his honour. Run in February, it has proved to be a good trial for Cheltenham aspirants, the best of which were Salmon Spray (1965), Coral Diver (1970), Comedy of Errors (1976–77), Birds Nest (1979), Beech Road (1989) and the brilliant French hurdler Baracouda (2001). Comedy of Errors was a dual Champion Hurdle winner (1973, 1975), owned by Ted Wheatley and trained by Fred Rimell (who rode his first winner at Fontwell in 1933), but he won the National Spirit Hurdle *after* his Cheltenham triumphs, whereas Salmon Spray and Beech Road won en route to the Festival.

Another champion to win at Fontwell in his twilight years was Tingle Creek, who won as an eleven-year-old carrying 12st 7lbs. Other classy horses who made appearances at Fontwell include Pas Seul, Pendil, Linwell, Crudwell, What a Myth and Kilmore; but the most prolific winner was the moderate Certain Justice, who won at the course 14 times. He won a Hereford Selling Chase after a string of failures in his younger days and his owner Major Pardoe must have been quite relieved to get 600 guineas for him at the resulting auction. His new owner was Kent trainer Albert Neaves,

who still managed only one win with him from 18 starts the following season. At the start of the 1961–62 season he offered the ride to amateur Bob McCreery and they went on to win seven consecutive races, three of them at Fontwell. Certain Justice was proof of the saying, 'If at first you don't succeed, try, try again'. He ran in 112 races over eight seasons, winning 25 times (14 of them at Fontwell), and despite all that hard work he still lived to be 26 years old.

Finally, a heart-warming story concerning Bob Champion, who not only overcame cancer but astounded the nation by winning the 1981 Grand National on Aldaniti and went on to found the Bob Champion Cancer Trust.

When he was initially diagnosed with the disease, he set about his recovery with a course of chemotherapy of which the side effects were far more painful than the symptoms of the illness. After the course was completed he began to ride again but found it increasingly difficult to reach the standard required to ride in a race. It also left him very heavy, which limited him in the rides he could take. A year and a half passed without a winner.

At Fontwell on 23 September 1980 he rode Physicist for his boss Josh Gifford in the Portsmouth Handicap Chase. His main rival was Bold Saint and they pulled a distance clear of their four rivals. With three fences to jump, Bold Saint passed Physicist and went three lengths clear but Bob Champion urged his mount forward and gradually closed the gap and at the last fence was almost upsides. The crowd went wild and on the run-in Bob Champion and Physicist got up to win by half a length. He entered the winner's enclosure to a tremendous ovation, probably the most joyous scenes ever witnessed at Fontwell. With what happened in the next few months culminating in that day at Aintree, the fairytale was complete. Fontwell must be proud and honoured to have played a small part in it.

Galway races are run at Ballybrit, a mile east of the town. There was an attendance of approximately 40,000 on the opening day, 17 August 1869. Records of organised race meetings in County Galway go back to the mid-18th century and, according to local tradition, steeplechases were run annually at Kiltulla, east of Ballybrit, before flooding caused them to be transferred to Bushfield, near Oranmore. These were the forerunners of the Galway races.

That first day was an overwhelming success and ever since Galway races have gone from strength to strength. To measure the success, the same meeting today lasts seven days and has become one of the biggest events in Ireland – the Galway Festival – and for those intending to come for the week plenty of stamina is required.

Typically, two hundred thousand people will throng Galway during the week, yet the racing cannot be compared with meetings like Punchestown, Cheltenham and Aintree. There is a mixture of flat and jumps for maidens, novices and seasoned handicappers. There are only a handful of races that can be described as decent, the best of which is the Galway Plate, a handicap steeplechase over two-and-three-quarter miles. A standing dish in

Ansar, the course specialist and David Casey win the Hewlett-Packard Galway Plate in 2004.

recent years has been Ansar, who won the plate twice. Trained by Dermot Weld, he has appeared at the festival for ten consecutive seasons and won seven times. The only horse to win the Plate three times was Tipperary Boy (1899, 1901, 1902).

It is not just in the Galway Plate that Dermot Weld has excelled. His record at the festival has far exceeded that of his fellow trainers throughout its long history. Since he first came to Ballybrit in 1972 he has saddled an astonishing 238 winners and has been leading or joint-leading trainer

27 times. His personal best was 17 in 2011, a record that may never be beaten except by himself.

Footnote: Towards the end of the week's Festival, a man was seen wandering around the town with a name tag tied around his neck which read: *'I'm English in Galway. After racing please return home. Address in jacket pocket.'*

Huge crowds attend the annual Galway Festival in July. In 2013, it was not only the horses and jockey who were racing. The ladies were invited to don their wedding dresses again and race up the straight as a charity kickstarter to the popular Festival.

Overleaf: Derek O'Connor endures a nasty moment as his mount Captain Dash rolls on top of him after falling in the Perfect Pint Beginners Chase in 2011 – miraculously, neither were seriously hurt.

Goodwood racecourse is the most idyllic course in the British Isles. Nestling high among the hills of the South Downs in West Sussex, it could even be described as the most beautiful in the world. On a clear day the backdrop of Chichester Cathedral, Chichester Harbour and, beyond that, the Solent constitutes a perfect setting.

Goodwood estate was purchased in 1695 by the 1st Duke of Richmond, the illegitimate son of Charles II and Louise de Kérouaille, Duchess of Portsmouth. It was his grandson, the 3rd Duke, whose idea it was to introduce racing at Goodwood in 1801. He organised a private afternoon's sport for the officers of the Sussex Militia, of which he was Colonel. (He was also a Field Marshal, a former Cabinet Minister and British Ambassador to

Goodwood then and now. The grandstand today and, below, the view from Trundle Hill in the 1930s.

116

Lord George Bentinck, as characterised by James Tissot in Vanity Fair, *August 1871.*

and the number board indicating the runners, and gave orders that the runners should parade in front of the stands. He also gave the track its present configuration, which came into use in 1829. Goodwood became the most modern racecourse in the country.

Bentick was responsible for another notable invention: the horsebox. In 1836 his horse Elis raced in the Goodwood Cup (coming second) and was due to run in the St Leger just days later. Thanks to the horsebox, he made it to Doncaster and duly won, landing a huge coup.

In 1812 the meeting was moved to May and, two years later, to the end of July, where it has remained. For many years it was Goodwood's only meeting and as it grew more popular as a midsummer fixture it became known as the 'Glorious Goodwood' meeting.

France.) He was so pleased with the popularity of that first two-day meeting that he laid out a proper course for a three-day meeting under Jockey Club rules the following year, which would be open to the public.

The inaugural meeting took place on 28 April 1802 and among those attending was the Prince of Wales, later King George IV. The opening race was the Hunting Club Subscription, run in the best of three two-mile heats and won by Pantagruel. The Duke won on the first day with his horse Cedar, but on the third day Cedar was beaten by Trumpator, owned by the Prince of Wales.

It was not until the 5th Duke inherited the estate in 1819 that the course's early development took place. His close friend, Lord George Bentinck, an MP and member of the Jockey Club, brought many innovations to Goodwood which would later become common practice on other courses. As well as railing off a lot of enclosures, including one for cigar smokers, he reformed the method of starting by equipping the starter with a flag instead of him simply having to shout the word 'Go'. He insisted that every horse displayed a number cloth corresponding to the racecard

Goodwood Cup

In May 1812 the first Goodwood Cup was run, over three miles and the meeting's most important race. It was not until 1831 that the race was won by a great horse in Priam, who had won the Derby the previous year. He went on to win the Cup again in 1832 and became the first horse to win it twice. Many top-class horses have since won the Goodwood Cup, and among the best in the 19th century were Virago (1854), Kincsem (1878), Isonomy (1879) and St Simon (1884).

Virago was the most versatile of fillies, winning the Goodwood Cup as a three-year-old by 15 lengths. Two days later she was brought out again to win the Nassau Stakes. Even in those days she had completed an exceptionally demanding programme during the first half of the season. In April she had won the two big handicaps at Epsom – the City and Suburban and the Great Metropolitan – on the same day and later in the month two valuable races on consecutive days at York, before winning the 1,000 Guineas at Newmarket the following week.

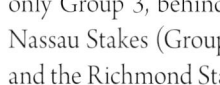

The Hungarian mare Kincsem was the most successful thoroughbred ever, being unbeaten in 54 races racing in five countries against the best European opposition. Already a household name, she won the Goodwood Cup in her only race in England, although she might never have won a single race if she hadn't been accompanied by her favourite cat, without whom she refused to travel.

Isonomy became the first horse to win the Stayers Triple Crown – the Ascot Gold Cup, Goodwood Cup and Doncaster Cup. St Simon completed his unbeaten career as a three-year-old by beating just two opponents in the Goodwood Cup at odds of 7/100 by 20 lengths. (He also made his racecourse debut as a two-year-old, winning the Halnaker Stakes at Goodwood in a canter. He was turned out again the following day and won the Maiden Plate. He was ridden by Fred Archer on both occasions).

During the 20th century the most notable winners were Brown Jack (1930), who had finished second in 1929 (beaten by a short head to Old Orkney), the French-trained Marsyas (1946), Tenerani (1948), Alycidon (1949) (who also won the Ascot and Doncaster Gold Cups), Predominate (1961), who won at the record age of nine, Le Moss (1979, 1980), Ardross (1981) and Double Trigger (1995, 1997, 1998), who is the only horse to win the race three times. One great stayer missing from this list is Bayardo (1910), who was amazingly beaten at odds of 1/20.

The original distance of three miles was soon reduced to two miles five furlongs, and in 1991 it was reduced to two miles. Races like the Goodwood Cup used to be the natural target of all the best horses including classic winners, but nowadays races over shorter distances have become more attractive for breeders and stud value. This trend was confirmed when the Pattern races were introduced in 1971. The Goodwood Cup was ranked only Group 3, behind the Sussex Stakes (Group 1), the Nassau Stakes (Group 2, promoted to Group 1 in 1999) and the Richmond Stakes (Group 2). However, when the

Goodwood Cup was shortened to two miles in 1991 it was promoted to Group 2.

Sussex Stakes

The Sussex Stakes was first run 1841 and was originally for two-year-olds, but after a series of uncontested races including 14 walkovers the conditions were changed in 1878 to become a race for three-year-olds only. It was not until 1960 that four-year-olds were allowed to compete, with five-year-olds and upwards following in 1975.

It is now one of the most prestigious mile races in Europe and is certainly the highlight of Goodwood's season, having at one time been the only Group 1 event. Early winners include Paradox (1885), Orme (1892) and King Edward VII's Derby winner Minoru (1909). In those days, however, the Goodwood Cup and the Stewards Cup were regarded as more important.

It was not until after the Second World War that the Sussex Stakes came to the fore. Two-Thousand Guineas winners to triumph in the Sussex Stakes were My Babu (1948), Palestine (1950), Brigadier Gerard (1971), Bolkonski (1975), Wollow (1976), Rock of Gibraltar (2002), Henrythenavigator (2008) and Frankel (2011). Frankel, owned by Prince Khalid bin Abdullah and trained by Sir Henry Cecil, beat the previous year's winner Canford Cliffs by a staggering five lengths and in so doing brought his unbeaten sequence to eight. Three fillies have landed the 1,000 Guineas and Sussex Stakes in the same season – the great Petite Etoile (1959), Humble Duty (1970) and On The House (1982). The roll of honour does not end there, as great milers that failed narrowly in the Guineas but won the Sussex Stakes were Kris (1979), Chief Singer (1984), Warning (1988) and the Kentucky-bred Giant's Causeway (2000). One of the greatest duels in the history of the Sussex Stakes occurred in 1992 when Edmund Loder's filly Marling, trained by Geoff Wragg, beat Selkirk, trained by Ian Balding, by a head after a titanic battle over the last two furlongs. Marling herself had been beaten a head in the 1,000 Guineas and then won the Irish 1,000 Guineas, followed by the Coronation Stakes at Royal Ascot, while Selkirk was the champion miler of the previous year – it was indeed Goodwood's race of the century.

King George Stakes

Another race to savour is the five-furlong Group 3 King George Stakes, named after King George V following his Coronation in 1910. Many fast horses have won this event but possibly the greatest was Abernant (1949, 1950) trained by Noel Murless and ridden by Gordon Richards, whose two victories came during a period of six consecutive wins in the race for his trainer from 1947 to 1952. Other dual winners were Tetratema (1920, 1921), Stingo (1930,

The Group 3 Oak Tree Stakes (originally called the New Stand Stakes and run since 1980 during Glorious Goodwood) was renamed in 1981 as it took place on the same day as the wedding of Prince Charles and Diana.

1931), Veuve Clicquot (1936, 1937), Right Boy (1958, 1959) and Lochsong (1993, 1994).

The big handicap at the July meeting is the Stewards Cup over six furlongs, described by many as a cavalry charge. First run in 1840, its name was derived from the fact that the trophy was a gift from the Goodwood stewards, the 13th Earl of Eglinton and Colonel Peel. The first winner was Epirus, trained in Malton by John Scott and ridden by the trainer's brother, William (Bill), who had a fondness for the bottle and was frequently so drunk that he was unfit to ride.

John Scott was also responsible for the 1860 winner Sweetsauce. It was the most remarkable training performance in that the three-year-old colt carried 7st 1lb to victory by three-quarters of a length in a field of 37, and two days later he romped home by ten lengths against high-class rivals in the Goodwood Cup over two-and-a-half miles. John Scott still holds the record for the most domestic Classic victories (40), but this was his greatest achievement.

The first winner of real note was Peter (1879), who had taken the previous year's Middle Park Stakes at Newmarket and was well fancied for the Derby before his nomination was voided upon the death of his owner, General Peel. Sir John Astley acquired the horse, which went on to win the Royal Hunt Cup and Hardwicke Stakes at Royal Ascot in 1881 under Fred Archer. Marvel (1890, 1892), trained by Richard Marsh, was the first horse to win the Stewards Cup twice. Owned by the 8th Duke of Devonshire, he was so badly deformed as a foal that he was nearly put down – he was appropriately named. There have been only four others dual winners: Golden Rod (1910, 1912), Lord Annadale (1913, 1914), Sugar Palm (1942, 1943) and Sky Diver (1967, 1968). Three champion sprinters to win were Mediant (1909), the French champion Epinard (1923) and Arcandy (1957);

American Express Royal Wedding Day Stakes Wednesday 29th July 1981 Goodwood
Official Programme 30p

Photgravura picture of the lawn at Goodwood in 1886. In the foreground – in his lounge suit – is the Prince of Wales, with his mistress, Lilly Langtry, seated at a discreet distance to the left.

two other notable winners were Closeburn (1947), who was trained by Sir Noel Murless and became his first major winner, and the filly Soba (1982), who made all the running to record one of 11 victories that season.

Richmond Stakes

The top two-year-old race is the Richmond Stakes, which was an immediate success as a pointer for the following season's classics. Janette, winner of the inaugural running in 1877, went on to win the Oaks and St Leger; the second winner, Wheel Of Fortune, completed the double in the 1,000 Guineas and the Oaks; and the 1881 winner, Dutchoven, landed the St Leger. (Fred Archer rode first four winners of the Richmond Stakes). Persimmon, a son of St Simon, won the Richmond Stakes in 1895 for the Prince of Wales before winning the 1896 Derby. Other Richmond Stakes/Derby winners were Bend Or (1879), Pommern (1914), Manna (1924) and Mahmoud (1935), but only two colts have completed the Richmond Stakes/2,000 Guineas double – Colombo (1933) and Palestine (1949). No Derby winners have emerged from the race for more than 70 years.

In 1895, on the day Persimmon won the Richmond Stakes, his owner the Prince of Wales caused quite a stir when he arrived dressed in a lounge suit. For nearly a hundred years the Richmond family and their friends had always attended Goodwood in morning dress. That day, the future King had set a new trend, transforming Goodwood into a less formal occasion, and from then on a holiday atmosphere prevailed. He explained that 'Goodwood should be a garden party with racing tacked on'. We can thank Lord John Bentinck and Prince Edward for putting the 'Glorious' into Goodwood before the end of the 19th century and making it one of the jewels in British racing's crown.

Another innovation that derived from Goodwood was the installation of the first public address system in 1952, thanks to Clerk of the Course Ralph Hubbard. Loudspeakers were positioned around the enclosures for the public to hear commentaries of the race and any other information.

It is a pity they had not been installed in time for the 1861 Stewards Cup. There was utter chaos, as 45 runners

were due to face the starter but with a severe shortage of jockeys. Many were unable to run and most of those that did were partnered by incompetents. To make matters worse, the winner, Croagh Patrick, was the subject of a huge gamble. It could have been the biggest coup of all time so the bookmakers refused to pay out. There was an objection six weeks later, giving the Stewards quite a headache and taking nearly ten months to resolve – eventually allowing the result to stand.

Wouldn't it have been nice for the public to hear those magic words over the loudspeakers, 'Weighed In'?

Runners in the Lillie Langtry Stakes in August 2012 race around the furthest point of the track at Goodwood. The winner was Wild Coco, who won the race again in 2013.

Gowran Park in County Kilkenny is a most attractive racecourse, with a splendid tree-lined paddock similar to the one at Haydock Park in England. This dual-purpose course opened on 16 June 1914 and enjoyed immediate success. The opening meetings consisted of flat races and steeplechases for moderate prize money, but they were popular with the local community as two local racecourses had closed in Danesfort and at Jenkinstown Park (known as the Goodwood of Ireland), and racegoers were eager to welcome a replacement. Gradually, the standard of racing improved and they were rewarded in 1952 when Gowran Park became the first racecourse in Ireland to have commentary. It was also the first course to include the Tote Jackpot in 1966.

Flat racing was not as popular as National Hunt racing but Levmoss, owned and trained by Seamus McGrath, made a winning debut here before landing a unique double in winning the 1969 Ascot Gold Cup and the Prix de l'Arc de Triomphe.

The facilities at Gowran Park were extensively upgraded with the support of Horse Racing Ireland, and the new grandstand and other facilities were officially opened in 2003. In 2006 Gowran Park not only staged its first ever Group 3 Flat race but was also re-classified as a Grade 1 course for National Hunt Meetings for prize money purposes.

The two biggest National Hunt races here are the Thyestes Chase (named after a figure from Greek

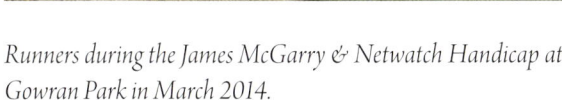

Runners during the James McGarry & Netwatch Handicap at Gowran Park in March 2014.

mythology) and the Red Mills Hurdle, both providing good trials for Cheltenham. Arkle, Flyingbolt and Brown Lad were all winners of the Thyestes Chase. Arkle ran here four times and was never beaten. In October 1962 he won the President's Handicap Hurdle with just 10st 5lbs, and in October 1963 the Carey's Cottage Handicap Chase with 11st 13lbs; he followed this in January with the Thyestes Handicap Chase (12st) and the Carey's Cottage Chase again in October 1964 (12 st).

Pat Smullen, the six-time Irish Flat Racing champion jockey, can be more than satisfied with his appearances at Gowran Park, on two separate occasions – in April and August of 2014 – riding four winners, all but one of them on horses trained by Dermot Weld, who himself holds the record for the most winners trained in Ireland

A P McCoy rode his first winner over hurdles at Gowran Park on 20 April 1994. In the Thomastown Maiden Hurdle he won by a distance on American-born Riszard, who had won the Queen Alexandra Stakes at Royal Ascot the previous year, for trainer Jim Bolger.

So Gowran Park has played host to the greatest steeplechaser and the greatest National Hunt jockey of all time. It doesn't get much better than that.

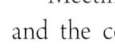

The earliest record of a meeting at Hamilton was on 6 August 1782, and its early days were not without their difficulties. One meeting in 1793 attracted only three runners and a farcical meeting in 1800 saw four walkovers and a mule race. After the Royal Caledonian Hunt Club staged a meeting in 1811, Hamilton closed until 1888. It was at this time that a new course was laid out by a group of whisky magnates. It was a round, right-handed course of one and a quarter miles with a five furlong straight, close to the banks of the River Clyde.

At the inaugural meeting on 12 July 1888 the first race, a Maiden Plate worth £200, was won by Wild West II, owned by Mr Jos Jameson and ridden by George Barrett. His trainer was Bob Armstrong, who trained at Penrith, Cumberland. (Bob was the father of Sam Armstrong and grandfather of Robert Armstrong, whose sister Susan married Lester Piggott). Bob Armstrong would later complete a most unusual double.

Meetings still did not prosper, Flat or National Hunt, and the course closed again in September 1907. The swansong was a National Hunt meeting at which Jim Storie rode the first and last winner. Another reason for the closure was that the owner of the land, the Duchess of Hamilton, refused to renew the lease on the grounds that gambling was bad for the lower classes; but the real reason was that the ground was sinking after mining operations and a new location was sought on higher ground. (The site of the old course is now occupied by a golf course and the Hamilton Services area on the M74 motorway).

It was 19 years before the present course opened in 1926, a mile from the old course on higher ground, during which time fixtures were allocated to the new course at Ayr. Those responsible for the revival of Hamilton Park were Lord Hamilton of Dalzell, Colonel Robertson-Aikman and Sir Loftus Bates, who spent lavishly on the course and amenities. Because of the limited space available on which to build a new course they laid it out with a loop similar to Salisbury.

The opening fixture on 16 July 1926 attracted a crowd of over 40,000 and the first race, the Cambusnethan

Handicap Plate over a mile, was won by Impress, ridden by Joe Thwaites. The winning trainer was again Bob Armstrong, thus completing an unusual but unique double, having also won the first race on the inaugural day on the old course in 1888. He died at Middleham in 1956, age 93. Racing at Hamilton was given a tremendous boost in 1947 when they staged the first evening meeting in the modern era in Britain. A crowd of 18,000 enjoyed this historic event from 6 pm on 18 July. Hamilton Park was also the pioneer for the first morning meeting, on 8 May 1971. The date was arranged to avoid clashing with the FA Cup Final (between Arsenal and Liverpool) that afternoon, but subsequent mornings proved unpopular and the practice was discontinued.

Hamilton Park in 1927, and in 2013. It is now owned by Hamilton Park Trust, who have put the course on the map as a venue for top-class racing and celebrity concerts.

Haydock Park hosts both Flat and National Hunt racing and, to its immense credit, the quality under both codes is among the best. Once in Lancashire but now in Merseyside, its location between Liverpool and Manchester suggests that the course is marooned in the midst of an industrial area but it is in fact a most picturesque location, with its tree-lined paddock a particular attraction.

It would be fair to say that the excellent racing all year round is probably dominated by jumping, so it is appropriate that it began proceedings on 10 February 1899 with a National Hunt fixture. The meeting was delayed for a week because of bad weather, although nobody would deny it was worth the wait. The opening flat fixture did not take place until May.

It all began following the closure of Newton races, two miles from the present course, where racing had started on 6 May 1751 on an extensive stretch of common known as Golborne Heath. The Old Newton Cup, first run in 1807 (the same year as the inaugural Ascot Gold Cup), is the last surviving link between the old course and Haydock Park and it remains one of the big handicaps in Haydock's flat season. National Hunt racing was not introduced at Newton until 1883, and lasted only 15 years until its closure on 13 July 1898.

The history of the Old Newton Cup is almost synonymous with that of flat racing in Lancashire and the names of the various winning jockeys read almost like a recital of the great figures of the last 200 years. Among those who rode in the Newton Cup races on the old course are Jem Snowden, Tom Challoner and John Osborne. Undoubtedly the greatest of them all was Fred Archer, champion jockey for 13 years in succession, who had a great win at Golborne Heath on a horse called Anchorite. The Newton era ended in 1898 and the fixtures were transferred to the new course at Haydock Park, where the first to win the trophy in its new surroundings was W J Wiling's Arsenal, ridden by Tommy Weldon and trained by William Elsey, father of the great Charles Elsey who trained at Malton. The first horse to win the race on two occasions was Sir Charles Hynd's Grease Paint, a son of Gainsborough, which won in 1930 with Australian jockey Brownie Carslake in the saddle and again in 1932 when ridden by A Burns. In 1936 and 1937 the feat was emulated by Mr G Ashworth's Pegasus, ridden on the first occasion by the Queen's jockey Harry Carr and on the second by the popular Lancashire jockey Billy Nevett.

Another notable feat was that of Fred Armstrong in training three successive winners – Preciptic (1948), Teacko (1949) and Courier (1950). To commemorate this achievement Armstrong was presented with an inscribed cigar box by the Haydock Park Directors.

The most prestigious flat race is the Sprint Cup, formerly the Vernon's Sprint, first run in November 1966 and won for the first two years by Sir Peter O'Sullevan's fine sprinter Be Friendly as a two- and three-year-old. He was denied the hat-trick by fog in 1968 and the race was later moved to September. Some flying machines have won the race, notably Lady Beaverbrook's Boldboy (1977) at the ripe old age of seven, Moorestyle (1980), Habibti (1983), Green Desert (1986), Ajdal (1987), Dayjur (1990) and Sheikh Albadou (1992). The race obtained Group 1 status in 1987.

The only other flat races of note are the Rose of Lancaster Stakes and the Lancashire Oaks. The latter was inherited from Manchester when it closed in 1963. Sadly, this race has never reached the high status of the Yorkshire Oaks and seems to attract only Epsom also-rans.

National Hunt racing by far outshines its flat counterpart at Haydock, with many high profile races. National Hunt has never looked back from that first February day in 1899 when the four-year-old Snarley Yow won the opening maiden hurdle and Imbroglio, trained by J G Elsey, won the feature race, the Warrington Handicap Hurdle, worth £136 (a big prize in those days).

Many Grand National hopefuls run at Haydock, as the fences are somewhat similar to those at Aintree; a left-handed course and with a slight drop on landing.

Many trainers take advantage of the sponsored Grand National Trial in February, and there can be no finer recommendation than Red Rum's participation in this race every year he ran at Aintree. In all he ran 18 times at Haydock, winning twice, and even ran his final race here in the Grenall Whitney Breweries Handicap Chase on 4 March 1978, but his finest hours were behind him and he finished unplaced. Locally-born Tom Coulthwaite trained three Grand National winners, Eremon (1907), Jenkinstown (1910) and Grakle (1931). To train the latter, he delayed his retirement, and for his services the Haydock Park executive named a race after him. Neville Crump was another successful Grand National trainer with victories for Sheila's Cottage (1948) and Teal (1952) using the Haydock route.

Among other high-profile chases are the Tommy Whittle Chase, run in December since 1982 and named after the late chairman of Haydock Park; the Peter Marsh Chase, first run in 1981 in January and replacing the Tom Coulthwaite Chase; and the Betfair Chase, a Grade 1 race first run in 2005, which replaced the Edward Hanmer Memorial Chase which was named after a former steward who served for 45 years. All these races have over the years been won by chasers of the highest order.

The Edward Hanmer has been won by L'Escargot, Pendil, Bula (twice), Silver Buck (four times), Wayward Lad and Forgive and Forget (twice). There was an epic race in 1982 when Christine Feather's fine gelding Silver Buck (who later that year won the Cheltenham Gold Cup), beat Stan Riley's Burrough Hill Lad (1984 Gold Cup) by two-and-a-half lengths, with Master Smudge (1980 Gold Cup) third.

The Tommy Whittle Chase's roll of honour was highlighted by One Man in 1995, while the Peter Marsh Chase has been won by four Cheltenham Gold Cup winners in Little Owl (1981), Bregawn (1982), The Thinker (1987) and Jodami (1993, 1997), and one Grand

National winner (Earth Summit, 1995), plus a host of other class horses including Ashley House (1983), Combs Ditch (1986) and Nick the Brief (1990). The Betfair Chase, in its short history, has been dominated by Kauto Star (2006, 2007, 2009, 2011).

The hurdle races are also top-class, with a Champion Hurdle Trial in January, the Victor Ludorum for four-year-olds – often a rehearsal for the Triumph Hurdle at Cheltenham – and the valuable Swinton Handicap Hurdle in May.

Such is the high standard for National Hunt racing at Haydock that they were asked to play host for something completely different in 1997. The Grand National of that year had to be postponed at Aintree because of a bomb scare and was rescheduled for the following Monday. What happened to the 40 runners in the meantime? They – and their grooms, of course – were all treated to 'bed and breakfast' at Haydock

Back on the flat, and Fred Archer – a man who may have thrilled the crowds at the old course at Newton and the like of whom you are unlikely ever to see again, but

Kauto Star at the unveiling of his statue at Haydock Park on 24 November 2011.

on 18 August 1948 a young man, just 12 years old, by the name of Lester Piggott rode his first winner, The Chase, for his father/trainer Keith Piggott. Lester had ridden The Chase, owned by Mrs P Lavington, in all his races that year starting with his first ride in public at Salisbury in April, followed by runs at Bath, Kempton and Worcester. Never having been placed, The Chase finally won the Wigan Lane Selling Handicap over one mile at Haydock and Lester had the distinction of beating established jockeys Frankie Durr, Joe Sime and Billy Nevett for good measure. It was the start of a magnificent career lasting 46 years and 4,493 winners, so it was appropriate that he rode his final winner at Haydock as well – on Palacegate Jack for trainer Jack Berry on 5 October 1994, was typically by a cheeky short head. Haydock Park will always be very special to Lester Piggott.

So Haydock remains one of the top-class racecourses in the country for year-round racing, and the closure of Manchester in 1963 left Haydock Park and Liverpool as the only two courses flying the Lancashire flag. Until that year Haydock had its own railway station on the Liverpool to Manchester line, right outside the main entrance, but Lord Beeching's axe came down and the station no longer exists. Travellers now have to make do with stations at Newton-le-Willows and Warrington Bank Quay, both several miles away.

However, on 30 November 1929 Mrs Catherine Unsworth of Liverpool probably arrived by train at Haydock station to put herself into the history books. She became the recipient of the biggest-ever dividend paid out on the Tote. Looking through the list of runners, Mrs Unsworth noticed that in the Selling Handicap Hurdle horse no. 36, named Coole, had not a single backer. More out of pity than anything else she remedied the defect and placed 2/- each way. The horse won at the amazing odds of 3410/1 and over 100/1 for a place, and the starting price was only 100/8.

The splendid city of Hereford lies on the banks of the majestic River Wye and just a few miles from the Welsh border. It is a big tourist attraction for its 12th-century Cathedral as well as a centre for the cider industry and home of the famous Herefordshire red-and-white cattle that graze in the lovely Wye Valley surroundings. The racecourse, to the north of the town, featured only National Hunt racing in modern times but when the course opened on 27 August 1771 it was flat racing only. Hurdle racing did not commence until 1840, followed by steeplechasing two years later.

The highlight of flat racing at Hereford was, undoubtedly, the appearance of the record-breaking Fisherman. Owned and trained by Tom Parr, he won the Queen's Plate at Hereford on 28 August 1857, recording his 22nd win of the season from 35 starts. In 1856 as a three-year-old he won 23 times (still a British record)

and in 1858 he won 21 races. Before he retired he won 70 times from 121 starts, although many of them were uncompetive in terms of opponents (he walked over three times and several races contained only two or three runners). He won the Ascot Gold Cup twice, in 1858 and 1859, and 26 Queen's Plates.

Soon afterwards flat racing went into decline with a dreary collection of sellers, plates and poorly-endowed handicaps, and came to an end in September 1883. But National Hunt racing began to flourish up until the First World War, although on a modest level.

Between the wars a very popular steeplechaser to appear at Hereford several times was Dudley, owned by the 4th Earl of Londesborough and trained and ridden by the celebrated Harry Brown. He raced over nine seasons, winning 44 times and establishing a 20th-century record until Crudwell beat it in the 1950s. During 1924 and 1925 he won 18 times – 15 of them in succession – including the Grand Annual at the National Hunt meeting at Cheltenham two years in succession, and the valuable Victory Chase at Manchester. His jockey, Harry Brown, was quite a character. He rode as an amateur but he was also a first-class marksman and fisherman. He possessed charm and wit and some of his exploits were quite outrageous. He was champion jockey in 1919 and was the last amateur to hold this title. He finished second to Shaun Spadah in the 1921 Grand National on the 9/1 favourite The Bore, having remounted. You can understand his incentive to get on board his mount again quickly – it was later discovered that he had invested £500 each way on his horse.

The course was originally public land and was still controlled by the council in 1946 when sold to a newly-formed private company. At the time Hereford hosted just three meetings a year, but by the 1990s this had increased to 15, including several Bank Holidays. It was on one of these Bank Holidays that Hereford created an unusual record. On May Day 1975 they staged an evening meeting but, with 219 runners declared, several races had to be divided. This amounted to 14 races, which meant that what was intended as an evening meeting actually started at 1.30. It must have been a headache for the caterers.

Racing remained at a modest level and, despite being competitive, can only be described as run of the mill stuff – but a few big names have appeared from time to time. In 1983 Champion Hurdle winner Gaye Brief and Cheltenham Gold Cup hero Bregawn both won at Hereford in their final races before glory at the Festival. In February Gaye Brief won the Fred Rimell Hurdle, a race named in honour of his late trainer. Saddled by Fred's widow, Mercy Rimell, Gaye Brief (who was the last horse Fred Rimell bought) completed the double by winning the same race the following year.

On 5 March 1983 Bregawn won the Newent Handicap Chase by a distance just 12 days before he headed Michael Dickinson's historic first five in the Gold Cup. On the same card West Tip finished third in a Novices Handicap Hurdle, going on to win the Newent Chase himself in 1985 and, later that month, the Ritz Club Handicap Chase at the Festival, and finally the 1986 Grand National. Michael Dickinson had also saddled Silver Buck to win the Sean Graham Chase at Hereford two years before he landed the 1982 Gold Cup, proving that some trainers did like sending their class horses to Hereford sometimes, as a stepping stone to greater things.

David Nicholson had a distinguished career both as a jockey and a trainer. His fondest memories as a jockey were probably of riding Mill House in many of his races but in 1974, when he had already switched his attention to training, he would still ride one or two of his own horses if no other jockey was available. At Hereford on 3 April in the Kingstone Handicap Chase he rode the final winner of his career, aboard What a Buck for his long-time owner Lord Vestey, which no doubt gave him just as much pleasure.

Young jockeys can all dream that one day they will be champions and it's often a case of being in the right place at the right time. For two of them, Hereford played a small part in making their dreams come true. On 1 June 1995 a young Tony McCoy sat in the weighing room without a ride in the next – a three-mile Novice Hurdle – when he heard that Richard Dunwoody had been injured in a fall in the previous race. Dunwoody's mount Crosula was without a jockey. Tony was approached by assistant trainer Chester Barnes. 'Would you ride Crosula for Mr Pipe, jump out and make all?' he was asked. Tony McCoy's first ride for Martin Pipe duly won, beginning one of the most powerful combinations ever in National Hunt racing. (In 1996 Tony McCoy became stable jockey.)

Richard Dunwoody also set the ball rolling at Hereford, on 3 March 1984. As a 7lb claimer he rode four winners, one second (beaten a neck), and two thirds. Quite a feat for an apprentice, raising a few eyebrows in the process. So you could say two champions were born at Hereford.

The course was closed in 2012 following failure by the owners to agree a lease extension with the local authority and what might have been the last ever National Hunt meeting was held in December. But since then an increasingly popular series of Arabian race meetings have been held between May and September, organised by the Arabian Racing Organisation and featuring top-class Arab horses from around the world – particularly the UAE. In the meantime, it looks unlikely that the course will reopen for Thoroughbred racing.

Top: Alcea Rosea, owned and trained by John Wilson of Louth, Lincolnshire, leads her rivals onto course prior to winning the Wathba Stud Farm Cup Restricted Maiden Stakes in July 2014.

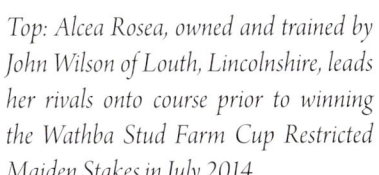

Right: Yakshi, owned and trained by Doreen Townsend of Leicester, in the Hereford Parade ring. before the same race.

HEXHAM

Racing first came to Hexham in 1721 when the sport was staged on Tyne Green, traditionally the town's fairground. The times were turbulent and racing here was intermittent thanks to thuggery, cockfighting and illegal meetings. It was said that such activities gave rise to vice, profanities and immorality. Ruffians in those days caused the demise of many minor courses.

Before moving to its present site at Yarridge Heights in 1869, Hexham had to overcome the rivalry of Wark races, which had opened four years earlier, and was, consequently, poorly attended and it closed for ten years from 1880. In the meantime, the owner of the course, Charles Henderson, had a new course laid and new fences built by his trainer Tom Coulthwaite (later responsible for three Grand National winners in Eremon 1907, Jenkinstown 1910 and Grakle 1931).

Hexham finally reopened on St George's Day 1890, but nearly all the jockeys were amateurs. One of only three professionals to ride that day was George Williamson, who, in 1899, had the distinction of partnering the great Manifesto to victory in the Grand National.

Hexham is known as the Heart of All England, although Hadrian's Wall is only a few miles away. The nickname is generally thought to have originated with King James VI of Scotland, who stopped at Hexham on his way to London to be crowned James I of England in 1603. He evidently thought he was at the halfway point of his journey, confirming his shaky knowledge of his new kingdom's geography. However, the description stuck and in 1907 'The Heart of All England Cup' was inaugurated, and remains Hexham's major race. Its first winner was the mare Redscar, who chalked up her fourth consecutive win in the hands of Mr C Pawson, by 30 lengths, in appalling weather.

Hexham has no grandstand and spectators watch the racing from a terrace giving a beautiful view across the Northumberland countryside. The course is 750 feet above sea level, comparable with Goodwood, and is well worth a visit. However, one visitor who could have a different view was the black boxer Jack Johnson. In May 1910, visiting Hexham for the first time with his wife, he was barred from entering the Club Enclosure by one of the stewards who was obviously unaware of his identity. A brave move in view of the fact he was the reigning world heavyweight champion.

There have been a few trainers who have excelled at Hexham over the years. As already mentioned, Tom

Coulthwaite started training athletes before training horses but had a lot of winners in the early 1900s. Neville Crump loved Hexham and his 1952 Grand National winner Teal ran here on his way to Aintree. More recently, the great Arthur Stephenson has been the most prolific trainer at Hexham. He used to concentrate on the smaller northern meetings and could have been described as the Martin Pipe of his day. He trained at Bishop Auckland and owned most of his horses himself, and after the Second World War had the distinction of being top owner after the Queen Mother. His motto in life was 'little fish are sweet', exemplified on 19 March 1987. His fine chaser The Thinker was running in the Cheltenham Gold Cup but Arthur preferred to saddle his seven runners at Hexham. So he sent his assistant and nephew, Peter Cheeseborough on the long journey to Gloucestershire. Arthur won just one race at Hexham, the Racing Post Handicap Chase with Succeeded, ridden by claimer Mr P Johnson. The Cheltenham Gold Cup had been delayed by a snowstorm, by which time the Hexham card had finished, so he had plenty of time to watch The Thinker storming to victory from the comfort of the members' bar.

Another trainer with special memories of Hexham is Bobby Renton, who also occasionally rode as an amateur. He is better remembered as the trainer of 1950 Grand National winner Freebooter, owned by Mrs Lurline Brotherton who also owned Red Rum for a short spell (whom Bobby Renton also trained). Bobby owned and trained nine-year-old Devon Peter, who was running in the £127 Sunniside Selling Hurdle on 30 September 1963. The morning papers had it that stable jockey, Johnny East, would ride (a strong jockey who rode a lot of winners in the 1950s and 60s, including Much Obliged in the 1957 Whitbread Gold Cup). For some reason, Johnny East was replaced by his owner/trainer Bobby Renton and the gelding finished seventh of the nine runners. Nothing unusual about this – except that Bobby was 75 years old, and thus became the oldest jockey in England ever to ride in a race.

Huntingdon, formerly a county town, is famous as the birthplace of Oliver Cromwell, who ruled the Commonwealth from 1649 and, as Lord Protector, from 1653 until his death in 1658. Even now, over 350 years later, a stand is named after him.

There is historical evidence of racing back in 1602 at Sapley, now part of North Huntingdon, and it is possible that steeplechasing may have originated here when horses were trained to jump against each other in matches arranged by courtiers in 1607. Formal racing was recorded on the flat at Portholme in the Parish of Brampton from around 1773 and moved to the present course at Waterloo Meadows in 1886.

The jockey Frank Buckle was a regular visitor to Portholme. He was born in 1766 near Newmarket and first rode in public at the age of 17, weighing 3st 13lbs. This seems a freakish weight, but it was quite common

at the time and he could still weigh out at 7st 11lb when he retired at the age of 65. Unlike many jockeys, Buckle did not have weight problems but, nevertheless, watched his diet until the end of each season, when he indulged in the curious habit of consuming a whole goose. Being local, Buckle rode frequently at Portholme and Stamford, as well as Newmarket. He rode 27 classic winners and was much sought after by the leading owners. He died just six months after his retirement.

Oliver Cromwell was not known for his approval of racing, but his grandson, Sir Henry Cromwell, played a small part in the inauguration of the present course. Sir Henry owned The George Inn and allowed a local man, John Goodliff, and six friends to hold a meeting in his establishment to discuss the opening of a new course. With the gradual decline of Portholme, they planned to hold a National Hunt meeting at a new site known as Waterloo Meadows. Their dreams were eventually fulfilled and the present course at Huntingdon opened on Easter Monday 1886. The first race was a three-mile chase, won by Catherine the Great.

Huntingdon's new fixture had a quiet introduction, with a yearly hunt meeting at Easter. Not until the 1920s did the National Hunt Committee grant them a second fixture, at Whitsun. In the meantime, Portholme closed through lack of interest. Facilities were poor at Waterloo Meadows and finances depended on the income from a hay crop mowed on the meadow. Thanks to two long-serving Clerks of the Course – Bob Lenton, who served for 25 years and Hugo Bevan, who served from 1974 – Huntingdon has prospered and can now stage close to 20 meetings a year.

Hugo Bevan was responsible for introducing some fine feature races to Huntingdon, in particular the Peterborough Chase, first run in 1978. Several equine superstars have won this race, especially since its Grade 2 rating, including Martha's Son (1994), Dublin Flyer (1996), One Man (1997) (who beat Viking Flagship in an epic battle), Edredon Bleu, who won it four times (1998–2001) and Best Mate (2002).

Credit is again due to Hugo Bevan for attracting Cheltenham-bound hurdlers to Huntingdon by way of the Sidney Banks Memorial Novices Hurdle and the Cambridgeshire Hurdle, many of whom go on to better things at the Cheltenham Festival. One famous Champion Hurdler to grace the turf at Huntingdon was Sir Ken (1954), who was never off the bit to win the Cambridgeshire Hurdle at odds of 1/6, and two years later another Champion Hurdler, Clair Soleil, won the same race. Cheltenham Gold Cup winner Burrough Hill Lad made his racecourse debut at Huntingdon in the Cromwell Three Year Old Hurdle in 1979 when trained by Jimmy Harris. He ran a promising race, ridden by Phil Tuck and finished eighth.

Parts of the centre of the course are of great historical interest. Forty-five acres of land towards the north end of the racecourse have been designated a Site of Special Scientific Interest. The area comes under the protection of the 1981 Wildlife and Countryside Act because the grasses, plants and herbs growing in the meadow are among the rarest in the country. They include the Green-Winged Orchid and the Blue Legged Mushroom.

Jockey Frank Buckle may not be a household name, indeed, very few people today would have heard of him had it not been for Lester Piggott surpassing his record of riding most classic winners. But the same certainly could not be said of a more recent jockey who made history at Huntingdon on 8 April 1985. The ever-popular John Francome decided to bring down the curtain on his career on this day and could not have written a better script himself. He bowed out with four winners – Julesian, Gratification, Rhythmic Pastimes and his very last mount, Gambler's Cup for his guv'nor Fred Winter, who had supplied so many of his 1,138 winners.

Since his first ride at Worcester in 1970. That first mount at Worcester, Multigrey, also won, so Gamblers Cup's success completed a very unusual double with John riding a winner with his first and last mounts, which I doubt has been achieved many times before.

Frank Buckle also ended his career at Huntingdon, in 1831. In those days jockeys were allowed to bet and would think nothing of having vast sums on themselves. However, it also led to many jockeys 'throwing' races, putting any of today's scandals in the shade. However, the esteem in which Frank Buckle was held was so high that he was regarded by everybody as being as honest as the day was long. For example, when he rode at Portholme in a two-horse race, Buckle got his mount home after a desperate finish to win by a neck, and it was later discovered that he had backed his rival.

KELSO

Kelso lies in the Borders Region of Scotland and is a charming town with cobbled streets and an elegant square surrounded by gracious buildings. It lies on the River Tweed and visitors from the south approach the town over a magnificent five-arch bridge built in 1803, the prototype for London's Waterloo Bridge. About a mile upstream is Floors Castle, home to the Duke and Duchess of Roxburghe, the largest inhabited castle in Scotland. It was James, 5th Duke of Roxburghe, who in 1822 was to play a major part in the opening of the present racecourse.

The earliest records of racing at Kelso were in 1751 at Caverton Edge, when the Caledonian Hunt presented a plate of 50 guineas. Racing was not continuous, however, mainly due to a shortage of runners – a four-day meeting in 1803 produced only three runners to contest four races, resulting in every race being declared a walkover. Having donated a Gold Cup to be run for in 1813, the Duke of Roxburghe also built a grandstand at Caverton Edge and erected some stables. The local gypsies soon took possession, however, causing a nuisance as well as stealing the odd sheep or two. Local farmers petitioned the Duke to take the buildings down and a change of venue was imminent.

By 1821 Kelso had a new course at Blakelaw, about three miles south of the town. In those days it was not difficult to transfer a meeting and little in the way of preparation was required. The course was not satisfactory, however, and was used only for two years. In the meantime the Duke had already made plans to purchase Berrymoss, a piece of land less than a mile north of the town, for Kelso's new and present racecourse.

There was still only flat racing at Kelso in 1822 when the Duke laid the foundations of the new grandstand at Berrymoss. The magnificent polished stone stand with its balustrades, balcony and elegant iron castings (a replica of a similar one at Doncaster) was ready for the opening fixture on 16 April 1823. It was described by many as the finest course in the British Isles. An immense crowd came for the opening but, sadly, the Duke was not among them. He died just before, at the age of 88, but Kelso will always be indebted to him for putting them firmly on the map.

In 1883 National Hunt racing came to Kelso courtesy of the United Border Hunt Steeplechases, which had previously held their meetings at nearby Stodrig and Wark. Races were held now under the title of the 'United Border Hunt' and continued so until 1951. Flat racing had come to an end in 1888 and, at the final meeting on 28 September, the winner of the Welter Plate was ridden by Mr M D Peacock, grandfather of trainer Dick Peacock.

Although National Hunt racing was confined to one meeting a year (increased to two in 1912 and three in 1935), it was very popular and was made more so by the presence of amateur rider Charles John Cunningham, who was 6ft 2in tall and weighed 12 stone. At the 1887 fixture he rode five winners from five rides. He was the most outstanding amateur of the era and his record at other northern courses was just as remarkable. He was born at Morebattle Tofts near Kelso in 1849 and began his brilliant career on the old Wark course. He rode on the flat but, because of his weight, mostly in Hunter Chases. (Cunningham had won the 1886 National Hunt Chase Challenge Cup on his own horse, Why Not.) His ambition to win the Grand National was always going to be difficult to achieve because of his weight but somehow he got down to 11st 5lbs to ride Why Not in 1889 – just failing to beat Frigate, ridden by Bobby Beasley, after leading for most of the race.

He rode Why Not again in the 1890 Grand National, finishing fifth, and in the 1891 Grand National, when he probably would have won if he had not been brought down by a loose horse two fences from home. Cunningham suffered terrible injuries, breaking a blood vessel in his head, splitting his leg from the knee downwards and falling with his wrists clenched and doubled under. This fall virtually finished his riding career. He died in 1906 of cancer, probably brought on by a series of bad falls. During his career he rode 417 winners from 952 rides, which represents an astonishing 44%. (Ironically he sold Why Not after the 1891 Grand National for £4,000; the horse went on to win the 1894 Grand National, ridden by Arthur Nightingall.)

Kelso continued to prosper into the 20th century, apart from a slight hiccup in 1912 when Suffragettes tried to burn down the paddock stand in order to stop racing. They were apprehended by police and escorted away.

In 1928 'The United Border Hunt Steeplechases (Kelso) Ltd' was registered under the Scottish Companies Act with the object of entering into a lease from the Duke of Roxburghe and carrying out further improvements to the course. One of these was the purchase of three adjoining

Above: Charles John Cunningham, the outstanding amateur of the 1880s.

Right: Kelso badges from 1928.

137

fields on the Hendersyde Park Estate; the chase course was extended over these fields and three jumps were constructed on them. One of the fields was still under the plough, as was customary in those days. The hurdle and chase courses at Kelso are still separated to this day.

The most prestigious race at Kelso is the United Border Hunt Steeplechase. Charlie Cunningham rode the winner 21 times (from 30 attempts), the first of which was his own horse Surprise in 1873. The best winner was Teal in 1951 – the year, incidentally, that the course reverted to the name of Kelso. (Teal went on to win the Grand National the following year).

On 27 April 1971, Arthur Stephenson joined a very select band of trainers to send out five winners at one meeting. His achievement was most unusual because his five winners were ridden by five different jockeys. The five races were won by Igloo Maid (8/1, ridden by G Griffin), Fandango II (11/10F, Mr C Macmillan), Interview II (4/1, R Thompson), Proud Percy (5/2, Tommy Stack) and Liscartan (3/1, J Enright) respectively. He was denied going through the card in the fifth race, the Mellerstain Novices Chase, when his runner Perchington, ironically the shortest price of any of his runners that day at 8/11, could finish only third to Turmo Tang, trained by Reg Lamb and the mount of Peter Ennis. (No trainer has ever gone through the card and Arthur Stephenson shared this record with seven other trainers until 2006, when Paul Nicholls broke the record by saddling six winners at Wincanton from a total of eight runners, although it was on a seven-race card.)

Two other more unusual records were created at Kelso when on 21 November 1990 Equinoctial, trained by Norman Miller and ridden by A Heywood, won the Grant's Whisky Handicap Hurdle at a British record SP of 250/1, and in the Sprouston Claiming Hurdle on 6 April 1992 the mare Countess Crossett was backed at 5000/1, the biggest price ever laid on a British racecourse. To the relief of those Scottish bookmakers, she finished ninth.

A sunny day at Kelso in October 2009.

With the closure of Alexandra Park in 1970, Kempton became the closest racecourse to London. Situated near Sunbury-on-Thames in what was once the county of Middlesex, it now represents the capital even though it is 12 miles from Hyde Park Corner – as the crow flies, at least. Londoners do, however, have easy access to Kempton by rail as the racecourse has its own station just yards from the enclosures.

The course was founded by S H Hyde, a textile businessman from Lancashire. Hyde had travelled south for the Epsom Derby in 1872 but, before returning home, took a leisurely drive in the country. He spotted a sign advertising the Manor of Kempton together with a park of 400 acres that had, according to the estate agent, the recommendation of being mentioned in the Domesday Book of 1086. He had found for himself and his family a home – and a racecourse.

The course was laid out for Flat and National Hunt racing but, on 18 July 1878, it was a Flat meeting that opened proceedings. The opening race, the Inaugural Plate over six furlongs, was won by Dunkenny, trained by John Porter and ridden by George Fordham, beating Mandarin, who went on to win the Royal Hunt Cup the following year. George Fordham was presented with a Silver Cup to mark the occasion. The event was run on the mile course as the infield was used in those days for hare coursing, a sport close to the heart of Mr Hyde.

The oldest race at Kempton is the Jubilee Handicap, first run in 1887 to commemorate Queen Victoria's 50th year on the throne. The first winner was Bendigo, ridden by John Watts, carrying 9st 7lb, who had won the inaugural running of the Eclipse Stakes at Sandown the previous year. He was now seven years old and had captured the public's heart, and was probably the most popular horse

of that era. In 1888 the race was won by Minting by three lengths carrying 10 stone, which remains a record for the race. (Minting was unlucky to be foaled the same year as the great Ormonde). The first dual winner was Victor Wild (1895, 1896). Owned by London publican Tom Worton, he was bought out of a seller at Portsmouth. In 1895 Worton spread the word all over London and cost the bookmakers a fortune at a generous price of 20/1. The following year another gamble was landed, but this time only 5/1 was available. Other high-class winners were Amphion, Polar Star and Wychwood Abbot and it was not unusual for classic winners to run in the race in the early days. Two trainers to dominate the race in later years were Atty Persse and Cecil Boyd-Rochfort, both of whom won the race six times, while trainer Eric Cousins took it four years in succession (1961–1964) with Chalk Stream, Water Skier (twice) and Commander in Chief.

Other major handicaps are the Queen's Prize, first run in 1895 over two miles, and the Rosebery Stakes (1932), run over the Jubilee course. The highest-profile race is the Group 3 September Stakes. For two-year-olds, there was the Imperial Produce Stakes, which produced a host of classic winners, the best of which was Mill Reef (1970). Sadly this race has disappeared from the calendar.

One regular patron at the end of the 19th century was the Prince of Wales. His chaser Fairplay won the Royal Handicap Steeplechase in 1882 but his finest winner was Ambush II, who won eight times, including the 1900 Grand National, and three times at Kempton. He did not run at all in 1901, as the new King was in mourning following the death of his mother. Ambush II – now owned by Edward VII – did return to Kempton in February 1902, winning the Stand Steeplechase. The King had been a great supporter of racing throughout his life and his ambition to win the Derby (as King) was fulfilled when his horse Minoru won at Epsom in 1909, just a year before he died. It was poignant that just hours before the King died in May 1910, his horse

Witch of the Air won at Kempton. The news was welcomed with a wry smile.

National Hunt racing began to gather momentum at Kempton and some of the best chasers won here, including Easter Hero and Golden Miller, who were both dominant in the 1930s. By the end of this decade, however, a new race emerged that was to become Kempton's greatest steeplechase – The King George VI Chase. The circumstances of its birth were highly unusual, as it was originally a selling chase. The Kempton executive had planned a tribute to King Edward VIII on his accession to the throne in January 1936, but when the new King abdicated later that year they were left with an embarrassing dilemma. So they renamed the Manor Optional Selling Chase as the King George VI Steeplechase in honour of the new monarch. It was first run under its new title in February 1937 and was won by Southern Hero. After a hiatus caused by the Second World War, the race was moved to Boxing Day in 1947, where it has remained since and the Grade I race has become Kempton's showpiece. Increasing its prize money and moving the race to its new date allowed prospective Cheltenham and Aintree horses more time and thus it attracts the best horses in the land. Run over three miles, it has become the second most prestigious steeplechase after the Cheltenham Gold Cup.

The list of King George VI Steeplechase winners since 1947 is nothing short of brilliant. The most popular winner was the lovable grey, Desert Orchid, who won it four times (1986, 1988–1990), but his record has since been bettered by the brilliant Kauto Star (2006–2009, 2011). His five-timer was completed at the grand old age of eleven, a record that will surely never be beaten. Wayward Lad, another popular horse from the northern stables of the Dickinson family, won it three times (1982, 1983, 1985), followed by dual winners Halloween (1952, 1953), Mandarin (1957, 1959), Pendil (1972, 1973),

Captain Christy (1974, 1975), Silver Buck (1979, 1980), The Fellow (1991, 1992), One Man (1995, 1996 – run at Sandown), See More Business (1997, 1999) and Kicking King (2004, 2005). Those to win it just once were Cottage Rake (1948), Limber Hill (1955), Mill House (1963), Arkle (1965), The Dikler (1971) and Burrough Hill Lad (1984).

Mill House and Arkle both won by wide margins, but the most remarkable win was by Captain Christy. Trained by Pat Taaffe in Ireland, in 1974 he led all the way to beat Pendil by eight lengths, but in 1975 he put up the most breathtaking performance with a superb display of jumping to beat Bula by 30 lengths. Arkle's win

in 1965 was marred by the fatal fall of Dunkirk, who had earlier that year won the Two Mile Champion Chase at Cheltenham. Owned by Bill Whitbread and trained by Peter Cazalet, he had shown tremendous speed over

Champion racehorse Desert Orchid in Hyde Park, London, celebrating the 50th running of the King George VI Chase at Kempton Park in December 2000. He is pictured with past winning owners and trainers (from left to right) Alison Begley, owner of Teeton Mill (1998 winner) holding the Chase trophy, Paul Barber the owner of l the 2013 winner See More Business, David Elsworth who is the trainer of four-times winner Desert Orchid. On the right is Desert Orchid's Stable Lass Janice Coyle.

two miles in all his races but it was a huge gamble to take on Arkle over three miles. He tried valiantly to match strides with him but fell heavily at the open ditch about six furlongs from home and broke his neck. (In those days the old Victorian stables on the far side of the course were still being used and were close to this obstacle. It is possible they may have been a distraction. In 1973 they were moved to a position near the paddock). Arkle himself suffered an injury in 1966, when beaten one length by Dormant. It transpired that he had raced with a fractured pedal bone of his hoof, but still battled on bravely. It was to be his final race and the end of an era.

National Hunt racing at Kempton was beginning to outshine the Flat, with other high-profile races such as the Racing Post Chase in February and, for the top hurdlers, the Christmas Hurdle and the Lanzarote Hurdle. Lanzarote was owned by Lord Howard de Walden and trained by Fred Winter. His finest hour was to win the 1974 Champion Hurdle, but at Kempton he was a standing dish. He was unbeaten here in eight starts between 1972 and 1976, including two Christmas Hurdles and the Imperial Cup (transferred from Sandown), carrying the massive weight of 12st 4lb. Throughout his career this tough performer won 20 of his 33 races, but sadly in the 1977 Cheltenham Gold Cup he broke a leg and had to be put down. Kempton have since proudly run the Lanzarote Hurdle in his honour.

Lady jockeys took centre stage at Kempton, but on the Flat, when they created history on 6 May 1972 with the running of the Goya Stakes over one mile one furlong, the first-ever ladies' race in Britain. It was won by Scorched Earth at 50/1, ridden by Meriel Tufnell and owned by her mother. Kempton was honoured with the appearance of Princess Anne riding in her first-ever steeplechase on 28 February 1987 (four months before becoming Princess Royal). It brought National Hunt racing to a new dimension and a large crowd came to see her. Riding her own horse Cnoc Na Cuille in the four-runner Portland Handicap Chase, she came a respectable fourth after leading for a long way.

Kempton underwent a massive change to their flat racing programme in 2005 by discontinuing all flat turf racing and building a new all-weather track. They were the fourth racecourse to embark on this type of racing but the first to build a right-handed track. The Jubilee course was scrapped altogether and the land sold. The new course was laid inside the National Hunt course, with two separate bends into the home straight. The last flat turf meeting was run on 2 May 2005 and amongst the winners that day was Her Majesty the Queen's Turnstile, who won the Amigo Handicap, trained by Richard Hannon and ridden by Ryan Moore.

The final race was, appropriately, the Jubilee Handicap, won by Mrs Pam Sly's San Antonio. Races like the Jubilee Handicap, the Rosebery Stakes and the Queen's Prize were to be retained when the new course opened ten months later.

On 25 March 2006 Kempton's inaugural all-weather meeting opened with an afternoon session, although floodlighting had also been installed with the intention of staging evening meetings all year round. The first race was won by Akona Matata, trained by Clive Brittain and ridden by Jimmy Fortune. The following month the first floodlit meeting took place.

Kempton may be the nearest racecourse to Central London but, until the renovations, it was not, perhaps, the most attractive, with a gloomy gravel pit occupying the centre of the course and beyond that the unsightly view of the Hampton Water Works. One person who didn't mind the outlook was a German prisoner of war housed there during the Second World War, who continued to live happily in the grandstand for a fortnight after the general repatriation.

Nobody stays after the last race these days.

Kilbeggan is located in County Westmeath in the centre of Ireland, about an hour from Dublin on the M6 motorway to Galway. The first recorded meeting was held on 9 March 1840. For 15 years racing was held at various places close to the town, including the present course at Loughnagore. These were difficult years, thanks to the combination of famine, land agitation, emigration and factional fighting. This all inevitably led to the end of the first phase of racing in the area in 1855.

On 17 April 1879 racing was revived when the first official meeting was held at Ballard, but this lasted only until 1885. The new century brought the third phase of racing at Loughnagore on 2 September 1901, and racing has continued here every year since with the exception of the Second World War.

From 1901 until 1947 only one meeting a year was staged. Always run in May, they were mixed cards of which the feature event was the Challenge Cup. Two trainers to dominate this period were Dick Cleary, who saddled 29 winners between 1903 and 1931, and James J Parkinson, who saddled 25 winners between 1907 and 1937.

Dick Cleary was a popular and highly-respected member of a Westmeath family all of whom were involved in racing. Dick had developed a career from horse breeding and training from as far back as 1883 and many good horses passed through his hands. The most famous were Shaun Spadah, who went on to win the 1921 Grand National when trained by George Poole, and Sergeant Murphy, who won the 1923 Grand National beating Shaun Spadah (two ex-Cleary horses finishing first and second).

Another prominent man in the history of Kilbeggan was Frank Barbour, who was one of the stewards for a number of years. He was a keen hunter and point-to-point rider who eventually turned to owning and training and had his first runner at Kilbeggan in 1913. He trained Shaun Spadah when he won the Loughnagore Plate in 1917, and in 1923 he also owned and trained Koko, who as a five-year-old finished third in a handicap hurdle. Koko went on to win the 1926 Cheltenham Gold Cup, still owned by Frank Barbour but trained in England by Alfred Bickley. Koko became the only Cheltenham Gold Cup winner to run at Kilbeggan. Frank Barbour won many

races in Ireland, including the Irish National with Punch in 1915, but his pride and joy was the brilliant Easter Hero. He will always be remembered for developing him from a moderate jumper (bought for only £50) to a superb chaser and the best in the British Isles.

A tragedy occurred in May 1952 when a young jockey, P F Conlon, riding Timber Topper, died from his injuries following a nine-horse pile-up in a mile and-a-half flat race. The 21-year-old appeared only slightly concussed at first but died in hospital later that evening.

On a brighter note, at the May meeting the following year Kilbeggan was in for a treat with the appearance of Prince Aly Khan (son of the Aga Khan), accompanied by the beautiful actress Gene Tierney. The sole purpose of their visit was for the Prince to ride in the last race, the bumper on a horse with the unpronounceable name of Ynys. The crowd eagerly awaited the race, backing Ynys down to 5/4 favourite, and he duly obliged, sending everybody home deliriously happy.

Nearby Mullingar closed in 1967 and Kilbeggan reaped the benefits. They discontinued flat racing and by 1971 had become the only racecourse in Ireland to stage National Hunt racing only. Recently, Punchestown and Thurles have followed suit.

Kilbeggan was voted Ireland's Racecourse of the Year in 1990.

The 2013 Irish Grand National winner Liberty Counsel parades at Kilbeggan.

The lakes of Killarney with the mountains in the background give this racecourse one of the most beautiful and natural settings in the world. Part of Killarney Park in County Kerry, the lake is known as Lough Leane and is overlooked by the heather-clad sandstone Purple Mountain; these, together with the McGuillycuddy Reeks, the Lakes of Killarney and Ross Castle and Killarney Cathedral, provide the most glorious backdrop. Race meetings were held in Killarney on three different racecourses between 1827 and 1901. Racing was resumed, at the present course, after a lapse of 35 years and soon established itself firmly, with a three-day May festival in 1947. Another festival in July has since been added, plus a two-day fixture in September.

The lovely town of Killarney and the surrounding areas are great tourist attractions, ensuring there are always large crowds at the festivals. In July 1991 they

The runners take the first hurdle at Killarney, with the Cathedral in the background.

were given a special treat when Lester Piggott made his first visit to the racecourse. Having recently returned to the saddle, he was riding three horses for his lifelong friend and old guv'nor Vincent O'Brien. (They all won.) When asked by the journalists after the meeting what he thought of their scenic racecourse he replied, 'I've seen worse'.

Many racecourses these days are also used for other functions, such as weddings, conferences, markets and car boot sales. The owners of this racecourse, the Killarney Race Company Ltd, lease one of the buildings for an unusual use – as a Driving Test Centre.

LAYTOWN

Laytown is situated in County Meath on the east coast of Ireland – literally. It is the only racecourse in Europe where racing actually takes place on the beach. Races are feasible only one day each year when the tide is at its lowest, which usually occurs around August, and the meeting takes place with the approval of the racing authorities.

Local folklore has it that it was the parish priest who in 1876 organised the first race meeting on Laytown's three miles of golden strand. It was held intermittently and did not become permanent until 1901, when local landowner Paddy Delaney established the meeting as we know it today. Nothing, not even two World Wars, has stopped it taking place since.

The enclosure consists of a three-acre field elevated above the beach. Steps have been built into the face of the sand dunes and these form the grandstand. Marquees are erected the day before the races and these are used to provide a weighing room, bars and refreshment areas. The only permanent building on the course is the Gents! Some railings are erected to form the paddock and unsaddling enclosure.

On the strand on the morning of the races a winning post is erected, plus about fifty yards of running rail with the remainder of the course marked by red flags on white poles. By the time of the first race the beach is thronged with people, creating a carnival atmosphere. The meeting has become quite a tourist attraction and among many

The scene in 1994 after the mayhem which left three jockeys injured and three horses dead.

celebrities to attend were the Aga Khan and his wife in 1950.

Some races used to be run on a round course that took the runners close to the edge of the sea. On one occasion a jockey lost control of his mount and forced another horse into the sea, causing him to drown. The rider of the unfortunate horse managed to jump off, as he was unable to swim. His claim of attempted murder was quickly rejected. There had been previous fatalities where horses had been injured when jumping pools of water, and nowadays all races are restricted to run over a straight mile. The U-shaped track was done away with and restrictions imposed on the number of runners (with only experienced riders allowed to race). Since then, too, vehicles and betting facilities have been banned.

Laytown attracts only moderate horses and it would not be unusual to see horses run twice. In 1957 Raleighstown won the first race under Mr Richard O'Connell and also the last, ridden by Johnny Wright.

Nobody takes racing at Laytown too seriously. If the weather is fine it is a lovely fun day out for the family. It is unique and not comparable with other racecourses, but it has something they don't have that works like clockwork – a first-class watering system that doesn't cost a penny.

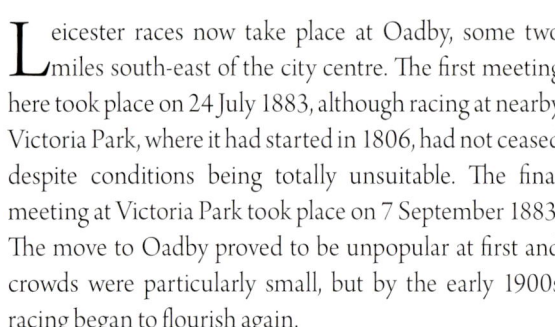

Leicester races now take place at Oadby, some two miles south-east of the city centre. The first meeting here took place on 24 July 1883, although racing at nearby Victoria Park, where it had started in 1806, had not ceased despite conditions being totally unsuitable. The final meeting at Victoria Park took place on 7 September 1883. The move to Oadby proved to be unpopular at first and crowds were particularly small, but by the early 1900s racing began to flourish again.

However, records show the earliest meeting in Leicester to have been on 23 March 1603, at a venue known as Abbey Meadow. This important date in the history of Leicester Races was somewhat overshadowed the following day with the grave news of the death of Queen Elizabeth I, after a reign of 44 years.

Leicester will long be associated with first successes of two racing legends. Golden Miller won his first-ever race at Leicester in the Gopsall Maiden Hurdle on 20 January 1931, ridden by Bob Lyall, who later that year won the

Grand National on Grakle. Ten years earlier, on 31 March 1921, Gordon Richards had ridden his first winner on Gay Lord in the Apprentices Plate for trainer Martin Hartigan. It was Gordon's third ride in public. Leicester provided another landmark for Richards when, on 10 November 1947, he rode Twenty Twenty to victory in the Stoughton Plate by a short head. It was his 260th winner of the season, beating his own record of 259 achieved in 1933. (The previous record of 246 had been set by Fred Archer in 1885). Gordon Richards finished the 1947 season on 269 winners, a flat record that still stands today.

Leicester became host to another legend on 15 October 1990, this time in the form of a comeback for Lester Piggott. He rode Lupescu in Division One of the Hare Maiden Fillies Stakes for Henry Cecil, finishing second on the 5/1 chance, beaten a short head. However, it was the return to riding after a five-year absence that thrilled the huge crowd. Lester had originally retired from the saddle in 1985 to take up training, but his new career

The 20-length maiden winner that never was: heavily-backed Flockton Grey (later identified as the experienced Good Hand) approaches the winning post in 1982.

had been interrupted by a brief prison sentence for tax evasion before making his comeback.

From heroes to villains and the story of an unraced grey two-year-old called Flockton Grey. In the Knighton Auction Stakes at Leicester on 29 March 1982, Flockton Grey won by 20 lengths, to the surprise of jockey Kevin Darley and trainer Stephen Wiles. From his stables at Flockton near Wakefield, Wiles had sent out his first winner on the flat after two years with a licence, and yet Flockton Grey returned as a heavily-backed 10/1 chance.

His owner Ken Richardson had bought the horse as a yearling and kept it on his farm. Two weeks before the race he brought the horse to Wiles' stables and asked him to declare Flockton Grey for the Leicester race, but kept him on his farm in the meantime, arranging to meet him with the horse at the races. The horse returned to Wiles' stables the day after the race, but Wiles was certain that this was not the same horse he had stood with in the winner's enclosure. The horse at Leicester had a scar on his off foreleg and this horse had not.

The Jockey Club launched an investigation and it eventually transpired that the winner was in fact an experienced three-year-old called Good Hand. The investigation continued for nearly five years, during which time both horses were kept in police custody at the taxpayers' expense.

Ken Richardson and two accomplices were sent for trial and found guilty of switching the horses, and Flockton Grey was disqualified. After the horses were released, Flockton Grey was bought by Robin Bastiman for 680 guineas in December 1986. He was now nearly a seven-year-old and still unraced. For the record he was a 20-length maiden winner that never was.

LEOPARDSTOWN

With the closure of metropolitan courses at Baldoyle in 1972 and Phoenix Park in 1990, Leopardstown is the only racecourse within the city of Dublin. Situated in the suburbs five miles south of the city at Foxrock, Leopardstown is older than its ex-neighbours, having opened on 27 August 1888.

The opening was very grand, with an attendance of over 50,000 and among them the Queen's Lord Lieutenant of Ireland, the Marquess of Londonderry. Another special occasion came in 1897 to celebrate the Diamond Jubilee of Queen Victoria, when she was represented at the course by the Duke and Duchess of York (who later became King George V and Queen Mary). The King George V cup (which first took place in 1911) was resurrected by Leopardstown racecourse and the British Irish Chamber of Commerce in June 2013 to recognise the strong racing ties of Ireland and the UK. Furthermore, the historic visit by Queen Elizabeth II and the Duke of Edinburgh to Ireland in May 2011, marked the centenary of the last visit of a British monarch to Ireland, which was the Queen's grandfather King George V in July 1911.

The winner of the inaugural King George V Cup in 1911, was Kirk Bloom, owned by a farmer Daniel Moloney from Knocklong. He was presented with The Farmer's Royal Cup by King George V and Queen Mary. In 2013, the family provided the original cup and it was competed for once again.

Leopardstown is modelled on Sandown Park, having been managed by a former assistant at the English course. When the course was reconstructed in 1971 it became the most modern racecourse in Europe and, although the Curragh is regarded as Ireland's premier racecourse, Leopardstown is the best dual-purpose one. There was at one time a separate six-furlong sprint course which opened in 1984 (another similarity to Sandown Park), but approached the winning post from the opposite direction. It closed, sadly, in 2002 to make way for the M50 motorway. Leopardstown was chosen to create a piece of racing history when, for a flat meeting on 21 July 1985, they staged the first-ever meeting on a Sunday in the British Isles.

National Hunt racing is of the highest order here, with the feature race being the Hennessy Gold Cup, run over three miles in February. Before 1991 it was known as the Vincent O'Brien Irish Gold Cup but since then under its new sponsor it has been won by some top-class horses. The most prolific winner was Florida Pearl, trained by Willie Mullins, who won the cup four times (1999, 2000, 2001, 2004). There have been two triple winners, Jodami (1993, 1994, 1995) and Beef or Salmon (2003, 2006, 2007). The latter, trained by Michael Hourigan, was practically unbeatable at Leopardstown but could not find the same form on English soil. Jodami completed the Hennessy–Cheltenham Gold Cup double in 1993, a feat also accomplished by Imperial Call in 1996. Other high class chases run at Leopardstown are the Lexus Chase (formerly the Ericsson Chase) and the Paddy Power Gold Cup, both run at the Christmas Festival.

The most prestigious hurdle race is the Irish Champion Hurdle, run in January. Triple English Champion Hurdle winner Istabraq added four Irish equivalents from 1998 to 2001, but by far the biggest betting race at Leopardstown is the Irish Sweeps Hurdle, once part of the four-day Christmas festival. It is now known as the Boylesports.com Hurdle, but the original race was run in 1969 (the first two runnings were at Fairyhouse during the redevelopment of Leopardstown) and won by Normandy, trained by Fred Rimell and ridden by Terry Biddlecombe. Other early winners were Persian War (1970), Captain Christy (1972), Comedy of Errors (1973, 1974) and Night Nurse (1975), but in 1976 the race became a handicap and it no longer attracted such classy horses. The title of the race changed to the Ladbroke Handicap Hurdle in 1987 and again in 2001 (until 2009) to the Pierse Handicap Hurdle.

The highlight of the flat season is the Irish Champion Stakes, run over ten furlongs in September. The race began as the Joe McGrath Memorial Stakes in 1976, when it was won by that year's Irish Derby winner Malacate. In 1984 the race was transferred to Phoenix Park and became the Phoenix Champion Stakes. The first running was the most valuable race ever run in Ireland and went to Sadler's Wells, then a top-class ten-furlong racehorse and later the most influential stallion until his death in 2011. After the closure of Phoenix Park in 1990 the race returned to Leopardstown, where it has produced an array of high-class winners – Suave Dancer (1991), Dr Devious (1992), Pilsudski (1997), Swain (1998), Daylami (1999), Giant's Causeway (2000), Fantastic Light (2001), High Chaparral (2003), Dylan Thomas (2006, 2007), New Approach (2008), Sea the Stars (2009) and So You Think (2011). One of the greatest finishes was Dr Devious, who had won the English Derby, and St Jovite, the Irish Derby winner. They were locked in a titanic battle all the way up the straight and the photo finish revealed Dr Devious had won by a short head.

Leopardstown has attracted all the best horses under both codes for many years and the list would not be complete without Arkle. He was unbeaten in five chases here between 1963 and 1966, including the Leopardstown Handicap Chase three times prior to his three victories in the Cheltenham Gold Cup. He had made an appearance here on 26 December 1961 as a gawky, backward four-year-old on his second visit to a racecourse in the Greystones Maiden National Hunt flat race. He finished fourth under amateur Mark Hely-Hutchinson, who also rode him to third place on his racecourse debut in a similar event at Mullingar. Mark's claim to fame was to be the only jockey that didn't win on Arkle but his contribution to the horse's education was priceless. Mark rode out for trainer Tom Dreaper twice a week before going to work and rode Arkle in his preparation regularly. He rode his first winner in April 1959 and had partnered Olympia to victory at Cheltenham. He was delighted to be asked to ride Arkle in his two bumpers and he gave him a patient, tender ride. He was instructed not to use the whip and he looked after him. Arkle became the greatest steeplechaser that ever lived and Mark Hely-Hutchinson must take an enormous amount of credit. He was one of racing's many unsung heroes.

LIMERICK

Limerick is Ireland's newest racecourse, having opened in October 2001. It is situated six miles south of the city centre at Greenmount, near the village of Patrickswell on an area of ground formerly used for point-to-point racing. It was the first racecourse to open in Ireland for nearly fifty years since Sligo opened their doors in 1955.

Until 1999 Limerick races had been held at Greenpark, close to the city centre and the River Shannon. They had raced here for 130 years but latterly there was a continual problem with flooding and a new location was needed. The final meeting took place on 21 March 1999 with the honour of the last winner going to Arthur Moore's gelding Well Ridden in the concluding bumper.

Racing in the Limerick area dates back before 1750, with meetings at Rathkeale, Lemonfield, Bruff and

Newcastle. The most established was at Newcastle, where in 1860 the meeting was attended by 30,000 racegoers. However, at the 1867, meeting it all went tragically wrong with appalling scenes of drunkenness and the horrific murder of a child by its father. The local press took a year to report on the dreadful scenes that marred the meeting but the landowner took immediate action and never permitted racing on his land again. The racing organisers had to find another location and in 1868 secured a lease on a site at Ballinacurra, two miles from Limerick City. It was here that they ran a Royal Plate of 100 guineas, but it proved to be the first and last plate at Limerick, as the following year it was transferred to the newly-opened Cork Park. The committee tried in vain to recover Newcastle but they had to look elsewhere and settled on

The old course at Greenpark, a far cry from the new facilities opened in October 2001.

Rain in Spain pulls away from Palace Storm in the first race of Limerick's inaugural meeting in 2001.

Greenpark, which became Limerick's home for the next 130 years.

The inaugural meeting at Greenmount was on Sunday 14 October 2001 and attracted a crowd of 18,000. The opening race, the Finucane Electrical Maiden Hurdle, was won by Edward O'Grady's Rain in Spain, ridden by Norman Williamson. (Rain in Spain was owned by Simon Tindall and was bought during the tea interval at a Lord's Test Match). The feature event was the Munster National Handicap Chase and the first running at the new course was won by the top-weight Foxchapel King in the hands of David Casey and trained by Mouse Morris. (The last winner of the Munster National on the old course at Greenpark in 1998 was Imperial Call, who had won the Cheltenham Gold Cup in 1996.)

Johnny Murtagh is thrown into the water trough by fellow Champions Barry Geraghty, Tony McCoy, Pat Smullen, Ruby Walsh and Declan McDonagh at the Limerick Charity Race Day in 2013.

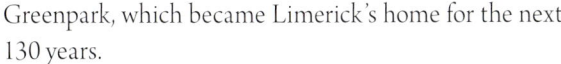

Racegoers today at Lingfield are constantly reminded of its close proximity to Gatwick Airport by the steady noise of aircraft ascending and descending above the enclosures. Ironically, Gatwick was a racecourse itself once until its closure in 1940 to make way for what would become London's second-largest airport. The racecourse stood where the South Terminal is today.

Lingfield Park opened on 15 November 1890 while Gatwick opened one year later, so they were neighbours for nearly 50 years. Gatwick made the better start by inheriting the fixtures from the recently defunct Croydon and also played host to three Grand Nationals during the First World War, while Lingfield's opening was a low-key affair with a National Hunt meeting. The first race was a Hunter Chase, won by Old Tatt. But Lingfield grew in popularity and four years later it held its first flat meeting on 16 May 1894, attended by the Prince of Wales.

In 1915 Fred Wilmot was appointed Clerk of the Course and put Lingfield firmly on the map with his brainwave of staging a Derby trial because of the similarity of the course to Epsom. The inaugural running of the Lingfield Derby Trial, as it became known, was in 1932. It was won by April the Fifth, owned and trained at Epsom by Tom Walls, who was more famous for his career as an actor.

April the Fifth had been quite unfancied at Lingfield, having won only a mile maiden at Gatwick the previous week and, even after winning the trial by six lengths, he was still not regarded as a serious candidate for Epsom. However, he won the Derby at 100/6, ridden by Fred Lane and beating, among others, the 2,000 Guineas winner Orwell, who started 5/4 favourite and was regarded by many as unbeatable. The success of April the Fifth, who incidentally became the first winner of the Derby to be trained at Epsom for 94 years (the previous one was Amato 1838), gave a huge boost to the new Lingfield Derby trial.

Inspired by this success, in 1933 Fred Wilmot introduced the Oaks trial, with the first running being won by Lookalive (6/1), trained by Cecil Boyd-Rochfort and ridden by Gordon Richards. With both trials now firmly established, they became, probably, second in status only to the Guineas. The Derby trial produced more Epsom winners than the Oaks trial in early years. Those to land the Lingfield–Epsom double were Mid-day Sun (1937), Tulyar (1952), Parthia (1959), Teenoso (1983), Slip

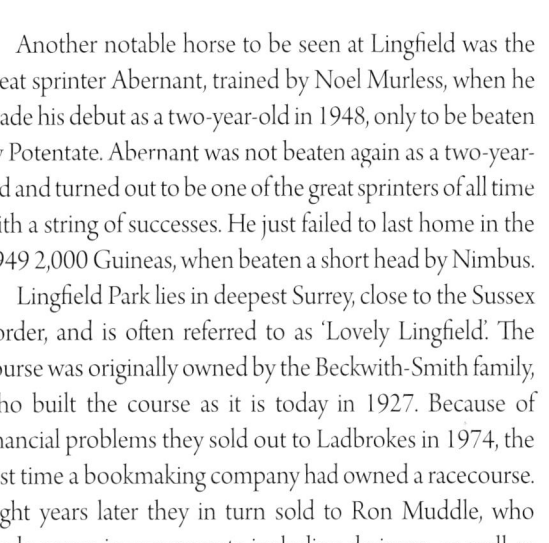

April the Fifth with jockey Fred Lane and trainer Tom Walls.

Anchor (1985), Kahyasi (1988) and High-Rise (1998). There have also been a few Epsom heroes who failed at Lingfield, notably Charlottown, who in 1966 finished second to Black Prince II in the Derby trial having been left twenty lengths. Blakeney (1969) and Snow Knight (1974) were also beaten at Lingfield.

Probably the best horse to win the Derby trial was Alcide in 1958, trained by Cecil Boyd-Rochfort. Alcide was a hot favourite for Epsom but a few days before the race was got at and had to be withdrawn. Let's also give a mention to Morston (1973), who won the Derby in only his second race. He had made a winning debut at Lingfield, not in the Derby trial but in the ten-furlong Godstone Plate.

Lingfield Oaks trial winners have been less successful in the Epsom race, with the exception of Sleeping Partner (1969), Ginevra (1972), Lady Carla (1996) and Ramruma (1999). Ark Royal won the Oaks trial in 1955 for trainer George Colling but had the misfortune to meet the exceptional filly Meld in the Oaks. She finished a creditable second, beaten six lengths; Meld went on to win the fillies' Triple Crown.

Another notable horse to be seen at Lingfield was the great sprinter Abernant, trained by Noel Murless, when he made his debut as a two-year-old in 1948, only to be beaten by Potentate. Abernant was not beaten again as a two-year-old and turned out to be one of the great sprinters of all time with a string of successes. He just failed to last home in the 1949 2,000 Guineas, when beaten a short head by Nimbus.

Lingfield Park lies in deepest Surrey, close to the Sussex border, and is often referred to as 'Lovely Lingfield'. The course was originally owned by the Beckwith-Smith family, who built the course as it is today in 1927. Because of financial problems they sold out to Ladbrokes in 1974, the first time a bookmaking company had owned a racecourse. Eight years later they in turn sold to Ron Muddle, who made many improvements including drainage, as well as improving the notorious bend into the straight. The course was sold again in 1988 to Arena Leisure Investments.

In 1989 Lingfield made racing history when it opened its all-weather track. The Equitrack surface was laid out inside the turf course of about nine furlongs circumference for flat and hurdle races throughout the winter, although hurdling was later abolished. The first ever all-weather meeting took place on 30 October 1989, a flat meeting comprising twelve races which started at 11.00 am. The opening race was a one-mile claimer won by Niklas Angel, the 7/2 favourite, ridden by Richard Quinn. The first National Hunt all-weather meeting at Lingfield took place on 16 November that year, although Southwell, the only other course with an all-weather track at the time, had hosted the inaugural meeting of this type fifteen days earlier.

One final footnote in Lingfield's history concerns a then unknown apprentice jockey having his first ride in public on 16 October 1920. He rode a horse called Clockwork for trainer Martin Hartigan in the five-furlong October Nursery Handicap. He finished fourth at 25/1. The jockey's name was Gordon Richards.

Listowel is renowned for its festival in late September which since 2002 has stretched to seven days. The meeting was originally known as the North Kerry Hunt Steeplechases and dates back to 1858. Racing lapsed the following year, but recovered quickly to hold a two-day festival in 1861.

Racing in the area was previously located on the beach at Ballyeigh near Ballybunion but it was often the scene of factional fighting – which resulted in twenty deaths in 1834 – and racing eventually moved to Listowel. The course is close to the town on an island bounded on two sides by the River Feale, so flooding can be a concern, but nothing else prevents the festival taking place with strong support from the local community and for over 150 years it has been the working man's festival.

Although a three-day holiday meeting is now held at the beginning of June, it is the September festival that means so much to the locals and an average of 15,000 attend each day. Since 1976 it has been run in conjunction with the harvest festival, and the sizeable proportion of the locals who are farmers can celebrate the result of a rich yield or get away from the stress of a disappointing season.

The feature race at the festival is the Kerry National, which confirms that National Hunt racing is preferred here. The 1975 Grand National hero and dual Gold Cup winner L'Escargot finished second in the Kerry National after his Aintree success, and 2003 Grand National winner Monty's Pass ran in four Kerry Nationals, finishing second in 2001 and winning in 2002. Michael Hourigan's star Dorans Pride also won the Kerry National in 1997 carrying 12 stone under Richard Dunwoody, while Bregawn, winner of that historic 1983 Cheltenham Gold Cup and owned locally by the Kennelly brothers, won a flat race here under Tom Mullins two years later.

The Listowel festival is a wonderful week of typically hectic Irish racing and plenty of stamina is required. Visitors are very welcome but don't worry if you cannot find accommodation – nobody goes to sleep anyway.

Left: runners pass the Kerry Food plant, and below, in the Helena Sheahan Memorial Maiden they round the final bend, with the Listowel Arms Hotel in the background.

The history books show the oldest racecourse in the British Isles to be Chester, which opened in 1540, but it could be argued that Ludlow is older.

The present racecourse is at Bromfield just less than two miles north of the town. It is well documented that officers garrisoned at Ludlow Castle matched their horses on the Old Field Bromfield during the 14th century.

It would be fitting if Ludlow could boast that it is the oldest racecourse because the town, often called 'the perfect historic town', is a sheer delight. Ludlow Castle, built by the Normans around 1090, was one of a line of castles along the Marches to keep the Welsh out. Its long history has included associations with some of the greatest families in the land. It was also briefly the home of King Edward V who, in 1483 at just twelve years old, set off from here for his coronation in London along with his eleven-year-old brother the Duke of York. They were seized before they reached London and imprisoned in the Tower of London where they later died, supposedly murdered.

There are also nearly 500 listed buildings in the town and the medieval street pattern survives almost intact. Among one of the many ancient properties is the world-famous Feathers Hotel where once you could stable your horse for five shillings, including hay and straw. *The New York Times* once described this 17th-century inn as 'the most handsome in the world'.

Despite claims that the racecourse is older than Chester, it can alas only be described as courtyard gossip, as the earliest recorded meeting at Bromfield was not until 27 August 1729 and it was a flat meeting. National Hunt racing was not introduced until the early 1850s and Bromfield became exclusively a National Hunt venue by 1868.

One lovely feature of the racecourse is the open-topped Edwardian Grandstand, erected in 1904 and giving a superb view not only of the whole course but also of the beautiful surrounding area and, in particular, Clee Hill.

The racecourse is shared with the local golf club and while this can incur hazards to the course such as divots, nothing compares with the fact that there are seven road crossings – for which huge mats are provided, though this has discouraged some trainers from sending their better horses to Ludlow.

Racing at Ludlow was given a tremendous boost in 1932 when Forbra won the Grand National at Aintree. He was owned by a local retired bookmaker, Bill Parsonage, and his victory gave the town of Ludlow one of its proudest moments. Parsonage had tried on five previous occasions to win the Grand National and in 1928 his horse Master Billie had started favourite. But it was not until four years later that his seven-year-old Forbra fulfilled his lifetime ambition.

Ridden by Tim Hamey and trained at Kinnersley in Worcestershire by Tom Rimell (Fred Rimell's father), he won at 50/1, although he was readily available at twice those odds the week before. Of the 36 runners, Forbra was one of only eight to finish. He had the distinction of never falling in a race and among his victims at Liverpool were the high-class Heartbreak Hill from Ireland, Gregalach (1929 winner) and Grakle (1931 winner).

Forbra had won at Taunton and Newbury and had finished third in the National Hunt Steeplechase at Cheltenham, so his odds of 50/1 were quite generous considering he was carrying only 10st 7lbs. He was a skinner

for the bookmakers on the course and all over the country, except perhaps for one or two local street bookmakers who may have caught a bit of a cold. Nevertheless, to commemorate the great occasion the Forbra Gold Cup is now run at Ludlow every March.

The other feature race at Ludlow is the Prince of Wales Challenge Trophy Handicap Chase for Amateur Riders run in November. Prince Charles has had a great affection for Ludlow since he rode here on 24 October 1980 on his own horse Allibar in the Clun Amateur Riders Handicap Chase over three miles. Riding in only his third chase, he finished second, beaten six lengths by Hello Louis, ridden by Mr Keith Reveley and trained by his mother, Mary Reveley.

The Prince made up an enormous amount of ground in the home straight, overtaking several of his rivals. The closing stages caused quite a degree of excitement to one young lady in the stands, shouting encouragement to the Prince at the top of her voice. Her identity was revealed as Lady Diana Spencer.

Prince Charles and Allibar in the 1980 Clun Amateur Riders Handicap Chase, in which they came second. Among the spectators were both the Prince's wives-to-be, Lady Diana Spencer and Camilla Parker-Bowles.

Market Rasen is delightfully situated on the west slopes of the Lincolnshire Wolds and over the years has had at least three racecourses. The first was at Hambleton Hill, where the earliest meeting is reported to have been in March 1859, and this survived thanks to the patronage of the Union Hunt, whose annual feature was the Union Steeplechase. The venue changed to Walesby in 1875 but for over thirty years meetings were not regular.

The present course opened in 1924 thanks to a consortium of local gentlemen headed by Wilfred Cartwright and James Nettleship, who decided to lay out a new course on land purchased by the group. They were granted two fixtures, the first of which took place on Easter Monday 1924. The inaugural day belonged to Bob Lyall, who owned, trained and rode the winner of the first race, a Selling Chase worth £50, with the odds-on favourite Have a Care. He completed a double by also winning the last race, the Town Hurdle, with the evens favourite Honeysuckle. Bob Lyall's claim to fame in later years was to partner Golden Miller in his first victory, and he also won the 1931 Grand National on board Grakle. After he retired he worked for the BBC as a commentator, starting

with Reynoldstown's victory in the 1935 Grand National.

Market Rasen was transformed after the Second World War thanks to Victor Lucas, who in 1946 was appointed Clerk of the Course. The first meeting after hostilities ceased came on Easter Monday that year and a reported crowd of 20,000 crammed into the primitive stands. This was not an overpopulated part of Lincolnshire and to attract a crowd of this magnitude gave Victor Lucas the incentive to put many of his ideas and innovations into practice.

His task was enormous, having inherited a few wooden buildings and a run-down track. He began by creating a separate hurdle and chase track, as well as rebuilding the bends to make them easier. He also provided a landing strip for light aircraft in the centre of the course.

It was not until the 1960s that money was available (with some help from the Levy Board) to build two new stands and ,at the same time, he positioned the parade ring in front of the stands so that even those in the cheaper enclosure could survey the runners. (Market Rasen became the first racecourse to adopt this idea; some other courses followed suit.) With the closure of the course at

Market Rasen's influential Clerk of the Course, Victor Lucas.

excitement by winning the first two races on Wayward Wind and It's Unbelievable, but then when Bobby Socks and Logical Sun were beaten it became mathematically impossible for him and Richard Dunwoody was crowned champion with 198 winners. It was a thrilling night for the huge Lincolnshire crowd.

But the jubilant scenes on that warm summer evening in 1994 can quickly be forgotten when tragedy strikes this sport we all love. Highs and lows of National Hunt racing could not be better illustrated than when, on 3 July 2005, Tom Halliday, a 20-year-old conditional jockey based with Sue Smith in Yorkshire, was killed in an horrific fall here. Riding Rush'n'Run for his boss in a novices handicap hurdle, he was unseated approaching the third-last flight but held on to the reins when the horse became unbalanced and fell heavily, landing on the young rider. Tom, a jockey with a very bright future who had ridden just four winners in his short career, all for Sue Smith, lost his life doing what he loved most and the racing world was devastated.

Jockey John Buckingham will remember Market Rasen well for his involvement in an unprecedented incident in the course's history in March 1966. Riding the mare Lira for trainer Edward Courage in the three-mile Cox Moore Sweaters Handicap Chase, the field of ten approached the tenth fence, which was divided to make two obstacles – an open ditch on the stands side and a plain fence on the other. John took his mount over the plain fence while his nine opponents took the ditch. The spectators assumed John and Lira had made a mistake and so did his fellow jockeys, who shouted at him to pull up. Lira finished second to Hyanna, ridden by George Lee, but John knew he would either win or be disqualified. John was right and was awarded the race. He certainly knew what he was doing and he knew his way around Aintree as well –a year later he rode Foinavon in the 1967 Grand National.

neighbouring Lincoln in 1964, Market Rasen is now the only course in Lincolnshire. Victor Lucas and his team must take enormous credit for all their hard work in making this racecourse so popular. On his retirement his son John took over the reins, but in March each year the Victor Lucas Long Distance Hurdle is proudly run in his honour.

Bank Holiday fixtures continue to be popular, along with many evening meetings, some of which are on Saturday nights. Not long ago on such a night Market Rasen used to bring down the curtain on the National Hunt season in June. The 1993/1994 season ended at Market Rasen with the jockeys' title going to the wire. Richard Dunwoody and Adrian Maguire were locked together, both of them riding at Stratford in the afternoon and Market Rasen in the evening. Dunwoody rode a treble in the afternoon, leaving Maguire needing to go through the card in the evening. He sustained the

MUSSELBURGH

usselburgh lies five miles east of Edinburgh Castle on the south shore of the Firth of Forth. The racecourse is the lowest in Britain, with a high tide mark in the centre of the course.

The centre of the course has its own piece of history as it is the home of Musselburgh Links Golf course, the oldest surviving golf course in Britain, dating from 1567, which staged the first British Open Championship in 1874. Among its early patrons were Mary Queen of Scots and James VI of Scotland, who became James I of England. The links are on common land for the people of Musselburgh, a situation that also occurs on the downs at Epsom.

Until the beginning of 1996 the racecourse operated under the title of Edinburgh Racecourse but, with a little persuasion from East Lothian District Council, they raced for the first time under the new banner of Musselburgh for the National Hunt meeting on 12 January 1996.

Racing had begun closer to the city centre in 1504 on Leith Sands, so Edinburgh could claim to be one of the oldest meetings in the world. Leith race week was a carnival for the citizens of Edinburgh and caused a partial suspension of work and business. Many of the huge crowd would watch from the pier, which became a temporary grandstand, but over subsequent years the location created many problems. Sometimes the tide would come in during the meeting, causing the final races to be run the following day – which was against Jockey Club rules. Ten years were lost altogether during the reign of George II, who put a restraint on owners entering more than one horse in a race. By 1805 the situation had become worse – attendances were low and entries were poor, with hardly any from England. Horses were running fetlock deep in heavy, wet sand, causing many to break down.

In 1816 racing was transferred from Leith Sands to Musselburgh Links, the present site of the course. The inaugural meeting on 7 October lasted six days and the first race, the King's Plate over four miles, was won by the Marquess of Queensberry's Epperston. The following year the Edinburgh Gold Cup was first run over three miles with a prize of 100 guineas. It is still run today in June, but over a mile and a half. In 1821 a race known as the Scotch St Ledger was first run but was not continuous, carrying the conditions of being open only to Scottish-bred horses, and gradually fell by the wayside.

However, racing did prosper at its new venue and the only interruption came in 1832 when, owing to a cholera scare in the Edinburgh area, the races were transferred to Gullane, which was then known as the Newmarket of Scotland.

Musselburgh has never attracted top-class horses but there have, nevertheless, been several favourites with racegoers. In 1866 a filly by the name of Contract ran three times at Musselburgh, winning on the final occasion. There is nothing special about that, except that she raced a total of 63 times, many at Musselburgh, winning 12 times in her career. That was excellent, but still not record-breaking. That came in 1893 when, at the age of 31, she produced a live filly foal – which is still a world record.

Another old timer to grace the Musselburgh Links is Le Garcon d'Or, who was foaled in 1958 and was still racing at the age of 15. Le Garcon d'Or is the joint holder of the record for winning the most flat races in Britain since 1900. He won 34 between 1960 and 1972, equalling the tally of High Stakes. Le Garcon d'Or achieved five of his wins at Musselburgh, more than at any other course, and his memorial race is run at

the Scottish venue because it was there that he equalled the record with his last victory, at the age of 14, in a selling handicap in June 1972. Le Garcon d'Or ran in a total of 181 races, and 15 of his wins came in sellers. He was trained throughout his career by Jack Ormston at Richmond, North Yorkshire, and his most regular jockey was Alec Russell, who partnered him to eleven victories, including his last. He died in 1986, aged 28.

On 6 October 1905 the 6th Earl of Rosebery visited the course for the first time and his runner Caraval, ridden by Willie Higgs, duly obliged. From that day Lord Rosebery was an enthusiastic supporter of Musselburgh and patronised the course until his death in 1974. His familiar colours of primrose and rose hoops were seen for nearly seventy years. In 1963 the Levy Board wanted to close Musselburgh but Lord Rosebery, himself a member of the Jockey Club from 1932, stood firm and rejected any suggestion of closure; the very existence of Musselburgh today is thanks to him.

The course's close proximity to the shoreline means that the prospects of snow and frost are slim and, together with the sandy soil, this led to a National Hunt course at Musselburgh being given the thumbs up; Jonjo O'Neill officially opened the new course on 5 January 1987. The introduction of jump racing was widely acclaimed by trainers because, even throughout the hardest of winters, Musselburgh could nearly always guarantee good ground. Unlike most other National Hunt courses the fences are mobile and can be dismantled during the flat season, while the hurdles are taken away to Perth for their spring and autumn fixtures.

Recent developments at the track have included integrating a strip of fibres and all-weather surface into the jumps turf track around the winning post bend. At least they didn't have to go far for the sand.

NAAS

In July 1922 local merchant Thomas Whelen persuaded thirty businessmen and farmers to invest £200 each to commence racing at Naas in County Kildare, about 20 miles from Dublin. The course is left-handed with an uphill finish and a long run-in. The first meeting took place on 19 June 1924.

It was not an ideal time to be making such an investment, as Ireland was entering an economic depression. Naas racecourse would also be very close to the Curragh, headquarters of Flat racing, and Punchestown, the leading National Hunt course. Furthermore, in late 1926 the Irish government imposed a new betting tax, which coincided with the Naas November meeting.

Naas has survived despite these challenges and among many famous horses to have run here were Cottage Rake, Prince Regent, Mill House, Arkle, Early Mist, Nicolaus Silver, Kilmore and Team Spirit.

Cottage Rake, triple Cheltenham Gold Cup winner, won here on the flat in the 1946 Naas November Handicap. Prince Regent, the best chaser in Ireland during the Second World War, also won on the flat here in 1940 before accumulating eighteen wins during his career over fences.

Mill House was bred locally by Mrs B Lawlor, whose family owned the famous Naas hotel, Osberstown House. (The dam of Mill House, Nas Na Riogh took her name from the Irish version of Naas). Mill House ran his first two races at Naas, winning the second, a novice hurdle in March 1961, ridden by Pat Taaffe who also partnered Arkle in the second win of his career in a handicap hurdle the following year.

Navan Racecourse in County Meath was known as Proudstown Park when it opened on 17 September 1921. It was the enterprise of the breeder Albert Lowry, a legendary gambler and raconteur from a local firm of auctioneers and livestock dealers. Its first grandstand was purchased for £50 from a racecourse in Wales which was closing down.

The course was beautifully made and has been described as the perfect course for jumping, with wide sweeping bends, well-built fences and a stiff uphill finish.

It is ideal for its major race, the Troytown Chase, run in November over three miles. It is named after the 1920 Grand National winner, who was owned and bred locally by Major Thomas Collins-Gerard. Troytown might have been the greatest-ever winner of the Grand National at the age of seven but the following season he broke a leg in a fall at Auteuil in France and had to be put down. He was trained by Algy Anthony and ridden in all his races by top amateur Jack Anthony, who likened him to riding a steam engine. An example of this came in the 1920 National when, in atrocious conditions of driving rain and high winds, he slipped and completely demolished the fourth-last fence, losing the lead by several lengths, yet pulled himself to the front again by the next obstacle. He was so powerful this mishap made little difference and he eventually won by 12 lengths, to the delight of the Irish who regarded him as unbeatable – and yet he was allowed to start at the generous price of 6/1.

A few decades later Navan played host to another Irish idol on 20 January 1962, but at the time nobody had heard of a bay five-year-old gelding by Archive and owned by Anne, Duchess of Westminster called Arkle. In only his third race (having previously run with promise in two bumpers) he contested the 27-runner Bective Novices Hurdle. Trained just 20 miles away by Tom Dreaper, among his opponents was his stable companion, the mare Kerforo, the even money favourite ridden by Pat Taaffe, already a winner of three chases, and also Blunt Cross. The ground was heavy and with four flights to jump Blunt Cross and Kerforo seemed to have the race between them, but Arkle had them in his sights and in the hands of Liam McLoughlin swept by them both, winning at 20/1. His rider said afterwards, 'He was travelling so well I just gave him a kick and he took off'. Pat Taaffe said, 'When he passed me he was flying. We were at the end of the race, but it was as if he'd just started'.

The Tote paid £6 4s 6d for a stake of 2s 6d (odds of 49/1). If only we had just a whisper; but at least it was an historic day for Navan.

NEWBURY

Newbury is without doubt the finest dual-purpose racecourse in the south of England today. It owes everything to founder John Porter, who had already achieved stardom as a trainer and must rank among the finest during the 19th century. Born in 1838, he began his career as a jockey but before he was 30 he switched his attention to training from his stables at Kingsclere. He trained seven Derby winners, the best of whom were the unbeaten Ormonde (1886) and Flying Fox (1899).

He travelled regularly by train from Newbury to London and in 1904 he stared from his carriage window and imagined an ideal place for a racecourse between Greenham Common and the railway. He formed a syndicate with the owner of the land and they sent their plans to the Jockey Club for approval. The plans were rejected but, after consulting King Edward VII, who was a past owner, Porter was persuaded to submit again and with the King's support the plans were approved at the second attempt.

So Newbury opened its doors with a two-day meeting on 26–27 September 1905. 15,000 people watched the inaugural race, the five-furlong Whatcombe Handicap worth £160. Twenty-seven runners went to the start and the race was won by Mr D J Pullinger's Copper King, ridden by 'Hellfire Jack' Charlie Trigg and trained by Charles Marnes at Newmarket. Marnes was presented with a silver cup valued at £25 and Trigg received a gold-mounted whip valued at £10.

Jockey John East rode two winners on the opening day, thereby becoming leading jockey at Newbury for a day; three of the winners over the two days were owned by the 5th Earl of Carnarvon, including the most valuable handicap with Missovata ridden by Joseph Plant. The race was worth £1,375, which would equate to nearly £80,000 these days.

Two other jockeys to ride at that opening meeting were Walter Griggs, who rode a winner on the first day, and Bernard Dillon. Walter Griggs was one of the most successful lightweights of that era, riding at 7st 1lb. Earlier that year he had won the Lincoln, a huge betting race in those days, on Sansovino. Bernard Dillon was among the best jockeys in Europe for over ten years, winning the Grand Prix de Paris on Spearmint in 1906 and the Derby on Lemberg in 1910. However, his greater claim to fame was to marry Marie Lloyd, the great music hall artist, becoming her third and final husband.

On the second day the Regulation Plate was won by Zelis, trained by John Porter, but, sadly, this was the only race won by Porter at Newbury as the course's founder retired from training at the end of the season. He was a splendid ambassador for the sport, enjoying a happy retirement until his death in 1922.

On 30 October 1906 the first National Hunt meeting at Newbury took place in front of 6,000 people. The inaugural race, a chase over an extended two miles, was won by future Grand National winner Eremon, trained by Tom Coulthwaite and ridden by Edward Lawn. He beat fourteen opponents for the £147 prize.

It is amazing that Newbury still exists considering the havoc wreaked during the First and Second World Wars. As a result of a compulsory possession order, in August 1914 the course became a prisoner-of-war camp, a munitions depot and a tank testing site and did not reopen until 1919. During the Second World War it fared no better, as the United States Armed Forces took up residence and made Newbury their main British supply depot. John Porter must have turned in his grave to see his famous turf being covered in concrete and 37 miles of railway tracks criss-crossing the course. The stables housed prisoners of war and the main bar was used as the Officers' Mess. Newbury was not able to race again until three years after the war and it is to the owners' immense credit that it has never looked back since that first post-war meeting in 1949, with some high-class racing, both Flat and National Hunt.

The oldest flat race of any importance is the Greenham Stakes, first run in 1906. It received a tremendous boost in 1909 when the race was won by Minoru, owned by King Edward VII. Minoru went on to win the Derby that year and remains the only horse owned by a monarch to win the Blue Riband. The Greenham is more recognised as a trial for the 2,000 Guineas, originally run over a mile, although since 1949 it has been reduced to seven furlongs. The greatest winner of the race was Mill Reef in 1971, before classic glory and a brilliant career. It is run in April alongside the Fred Darling Stakes, the equivalent race for fillies.

Other Group races are the John Porter Stakes, first run in 1928 honouring the founder, the Hungerford Stakes and the Lockinge Stakes, run over the straight mile. The Lockinge Stakes, first run in 1958, has attracted some top-class milers. The first two runnings were won by the Queen's Pall Mall, and his picture was on the front cover of the race card for many years. Other first-class winners were Silly Season (1966), Habitat (1969), Welsh Pageant (1970, 1971), Brigadier Gerard (1972), Boldboy (1974), Kris (1980) and Selkirk (1992). In 1995 it deservedly reached Group 1 status when it was won by Soviet Line, and the most impressive winner since its conception was Hawk Wing (2003), who spreadeagled a high-class field by eleven lengths.

The Horris Hill Stakes in October represents the best of the two-year-old races but maiden races at Newbury have proved to be far more informative as far as the future is concerned. Some of the fields used to be enormous before safety limits were applied (the Beckhampton Plate in 1937 set a record when 51 runners went to the start).

The immortal Brigadier Gerard made his racecourse debut on 24 June 1970 in the Berkshire Stakes over five furlongs, winning by five lengths in the hands of Joe Mercer at the amazing price of 100/7. Two future Derby winners to make winning two-year-old debuts here were Shergar (1980) and Lammtarra (1994).

It was also at Newbury that one of the greatest steeplechasers of the last century, Golden Miller, made his chasing debut on 4 December 1931 in the Moderate Chase. He finished first, only to be disqualified for carrying the wrong weight, and the race was awarded to Forbra, who went on to win the Grand National the following year. Golden Miller quickly made amends by winning the Reading Chase later that month and the Sefton Steeplechase in January.

National Hunt racing at Newbury has been dominated over the last 50 years by three major races – the Hennessy Gold Cup, a handicap chase over three and-a-quarter miles run in November; the Betfair Gold Trophy (still referred to by some as the Schweppes Gold Trophy, its original sponsor) run in February; and the Game Spirit Chase. However a small piece of history was made at Newbury when in December 1994 it was host to the Welsh Grand National following the abandonment of Chepstow, which was waterlogged. The race was won by Master Oats, trained by Kim Bailey and ridden by Norman Williamson, and was the only occasion on which the Welsh Grand National has been run in England.

Hennessy Gold Cup

The Hennessy Gold Cup was first run in 1957 and is the longest-surviving sponsored race. For the first three years it was run at Cheltenham and the inaugural running was won by Mandarin, ridden by Peter Madden, who beat that year's Cheltenham Gold Cup winner Linwell. He was owned by Madame Peggy Hennessy herself (guaranteed sponsorship for a few years at least) and was the first of seven winners trained by Fulke Walwyn. In 1958 the winner was Taxidermist, a second win for Fulke Walwyn, owned by his wife Cathy and ridden by the only amateur to win the race, John Lawrence (later Lord Oaksey). Ten lengths behind at the last fence in fifth place, he produced an amazing turn of foot to catch the mare Kerstin on the line. Kerstin won the race the following year, having won the Cheltenham Gold Cup in the meantime.

In 1960 the race moved to Newbury and was won by Knucklecracker, trained and ridden by Derek Ancil; the following year the winner was again Mandarin (ridden this time by Willie Robinson), who became one of only three horses to win the race twice. The 1960s turned out to be vintage years in the history of the Hennessy Gold Cup and established it as one of the finest handicap chases of the National Hunt season. In 1963 it saw the first meeting of Mill House and Arkle, with Mill House emerging the winner. Arkle slipped on landing at the third-last, handing the race to the giant from Fulke Walwyn's stable. It turned out to be the only time that Mill House would finish in front of the Irish star. In 1964 Arkle gained revenge, with Mill House only fourth, and again in 1965 Arkle beat a field of eight, giving over two stone to all his rivals. 1966 was an astonishing race with Arkle, carrying 12st 7lb, going for the hat-trick, only to be caught in the dying strides by Stalbridge Colonist, carrying 10st ridden by Stan Mellor and trained at Compton by Ken Cundell. The Newbury crowd were stunned but the weight concession proved to be just too much, even for Arkle.

These races laid the foundation for the race and the quality has remained with winners like Rondetto (1967), Spanish Steps (1969), Charlie Potheen (1972), Diamond Edge (1981), Bregawn (1982), Brown Chamberlin (1983), Burrough Hill Lad (1984), One Man (1994), Suny Bay (1997), Trabolgan (2005) and Denman (2007, 2009).

Besides training seven winners of the Hennessy Gold Cup, Fulke Walwyn was responsible for many other winners at Newbury, none more popular than Game Spirit, owned by the Queen Mother. During the 1970s Game Spirit lived up to his name throughout his career of 21 victories. Though placed in the Cheltenham Gold Cup and the two-mile Champion Chase, he was best over two and a half miles at Newbury, where he won nine times including a Geoffrey Gilbey Memorial Chase and two Hermitage Chases (in the last of which, in 1976, he beat Bula). Sadly, after contesting the 1977 Geoffrey Gilbey, in which he finished fifth, he collapsed and died. The Game Spirit Chase over two miles is now run in his honour in February at the same meeting as the Tote Gold Trophy.

Schweppes/Tote/Betfair Gold Trophy

The fiercely competitive Tote Gold Trophy is certainly the hottest handicap hurdle at Newbury, if not the country. It began in 1963 as the Schweppes Gold Trophy and was first run at Liverpool, two days before Ayala won the Grand National. The inaugural race had quantity and quality; no fewer than 41 runners went to the start, including two Champion Hurdle winners (Merry Deal and Anzio) and another future winner (Salmon Spray). The tight turns of Liverpool were too much for forty-one runners and Stan Mellor sustained terrible injuries when his mount, Eastern Harvest, fell at the second flight.

The winner was Rosyth at 20/1, trained at Findon by Ryan Price and ridden by Josh Gifford, and the trio repeated their success the following year when the Schweppes was transferred to the more spacious track at Newbury. That first running at the Berkshire course brought controversy, as Rosyth seemed to make abnormal improvement compared with the second horse Salmon Spray. After an investigation by the National Hunt Committee Ryan Price and jockey Josh Gifford were temporarily suspended.

Rosyth, now in the care of Tom Masson, finished second to Elan in 1965 but Ryan Price was back in business in 1966, winning with Le Vermontois and in 1967 with

NEWBURY
MAY MEETING

Second Day — Saturday, May 14th, 1983
(Under the Rules of Racing)
Stewards
The Hon. JAMES MORRISON, T.D.
T. E. S. EGERTON, Esq.
The Hon. RICHARD STANLEY
Lord BUCKHURST
Lt. Col. C. H. F. COAKER
RUPERT LYCETT-GREEN, Esq.
C. L. LOYD, Esq., M.C.
A. J. MacDONALD-BUCHANAN, Esq.
D. J. R. KER, Esq.
Stewards' Secretaries —
Lt. Colonel R. T. S. INGLIS
Major J. S. KER
Handicappers —
(Three years old and upwards)
Major A. R. F. ARKWRIGHT, and Major R. H. F. DANGAR
(Two years old)
Mr. G. R. GIBBS
Starter — Capt. R. B. SMALLEY
Judge — Major C. G. WEMYSS
Clerk of the Scales — Major IAN MANNING
Veterinary Officer — Miss B. J. NEWSOME, B.V.Sc., M.R.C.V.S.
Veterinary Surgeons — Messrs. BRAIN, CULLEN & McCARTAN, Ms.R.C.V.S.
and Mr. M. B. O'GORMAN, M.V.B., M.R.C.V.S.
Hon. Surgeons —
Dr. W. ANDERSON, M.B., Ch.B. and Dr. R. J. G. WELLER, M.B.Ch.B.
Clerk of the Course — Captain C. B. TOLLER
Racecourse Manager and Secretary — Mr. F. W. OSGOOD
Club Secretary — Mr. F. W. OSGOOD
Commentator — Mr. C. G. MARSHAM

OFFICIAL RACECARD   **30p**

Published by authority of the Clerk of the Course.
Printed by Pentalith Ltd., Craven House, Craven Rd., Newbury, Berks. Tel. (0635) 42492

Hill House. Hill House caused a sensation, winning by twelve lengths having displayed no form at all and, on returning to the winners' enclosure, was greeted by boos from some very disgruntled punters. Things got worse when he failed a dope test and another lengthy enquiry developed. It transpired that Hill House produced the cortisol himself through a metabolic imbalance and he became well known as 'the horse that made his own dope'.

The controversy of the early years of the Schweppes Gold Trophy gradually faded and the race soon became established as one of the major events of the National Hunt season. Persian War provided a touch of class by winning in 1968, followed swiftly by three Champion Hurdles. It was not until 1997 that a second horse would win followed by the Champion Hurdle, when front running Make a Stand spreadeagled a big field by nine lengths. By this time the race was sponsored by the Tote and a trainer to follow into the next millennium was Nicky Henderson who, over a period of seven years, won the race four times with Sharpical (1998), Geos (2000, 2004) and Landing Light (2001). Geos' second victory was at the expense of the 2003 Champion Hurdle winner Rooster Booster by a short head. Since 2012 the race has been sponsored by Betfair.

Nicky Henderson continues to train plenty of winners at Newbury and one of his finest days was the completion of a five-timer on 18 December 2002, all ridden by his stable jockey Mick Fitzgerald. On a seven-race card his winners were Saintsaire, Iris Royal, Carracciola, Calling Brave and Royal Rosa.

Arabian Racing

The Arabian horse is recognised worldwide as the purest and oldest of all horse breeds. Hailing from the Middle Eastern deserts its stamina was an invaluable asset, ensuring it could carry its rider at speed across miles of open desert with little food or water. The Arabian Racing Organisation (ARO) is based at Newbury and is the sole organiser of Arabian racing in Great Britain. With the support of the British Horseracing Authority, it holds regular meetings at various courses between early May and October.

John Porter would be very proud if he saw Newbury today, particularly after the disruption caused during the two World Wars. An immense amount of credit should be awarded to a fine management team who have improved facilities to the highest standard, especially by way of building the Hampshire Stand in 1960 and, more recently, the Berkshire Stand, opened by the Queen Mother in 1992, to match the racing of the highest quality.

Finally, a special mention to some of the unsung heroes and heroines, without whom racing could not take place – the St John Ambulance Brigade. They can be seen on all British racecourses doing a wonderful job in response to any cry for help. It was at Newbury one day that a memorable incident occurred in the line of duty. Jockey Fergie Sutherland had lost his leg during the Korean War but continued to ride with a wooden one. His mount had fallen, landing on top of him, and the only way to extricate himself from the stricken horse was to unstrap his leg. When a young St John Ambulance girl arrived rushing to his aid, he stood up – minus one leg. The poor girl fainted and it was she that needed the first aid.

Shuwaiman al Kebir, a 7-year-old Bahraini-bred Arabian, with Swedish jockey Fanny Olsen, parade before the ARO Newbury Apprentice's Race in August 2014.

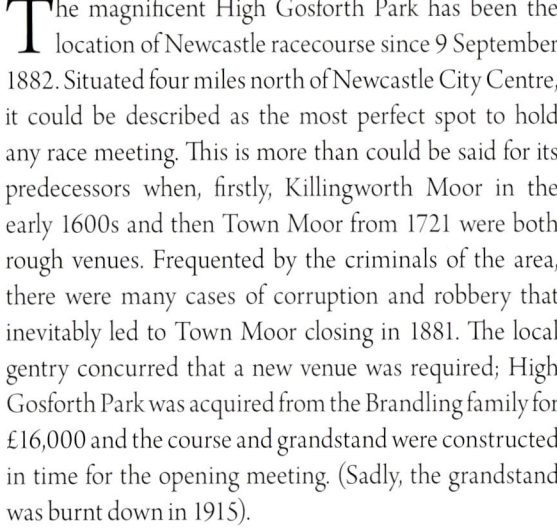

The magnificent High Gosforth Park has been the location of Newcastle racecourse since 9 September 1882. Situated four miles north of Newcastle City Centre, it could be described as the most perfect spot to hold any race meeting. This is more than could be said for its predecessors when, firstly, Killingworth Moor in the early 1600s and then Town Moor from 1721 were both rough venues. Frequented by the criminals of the area, there were many cases of corruption and robbery that inevitably led to Town Moor closing in 1881. The local gentry concurred that a new venue was required; High Gosforth Park was acquired from the Brandling family for £16,000 and the course and grandstand were constructed in time for the opening meeting. (Sadly, the grandstand was burnt down in 1915).

Given the bad reputation of Town Moor it is surprising that it survived as a racing venue for over 150 years. During this time a King's Plate was granted in 1740, enabling them to hold a five-day meeting. This led to a race week being founded in 1751 and it became the main meeting of the north, so prominent that in 1758 Secretary of State William Pitt imposed a tax on every winner over a certain amount and on every runner in a Plate.

Two of the most famous races to be held at Newcastle did originate from Town Moor – the Newcastle Gold Cup, which was discontinued when the meeting moved to Gosforth Park, and the Northumberland Plate (known locally as the Pitmen's Derby), which has survived and is run in late June or early July.

The Newcastle Gold Cup was the principal race at Town Moor and was won in four consecutive years from 1811 by XYZ (a handicap until recently run in his honour). Beeswing, one of the most prolific winning mares of the 19th century, won the Gold Cup six times, plus 18 other Gold Cups, winning a grand total of 51 races. (The Beeswing Handicap over seven furlongs is run in her honour). She was a daughter of Doctor Syntax, who also won the Gold Cup amongst his 38 victories.

The Northumberland Plate (a handicap run over two miles for all ages) was first run in 1833 when it was won by Tomboy. Early winners include top-class horses such as Cyprian (1836), who also won the Oaks, Mr Bennett (1838, 1839), Caller Ou (1863, 1864), who also won the St Leger, and the only triple winner Underhand (1857, 1858, 1859). In only its second year at Gosforth Park, Fred Archer won on Barcaldine and when Lord Derby's Princess Florizel won in 1905, she broke the world record for a two-mile race. During the Second World War the course was used as an army camp and the Plate was considered so important to the racing calendar that in

1946 a substitute race was run at Liverpool (Aintree). In 1952 the race was transferred to a Saturday and was won by Souepi, who was also the winner of the Ascot Gold Cup and Goodwood Cup, demonstrating that the race had retained its prestige. Trainer Noel Murless (who later saddled three Derby winners) won the race in three consecutive years with three different jockeys – Friseur (1954) with Gordon Richards, Little Cloud (1955) with Lester Piggott and Jardiniere (1956) with Doug Smith. In recent years the proximity of the Royal Ascot meeting has reduced the prestige of the race as the top stayers are unlikely to run with such a short interval.

When Willie Carson won in 1990 on Al-Maheb for trainer Alec Stewart it was the third winner of an incredible six-timer and he became only the third jockey in the 20th century to do so, following Gordon Richards (1933) at Chepstow and Alec Russell (1957) at Bogside. His winners were Arousal (for Dick Hern), Soweto (Gavin Pritchard-Gordon), Al-Maheb (Alec Stewart), Ternimus (Charles Elsey), Tadwin (Peter Walwyn) and Hot Desert (Dick Hern). He finished unplaced on his only other mount, Parliament Piece. It was Willie Carson's second win in the Northumberland Plate, having won the 1968 edition on the Earl of Derby's Amateur. To mark the occasion, the Newcastle executive presented him with a silver salver engraved with the names of the six winners. Not to be outdone, in 1992 on the Friday evening of the same meeting, Pat Eddery arrived from Newmarket to ride four winners from four mounts, including Piquant, owned by the Queen. Having already ridden three winners at Newmarket, it was a notable achievement to ride seven winners in a single day. This was marked by a joint presentation by both racecourses. (Frankie Dettori broke this record in September 1996, riding all seven winners at Ascot.)

There is a shortage of top two-year-old races at Newcastle now that the Seaton Delaval Stakes has become only a Class 3 Handicap. However, in 1961 a Grey Sovereign filly trained by Paddy Prendergast called La Tendresse showed blistering speed to win the Seaton Delaval before going on to win the Molecomb Stakes at Goodwood, followed by the Lowther Stakes at York by 12 lengths, topping the free handicap. Newcastle may have seen that day one of the fastest horses ever to cross the Irish Sea.

It was not until 1951 that National Hunt racing came to Newcastle, introduced by Major Ian Straker, a director of Gosforth Park Company. National Hunt racing blended in perfectly on this lovely racecourse and by the mid-1960s nine fixtures a year had been established. The most important is the Eider Chase, run over an extended four miles in February, an ideal rehearsal for the Grand National.

The most celebrated winner of the Eider Chase was Highland Wedding, who won it three times (1966, 1967, 1969) before winning the Grand National in the final year. Trained by Toby Balding, he was a most resolute horse who stayed extreme distances and loved the mud. His usual jockey, Owen McNally, was injured and the Irish jockey Eddie Harty deputised at Aintree and his victory completed a most unusual double. He was the only rider to have represented his country at the Three-Day Event (in the the 1960 Olympic Games in Rome) *and* win the Grand National.

1969 also saw the inaugural running of the Fighting Fifth Hurdle, a high-class trial for the Champion Hurdle at Cheltenham. The race is named after the Fifth Regiment of Foot, raised in 1674 during the Third Anglo-Dutch War in the reign of Charles II.

The first winner was Mugatpura, trained by Fulke Walwyn and ridden by Willie Robinson. He was a winner of seven races, including the Scottish Champion Hurdle. Other winners right out of the top drawer were Comedy of Errors (1972, 1973, 1974), Night Nurse (1975), Birds Nest (1976, 1977), Sea Pigeon (1978, 1980), followed by

Gaye Brief, Kribensis and Beech Road. All except Birds Nest were Champion Hurdle winners.

The 1975 race was a classic, although there were only four runners – Comedy of Errors, the reigning Champion Hurdler, plus future champions Night Nurse, Sea Pigeon and a complete outsider. Night Nurse, ridden by Paddy Broderick, beat Comedy of Errors by two lengths, with Sea Pigeon a further two-and-a-half lengths back in third. It was an incredible performance by Night Nurse, as he was only a four-year-old up against older rivals.

In the Fighting Fifth Hurdle in November 1983 tragedy struck, emphasising all too vividly the highs and lows of National Hunt racing. The Champion Hurdle winner of that year, Gaye Brief, was having a real battle with Ekbalco, a potential champion who was described as one of the most exciting hurdlers of his time, when Ekbalco (ridden by Jonjo O'Neill) fell at the penultimate

flight and had to be put down. When Newcastle played host to the Whitbread Gold Cup during the rebuilding on Sandown in 1973, the young jockey Doug Barrott died from head injuries sustained in a fall from French Colonist. These heartbreaking events are reminders of the risks that horses and riders take for the love of this sport, only to pay the ultimate price.

In spite of adversity, racing at High Gosforth Park has remained at the highest level and those bad days at Town Moor are but a distant memory. There have been many happy stories to remember, none more special than the 1904 Northumberland Plate won by the filly Palmy Days. She was tiny – not much bigger than a pony. She had a small appetite and was known as a 'shy feeder'. So before she left her stables that morning her trainer gave her a pint of the 'dog' – better known as Newcastle Brown Ale. Who needs oats, anyway?

Highland Wedding, ridden by Eddie Harty, seen here returning to the unsaddling enclosure after winning the 1969 Grand National at Aintree.

On 6 May 2000, the new Millennium Grandstand at Newmarket's Rowley Mile was opened by the Queen.

It was King Charles II who decided that Newmarket should become the headquarters of British flat racing. Newmarket today is a thriving racing town surrounded by three thousand acres of training grounds, over fifty racing stables, numerous studs, including the National Stud, and the home of the most prestigious bloodstock sales, a Horseracing Museum and two racecourses. During Charles's reign (1660–1685) he instigated many of the facilities we enjoy today. He also introduced the Newmarket Town Plate in 1664, run over four miles – and won the race himself on 14 October 1671. He became the first and so far only reigning monarch to ride a winner on his own horse (Woodcock) and repeated the feat, winning another plate in 1674.

It all began with his grandfather, James I, who visited the area on 27 February 1605 and recognised its potential as a sporting centre. He moved to the town, known then as New Market in part of the parish of Exning, where he could pursue his favourite hobbies of hunting and hawking. The first recorded race on the vast Newmarket heath took place on 8 March 1622 when two of James's courtiers, the Earl of Salisbury and the Duke of Buckingham, matched their horses for £100. Racing at Newmarket was born.

When James I died in 1625 he was succeeded by his son Charles I, who maintained the family devotion to racing and was himself a fine rider. He introduced the Newmarket Gold Cup in 1634 among other prizes but, before he could make any further improvements, he upset a few dignitaries, resulting in an appointment with the executioner on 30 January 1649.

Racing went into a decline during the Restoration but when the monarchy was restored Charles II soon had Newmarket alive again. He had a new palace built, near the site of what is now the Rutland Arms Hotel, with an adjoining secret passageway under the High Street to the house of his mistress, Nell Gwyn. As with his grandfather, affairs of State were neglected, allowing him to concentrate more on sports and pastimes. He became affectionately known as 'The Merry Monarch'.

Charles II died in 1685 but under his patronage Newmarket had become well and truly established as the headquarters of racing, so much so that when the Jockey Club was formed in 1750 as administrators of racing, their offices were built in Newmarket High Street and known as the Jockey Club Rooms. (The Jockey Club headquarters have since moved to Portman Square, London, but the elegant building in Newmarket remains, in front of which stands a beautiful bronze statue of the 1933 Derby winner Hyperion.)

Newmarket has two courses that share a stretch for about a mile from the furthest point from the stands before dividing into two separate straights. Between these straights lies the Devil's Dyke, an ancient earthwork inside which are reputedly buried the remains of armies who had fought with and against Boudica (Boadicea). The two courses are known as the Rowley Mile (named after Charles II's hack Old Rowley) and the July or Summer course. The straight on the July course is a mile long, while the Rowley course stretches two furlongs longer and is the longest finishing straight in Britain.

Racing takes place on the Rowley course in the spring and autumn and, predictably, on the Summer course in July and August. Newmarket's season opens with the Craven meeting in early April, followed by the Spring meeting (end April/early May), where the first two classics of the season are run, the 2,000 Guineas (first run in 1809) and the 1,000 Guineas (1814). The two main meetings in the Autumn feature the Cambridgeshire, a highly-competitive handicap over nine furlongs, the Middle Park Stakes and the Cheveley Park Stakes, both Group 1 races for two-year-olds. The second Autumn meeting, or Houghton meeting as it is sometimes known, featured the Champion Stakes (now run at Ascot), the Dewhurst Stakes (another Group 1 two-year-old race that is most important in terms of next year's classics) and the big handicap, the Cesarewitch over two and a quarter miles. (This and the Cambridgeshire form the famous Autumn Double.)

On the July course the main meeting is the July Festival, during which one of the best sprints is the Group 1 July Cup. The July course is far more relaxed, appropriate to the setting of lovely thatched buildings, beautifully-kept flower beds and a tree-lined pre-parade ring where spectators can watch the runners from the inside.

The 2,000 Guineas

The first classic of the season, the 2,000 Guineas, is for three-year-old colts and fillies over the Rowley Mile. It is also the first leg of the Triple Crown, which, over the last 200 years, only 15 horses have succeeded. To win the Triple Crown is the highest accolade for a racehorse on the Flat and the first to achieve it was West Australian (1853). Although he only won the 2,000 Guineas by half a length, his multiple-classic-winning trainer John Scott claimed he was the best he ever trained. John Porter holds the record for training three Triple Crown winners – the first, Ormonde (1886), was probably the greatest horse of the 19th century. Unbeaten in 16 races, his 2,000 Guineas win was a classic. His main rival was the favourite and champion two-year-old Minting, whose trainer Mathew Dawson had refused to accept the possibility of defeat. Ormonde went clear in the dip to win in a canter. John Porter's second winner was Common (1891), who was virtually a cripple as a two-year-old and never ran. He made his racecourse debut in the 2,000 Guineas and, despite becoming very nervous in the horsebox, won by three lengths. Flying Fox (1899) was Porter's third winner.

Other notable winners were Isinglass (1893), who as well as winning the Triple Crown won the Eclipse and the Ascot Gold Cup and only suffered one defeat in his career; Diamond Jubilee (1900); the filly Sceptre (1902), who also won the 1,000 Guineas, Oaks and St Leger; Rock Sand (1903) and the unbeaten Bahram (1935). Tudor Minstrel (1947) in the hands of Gordon Richards won the 2,000 Guineas by the widest margin of eight lengths (photographs show it was at least ten). He showed blistering early speed and was clear after three furlongs with his only serious rival, Petition, in his wake. He failed to stay in the Derby but was one of the finest milers of the 20th century. It proved to be his brilliant trainer Fred Darling's last classic winner, as he retired at the end of that season.

From one great trainer to another. Vincent O'Brien's first 2,000 Guineas winner came courtesy of Sir Ivor (1968), who his jockey Lester Piggott claimed was the best horse he ever sat on. Two years later O'Brien and Piggott teamed up again with the immortal Nijinsky (1970), who became the last horse to win the Triple Crown. Nijinsky was a massive horse who was unbeaten in five starts as a two-year-old. In the 2,000 Guineas he started 4/7 favourite, the shortest price since Colombo (1934), and won easily. He stretched his unbeaten run to eleven before defeats in his final two races, having contracted ringworm.

Only six runners went to the post for the 1971 2,000 Guineas, the smallest field in over a century but it turned out to be the race of the century. The race was expected to concern two top class two-year-olds from the previous season in Mill Reef and My Swallow who were involved in a titanic battle over the last two furlongs but along came Brigadier Gerard, making his seasonal debut, to swoop by them on the stand side to win by three lengths. Mill Reef just edged out My Swallow for second place; considering that Mill Reef was never beaten again, Brigadier Gerard's performance was all the more meritorious. The Brigadier stayed in training until he was four and was beaten only once in 18 starts. To keep him at his peak was a brilliant piece of training by Dick Hern

This performance was so high-class that no subsequent Guineas have raised the bar, but one that came close was with El Gran Senor (1984), trained by Vincent O'Brien (who else?), who fought off a field including Chief Singer, Lear Fan and Rainbow Quest. Since then other top-class winners to savour have been Dancing Brave (1986), Nashwan (1989), Zafonic (1993), Mark of Esteem (1996), Rock of Gibraltar (2002), George Washington (2006), Sea the Stars (2009) – who surely would have joined those other 15 immortal winners of the Triple Crown if he had been allowed to take his chance in the St Leger instead

Brigadier Gerard and Joe Mercer race home to take the 1971 2,000 Guineas, leaving Mill Reef and My Swallow in his wake.

of winning the Prix de l'Arc de Triomphe – and Frankel (2011), who won in breathtaking style reminiscent of Tudor Minstrel.

The 2,000 Guineas comes very early in the season for some horses, which alone is sufficient reason for victory to be a source of immense credit. Subsequent results later in the season prove that the best horse does not always win the opening classic, for various reasons. Some of the following near-misses can be regarded as shocks, or just unlucky.

- Caesar (1839) finished second, beaten a head at 1/7.
- Donovan (1889), winner of eleven races as a two-year-old, was denied by a head to Enthusiast of winning the Triple Crown at odds of 20/85.

- Bayardo (1909) was unfit and could finish only fourth to Minoru, but later proved to be a champion.
- Lemberg (1910) was beaten a short head by Neil Gow, but later won the Derby.
- Craganour (1913) won the Guineas but the judge made a mistake and awarded the race to Louvois.
- Coronach's defeat (1926) by Colorado denied him the Triple Crown.
- Abernant (1949) was beaten a short head by Nimbus.
- Prince Simon (1950), a big hope of Newmarket, was beaten a short head by Palestine.
- Venture VII (1960) was split by the width of the track and beaten a head by Martial.
- Pinturishio (1961), the hot 7/4 favourite, was probably doped.

Frankel, possibly one of the greatest racehorses ever, after his 2,000 Guineas win in 2011 with trainer Henry Cecil, jockey Tom Queally and owner Prince Khalid bin Abdullah. 'He's the best I've ever had, the best I've ever seen,' said Cecil.

- Crocket (1963), a leading two-year-old, finished last.
- Ribofilio (1969), already hot favourite for the Derby but the 15/8 favourite was virtually pulled up by Lester Piggott.
- Apalachee (1974), an Irish banker, could finish only third.
- Try My Best (1978), an even money favourite and another Irish banker, finished last.
- Nureyev (1980), a hot favourite from France, finished first past the post but was disqualified for interference two furlongs out and the race was awarded to Known Fact (more than a few fingers being burnt).

The 1,000 Guineas

For fillies only, the 1,000 Guineas was first run in 1814 and the inaugural running was won by Charlotte, who beat just four opponents. The winning jockey, Bill Clift (who won five Derbys during his career), and owner Christopher Wilson were also the successful combination when winning the inaugural 2,000 Guineas in 1809 with Wizard.

The 1,000 Guineas was not an immediate success, drawing small fields and contested mostly by local stables. Gradually, fillies outside Newmarket became interested with the next target being the Epsom Oaks – of which there were far more winners than their male counterparts. The Fillies' Triple Crown (1,000 Guineas, Oaks and the St Leger) has produced nine winners. The first was Formosa (1868), who also dead-heated in the 2,000 Guineas, followed by Hannah (1871), Apology (1874), La Fleche (1892), Sceptre (1902) – who also won the 2,000 Guineas – Pretty Polly (1904), King George VI's Sun Chariot (1942), whose Oaks and St Leger victories were run at Newmarket, Meld (1955) and Oh So Sharp (1985).

By far the best of these fillies' Triple Crown winners was Pretty Polly, who won 22 races from 24 starts.

She was trained by Peter Purcell Gilpin who, having moved from Dorset, had built the Clarehaven Stables at Newmarket, which he named after a mare on whom he had won a fortune in the 1900 Cesarewitch. Pretty Polly was unbeaten in nine races as a two-year-old, including an astonishing debut at Sandown, winning by ten lengths (many reckoned it was closer to 100 yards). As a three-year-old she won the 1,000 Guineas with ease in record time at 4/1 on, and ran up an unbeaten sequence of 15, including the Oaks, Coronation Stakes, Nassau Stakes and at Doncaster, the St Leger and the Park Hill Stakes. Afterwards, she met her first defeat in Paris, in bad weather after a long rail journey (she was stuck in a railway siding at Folkestone for hours). In the torrential rain and heavy ground she was unable to show her true form. She recovered to win the Coronation Cup, the Champion Stakes and the Jockey Club Cup the following year.

Other great winners of the 1,000 Guineas were Rockfel (1938), Godiva (1940), Petite Etoile (1959), Hula Dancer (1963), Pebbles (1984) and Miesque (1987), but the greatest filly of the 20th century was Pretty Polly.

The 'Headquarters' – a series of firsts

Now Newmarket was established as the 'Headquarters' of Flat racing, most champions would have appeared here at some time or another. One of the icons of the early 18th century was Flying Childers, who beat Speedwell in a match over four miles in 1721. The immortal Eclipse won here in 1769/1770 during his unbeaten sequence of 18, followed by Gimcrack (winner of 25 races), who made his final appearance here in April 1771. The 1872 2,000 Guineas winner Prince Charlie was never beaten at Newmarket in 12 outings. He was another prolific winner in mostly sprint races, winning 25 from 29, starts including an unbeaten sequence of 14.

In the early days very few horses ran under the age of five. It was not until 1727 that four-year-old races were

NEWMARKET

Flying Childers, a sketch by Peter Upton after a painting by James Seymour.

introduced, with three-year-olds following in 1756 and first two-year-olds in 1786 (with the first running of the July Stakes). Exercising its position as 'Headquarters', Newmarket experimented with yearling races from 1791 but these were abolished in 1859.

Newmarket was also the pioneer of many other new racing innovations which, depending on their success, were quickly copied by other racecourses. The most notable were the first use of starting tapes in 1897, the first installation of the Tote in 1929 (although this honour was shared with Carlisle), the first to have a patrol camera in 1930, the first to use photo finish in 1949 and, on 8 July 1965, an historic moment when starting stalls were used for the first time in a race in Britain (Track Spare won the five-furlong Chesterfield Stakes for two-year-olds). The trial was very successful and two years later the first classic using starting stalls was won by Royal Palace in the 2,000 Guineas. Other notable moments were when

the 2,000 Guineas and 1,000 Guineas were run on the same day in 1921 due to a miners' strike, and 7 May 1995 when the 1,000 Guineas was run on a Sunday with betting allowed. (Sunday racing in Britain began in July 1992 but betting on-course was initially prohibited. The 1995 1,000 Guineas, won by Harayir trained by Dick Hern, became the first English Classic winner on a Sunday.)

As mentioned earlier there are two racecourses at Newmarket, but during the 19th century there were as many as 18. Another, still used today, is the course for the Newmarket Town Plate over four miles, which starts beyond the July course. Newmarket had a National Hunt course, which was situated on the other side of the Cambridge Road, opposite the Rowley Mile grandstand. It opened in 1894 but never quite took off, lasting only 11 years before closing on 28 December 1905. The Rowley course experimented with a two-mile round course that joined the present course at about the five furlong mark. It was called the Sefton course, but was unsuccessful and used only between 1958 and 1973.

Wartime racing

During the First World War all the classics were transferred to Newmarket from 1915 until 1918. The Guineas remained on the Rowley course, accompanied by the St Leger. The Derby and the Oaks were run on the July course. During this period they witnessed three Triple Crown winners in Pommern (1915), trained by Charley Peck, and Gay Crusader (1917) and Gainsborough (1918), both trained by Alec Taylor. They all had easy tasks in the St Leger – Pommern beat six opponents at odds of 1/3, Gay Crusader (whose owner Alfred Cox also owned the great Bayardo) had just two opponents and it was no more than a canter at 2/11, while Gainsborough was another odds-on winner, beating four others at 4/11.

The classics in 1916 also produced two horses of exceptional ability. The filly Fifinella achieved a most unusual double by winning the Derby and the Oaks. She was a brilliant but bad-tempered filly; but for her temper she would also have won the 1,000 Guineas, but she sulked and ran on to take second place when it was too late. She was also a bit nervous in the Derby, but ran on resolutely towards the finish to put the colts in their place. Two days later she was a different filly in the Oaks and won easily. She was only the fourth filly to land this double and the sixth and last filly to win the Derby.

The 1916 St Leger was won by Hurry On, who remained unbeaten in six outings. He was the first classic winner to be trained by Fred Darling but he was so big and backward that he was unable to get him ready for the Derby (where he may have spoilt the party for Fifinella). Fred Darling described him as the best horse he ever trained – high praise indeed for a trainer who saddled 19 classic winners, including seven Derbys.

Throughout the Second World War both Guineas were run on the July course as well as the Derby and Oaks plus three St Legers, making a total of 27 classics. Two owner/trainer combinations dominated this period – the 17th Earl of Derby with Walter Earl, and King George VI with Fred Darling.

George VI almost swept the board in 1942 by winning the 2,000 Guineas with Big Game followed by the exceptional filly Sun Chariot in the 1,000 Guineas. Big Game failed to stay in the Derby, finishing sixth behind Watling Street (Lord Derby/Walter Earl), but Sun Chariot made amends by winning the Oaks and the St Leger to complete the Fillies' Triple Crown. Her victory in the St Leger was even sweeter by beating Watling Street by three lengths. At a time of war, to see the royal colours

successful in any classic would have been enough to lift the spirits of the nation but to win four was a huge boost to morale.

In the 1943 classics there were no outstanding horses but the races recorded some extraordinary results. The heroine of the year was Lord Rosebery's filly Ribbon, who must be a contender for the unluckiest filly of the century. When she was a two-year-old she was beaten first time out but then won her next four races, ending up beating the colts in the Middle Park Stakes. Trained locally by Jack Jarvis, she finished second in three classics, beaten a neck to Herringbone (1,000 Guineas), beaten a neck to Why Hurry (Oaks) and finally beaten a short head to Herringbone (St Leger). Both her jockey Eph Smith and Jack Jarvis were sure she had won the St Leger and both remained utterly convinced that Ribbon had been robbed. (Jack Jarvis was later quoted as saying that Ribbon had won the St Leger and he would take that result to his grave).

The 1943 St Leger was an extraordinary race. Despite the controversy over the result and the defeat of Ribbon, the race brought together the winners of the four previous classics that year – Kingsway (2,000 Guineas), Herringbone (1,000 Guineas) Straight Deal (Derby) and Why Hurry (Oaks). The 12-runner field also included Pink Flower, second in the 2,000 Guineas, Ribbon, second in the 1,000 Guineas and Oaks, and Umiddad and Nasrullah, second and third respectively in the Derby. It is very unlikely that, during the modern era at least, a year's four previous classic winners have ever faced the starter together in the St Leger. Records will show Herringbone won by a short head from Ribbon, with Straight Deal three-quarters of a length back in third. Quite a race.

Walter Earl won six wartime classics in the space of four years – Watling Street (1942 Derby), Herringbone (1943 1,000 Guineas/St Leger), Garden Path (1944 2,000 Guineas) and Sun Stream (1945 1,000 Guineas/Oaks),

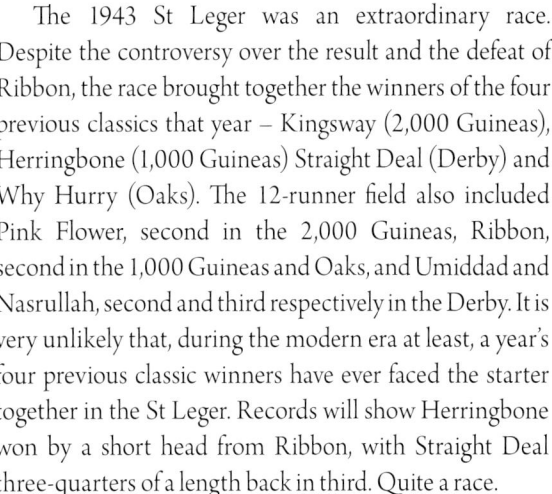

while trainer Fred Darling amassed seven classics during the war – Pont L'Eveque (1940 Derby), Owen Tudor (1941 Derby), Commotion (1941 Oaks), Big Game (1942 2,000 Guineas) and Sun Chariot (1942 Fillies' Triple Crown).

Remarkable feats

Newmarket is littered with other great races during the year, but the two huge gambling races in the autumn on the Rowley course are worth a mention – the Cambridgeshire and the Cesarewitch.

Lambourn trainer George Clement brought off a stunning coup in 1876 by landing both legs of the Autumn Double – with the same horse. Rosebery, a four-year-old maiden, was heavily backed for the Cesarewitch and won by four lengths. A 14lb penalty did not stop him in the Cambridgeshire a fortnight later, though he scored by only a neck. Those were the only two victories of his career. This remarkable double would not be attempted

these days, but two others to have emulated it were Foxhall in 1881, trained by William Day, and the French filly Plaisanterie in 1885.

A heart-warming performance concerns the 1966 Cesarewitch winner Persian Lancer. He had already finished third in the 1961 Cesarewitch when trained by Sir Gordon Richards, before breaking down badly and spending 18 months in convalescence. During this period he got loose and became stuck under a bus, which had to be lifted to free the poor animal. Amazingly no serious damage was done and his owner, Lord Belper, sent him to legendary trainer Ryan Price with a view to getting him racing again. Now a five-year-old, he had two unplaced runs before he broke down again and spent another two years on the sidelines. He then had six races over hurdles in which he stayed sound, so Price trained him for the Cesarewitch despite the fact he had not troubled the judge for five years. Ridden again by Doug Smith, the now eight-year-old, heavily backed from 33/1 to 100/7, won by three-quarters of a length. Persian Lancer gave Ryan Price one of his proudest moments.

The last word, literally, goes to Lester Piggott who, in 1992, rode his 30th Classic winner in the 2,000 Guineas on Rodrigo de Triano for his long-time friend Robert Sangster. At the age of 56, his record of riding more classic winners in Britain than any other jockey will surely remain for many years to come. On dismounting in the unsaddling enclosure he was surrounded by members of the press and racing reporter Brough Scott asked Lester, "How much longer can you go on?"

Lester replied with a wry smile, "I've still got a ride in the sixth".

Lester Piggott in 1992 on his last classic winner, Rodrigo de Triano in the 2,000 Guineas.

It was once traditional for Newton Abbot to open the National Hunt season in August but with the introduction of summer jumping it has lost that privilege. It does, however, play an important part in the summer jumping programme, thanks to the River Teign bordering one side of the course. This makes for good ground but can be a mixed blessing, as the river has caused flooding in the past. A large bank has been built in recent years to guard against this problem.

Newton Abbot first staged racing on 9 August 1866. It was called the South Devon and Newton Races and the racecourse was known as Teignmouth, with the initial contest being run for a prize of just 12 sovereigns. Racing continued without interruption apart from the two World Wars. Between 1914 and 1918, the course was occupied by troops and used as a prisoner-of-war camp, and during the Second World War only one fixture was staged. The end of the war was celebrated with a huge crowd of over 17,000 on August Bank Holiday 1946. It was not until 1969 that the track's main grandstand was built and opened by the Queen Mother.

Racing at Newton Abbot is largely of a moderate nature with no major races, but a few high-class horses have made their way to the Devonshire course from time to time, most of them during the early stages of their careers. None was better than the 1984 Cheltenham Gold Cup winner Burrough Hill Lad – the pride and joy of trainer Jenny Pitman. Burrough Hill Lad won his first chase at Newton Abbot on 16 February 1982, dominating the Rippon Tor Novices Chase by 30 lengths, ridden by Colin Brown. He followed this by unseating his rider at Haydock and falling in the Sun Alliance Chase at the Cheltenham Festival, before winning again at Liverpool at the Grand National meeting. He finished that season at Newton Abbot, winning the Foxwell Novice Chase by 12 lengths in the hands of Phil Tuck.

Two other Cheltenham Gold Cup heroes to win here in their early days were Bregawn and Cool Ground, but dual Queen Mother Champion Chase winner Viking Flagship did not show any promise for his new trainer David Nicholson in 1991, finishing only ninth of eleven in the Plymouth Handicap Hurdle and beaten 44 lengths. It would be an understatement to say that he improved later.

In contrast, the 1997 Champion Hurdle winner Make a Stand, trained by Martin Pipe, made a winning start to his hurdles career at Newton Abbot in May 1996. Making every yard of the running, he won the Limerick Maiden Hurdle unchallenged, ridden by David Bridgwater at the generous odds of 10/1. Martin Pipe performed a miracle with this gelding, having claimed him out of a flat race. He improved him enough to win half a dozen hurdles and a flat race including the Tote Gold Trophy at Newbury and finally the Champion Hurdle, where he demolished a high-class field in record time, all in the space of ten months.

Make a Stand, trained by Martin Pipe, seen here winning the 1997 Champion Hurdle.

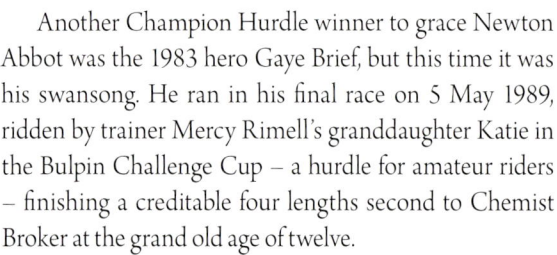

Another Champion Hurdle winner to grace Newton Abbot was the 1983 hero Gaye Brief, but this time it was his swansong. He ran in his final race on 5 May 1989, ridden by trainer Mercy Rimell's granddaughter Katie in the Bulpin Challenge Cup – a hurdle for amateur riders – finishing a creditable four lengths second to Chemist Broker at the grand old age of twelve.

West Country trainer Martin Pipe retired in 2006 having sent out nearly 4,000 National Hunt winners in a career which spanned over 30 years. He became the most successful National Hunt trainer of all time (having passed the record number of wins set by Arthur Stephenson) and, in addition to breaking many other records, he also saddled more winners at Newton Abbot than at any other racecourse.

Two champion jockeys to excel at Newton Abbot were Peter Scudamore and Tony McCoy. Peter retired in 1993 having ridden for the Pipe stable for nine years. He rode 127 winners at Newton Abbot, of which 111 were for Pipe. It was here on 14 February 1989, following wins on Wingspan and Let Him By, that he completed a treble for the Pipe stable by riding Avionne to victory to record the 1,000th winner of his career and became only the third National Hunt jockey to reach this milestone.

McCoy had a nice introduction to Newton Abbot, recording his first win in a chase on Bonus Boy for Bob Buckler on 4 October 1994. He first rode for Martin Pipe in 1995 and together they soon formed a formidable partnership. By the end of the 1995-96 season Tony McCoy had become champion jockey for the first time – a title he has yet to relinquish. Martin Pipe and Newton Abbot have certainly played their part in making him probably the best National Hunt jockey of all time – he has ridden over 200 winners at Newton Abbot, more than at any other racecourse.

Newton Abbot was honoured on 21 May 1981 when Prince Charles rode in his one and only hurdle race for his grandmother. Running in the Bulpin Challenge Cup Hurdle for amateur riders, his mount Upton Grey, trained by Fulke Walwyn, gradually lost his place to finish a distant ninth. On his return to the weighing room some senior jockeys were quick to offer him a word of advice – Don't give up the day job, Sir.

Controversy

There may be no major races at Newton Abbot, but on Bank Holiday Monday, 28 August 1978, there was a controversial one. The Hatherleigh Selling Handicap Hurdle was won by 20 lengths by a nine-year-old called In The Money, trained in South Wales by John Bowles. The gelding had not run for nearly three years, having shown no form at all in three outings during the autumn of

1975. It was reported that after his last race he had slipped and returned very lame. Although there were no strong betting patterns, the horse was a well-backed 8/1 chance and many bookmakers had him wiped off their boards at the off. On the evidence of his poor form he should have been a 100/1 shot.

At the time, the stables were owned jointly by Bowles and Taffy Salaman – an ex-jockey turned trainer. In 1976 Bowles and Salaman had a dispute over a horse's forged passport, for which they were both heavily fined. It transpired that Bowles had forged a vet's signature; Salaman was livid and had to be restrained in court. In January 1977, Salaman left the stables to set up on his own in Lambourn, taking some of the staff and horses with him. When he heard that In The Money had won so convincingly at Newton Abbot he could not believe it. He knew the horse well and knew that after his last race he had undergone an unsuccessful tendon operation and was still very sick. He had advised Bowles to have him put down but Bowles would not. Salaman was certain the horse could not canter 20 yards let alone win by 20 lengths. One of his staff confirmed the horse was a cripple in poor condition and had been sharing a corrugated iron shed with a cow.

Still incensed over the passport business, Salaman asked the Jockey Club to investigate the winner and advised them to go to Bowles' stables as he believed the horse to be a ringer. Four days later the Jockey Club arrived at the stables only to be told by Bowles that the horse had had to be put down having sustained a serious injury during the race.

One man who could throw some light on the mystery was racecourse photographer Colin Wallace, who had taken photographs of all the winners that day. He confirmed that the winner looked as sound as a bell, and the photograph showed him to have a small white blaze on his forehead – In The Money did not. In the Money had bad scars on his forelegs following the operation – the winner did not. Wallace also said the winner looked like a horse he once owned called Cobbler's March, who was a confirmed front runner, with five wins to his name.

Bowles was arrested and appeared at Exeter Crown Court in March 1980. He was found guilty by overwhelming evidence of defrauding Newton Abbot, bookmakers, the Tote, Weatherby's and other racecourse owners for declaring a horse that was not In The Money. He was jailed for 18 months.

The horse that was put down was probably Cobblers March, but it will probably never be known for sure what happened to In The Money.

Cobbler's March, with his distinctive white star, was passed off as In The Money in 1978 which resulted in an 18-month jail sentence for his fraudulent trainer, John Bowles.

Racing at Nottingham takes place at Colwick Park, two miles east of the city centre, and opened on 19 August 1892. Racing had been staged in Nottingham as early as 1689 during the reign of William III. A course was laid out at Basford Lings on the fringe of Sherwood Forest. It became an annual event for over 140 years with little interruption, during which time a Windsor-style figure-of-eight course was laid out in 1797 without success, followed by an orthodox mile-and-a-quarter circuit. Racing continued until 1831, when reform rioters threatened to injure the horses if racing went ahead. The meeting was abandoned as the riots intensified, during which Nottingham Castle was set ablaze. However the Reform Act was passed the following year and racing resumed.

In 1846 the land on the edge of Sherwood Forest was leased for racing and came under the control of Nottingham Corporation. It remained an annual event until 1853, when a second meeting was added, usually on the day after the

Grand National. The flat season commenced in February in this period.

However, by 1890 Nottingham Corporation were persuaded by nonconformists to close the course under the Public Health Act with reference to infectious diseases, but two years later Colwick Racing and Sporting Company set up a new course on the present site. The opening race was won by Delaval, a five-year-old ridden by Fred Rickaby. He won the one-mile-three-furlong handicap at odds of 4/1.

National Hunt racing began at Nottingham in 1867 and provided some excellent sport for nearly 130 years, the final meeting taking place on 29 February 1996. The decision to close was taken so as to provide better ground for flat racing, but many jumping fans, owners, trainers and jockeys were very much against it.

A fire in 1986 destroyed much of the Tattersalls stand, but a new stand offering a fine view over the wide finishing straight was opened in 1987 by Jonjo O'Neill. In 1992,

Nottingham celebrated its centenary with the completion of a new members' stand, this time officially opened by none other than Desert Orchid.

One memorable moment occurred in the Christmas Spirit Novices Chase on 18 December 1971 when Ouzo, a five-year-old trained by Harry Thomson-Jones and ridden by Stan Mellor, beat Ponty Pierre, ridden by David Nicholson, by five lengths. This gave Stan Mellor his 1,000th winner, the first National Hunt jockey to achieve this landmark. On returning to the winner's enclosure on the 4/6 favourite Stan was given a tremendous reception by the crowd.

Other National Hunt heroes to appear at Nottingham were the Queen Mother's Devon Loch, who made his debut in a maiden hurdle in October 1951. Devon Loch went on to fame for not winning the 1956 Grand National, collapsing yards from the winning post when well clear.

Red Rum was another National Hunt hero to run at Nottingham in his younger days. Having made his debut over hurdles at Cheltenham followed by a race at Market Rasen, he made his third appearance over hurdles at Nottingham on 18 November 1968 in the Merit Hurdle for three-year-olds, finishing third at 100/8 behind Soloning, trained by Fred Winter. Red Rum won his first hurdle race at Wetherby the following year and his second at Nottingham in the Bradmore Handicap Hurdle for four-year-olds ridden by Paddy Broderick. He produced a strong run after the last, getting home by half a length at 5/1. Red Rum made only one appearance at Nottingham, in a chase on 21 March 1972, finishing third to Nom De Guerre, but it was nevertheless a stepping stone to stardom.

Another National Hunt star to appear at Nottingham was Persian War, who ran in the City Trial Hurdle on 23 February 1970, finishing second behind Orient War, beaten a short head in heavy ground. He turned the tables on his victor three weeks later when winning his third consecutive Champion Hurdle at Cheltenham.

Flat racing at Nottingham has been immensely popular with trainers, especially for introducing their young horses. A good galloping course with gentle bends is often the perfect education. Two of Henry Cecil's classic winners, Slip Anchor and Oh So Sharp, won as two-year-olds at Nottingham in 1984, with Oh So Sharp in particular making an impressive winning debut there before going on to win the Fillies' Triple Crown the following year. To commemorate their wins both horses have had races named after them.

However, Henry Cecil may not wish to remember another of his horses, a three-year-old filly called Starlite Night, running in the Bridgeford End Stakes on 20 July 1985. Sadly, the horse, ridden by Paul Eddery, burst a blood vessel and finished unplaced. She was expected to start at odds of 1/20 but because of insufficient on-course betting no SP was returned – a lucky break for off-course backers, with all stakes on the race refunded. This highlights one of the oldest rules of racing – if you can't win, you can't lose!

Nottingham will always be remembered for the retirement of Lester Piggott on 29 October 1985. He planned to retire from riding at Nottingham with five rides, all of whom started favourite. He rode just one winner – Full Choke in the Willington Handicap for John Dunlop. The 15/8 favourite made all the running in typical Piggott fashion, dictating the pace and pulling out a bit more when challenged.

His final three mounts were all beaten, the last of which – Wind From The West for Patrick Haslam – finishing second, beaten four lengths by Tony McGlone on Gurteen Boy for Richard Hannon. After the last, Lester was cheered into the weighing room by a crowd of over 5,000 who came from far and wide to say farewell to their hero. Ironically, this momentous day became a premature piece of racing history – Lester returned to the saddle five years later at Leicester, following a brief prison sentence for tax evasion.

Perth is the most northerly of all British racecourses and stands in the beautiful wooded grounds of Scone Palace, built in 1803 on the site of several earlier ancient palaces. Since the 9th century Kings and Queens of Scotland have been crowned here on a special piece of sacred sandstone called the 'Stone of Scone' in an abbey in front of the palace. However, in 1296 the stone was stolen by Edward I and placed in Westminster Abbey, where it remained for over 700 years. It is now safely back in its native land, under guard in Edinburgh Castle.

The original course was on the South Inch of Perth, where the earliest reference to a meeting is in 1613, when a Silver Bell was run for. In 1784 the Perth Hunt Club took over and moved the course to North Inch; only flat racing was held on these two courses and, although run by the Caledonian Hunt, there were very few meetings. The Caledonian Gold Cup was first held in 1818 and boasted six days of racing and twelve races. Caledonian Hunt withdrew their patronage in 1890 but the racecourse retained the title of Perth Hunt.

The first meeting in Scone Palace Park, close to the River Tay, was a two-day affair on 23–24 September 1908, and the first race was the Cramock Handicap Chase over two miles, won by 5/1 shot Loch Sloy ridden by R Cowe. The jockey later received a gold-mounted whip from the Earl of Mansfield to mark the occasion. (Scone Palace is the Mansfield family seat.) The main race, the Fingask

Handicap Hurdle, was won by Obtruder, the 6/4 favourite, and the Mansfield Steeplechase by Rashiegrain, owned and trained by Adam Scott and ridden by Mr C R Pawson. The following day, Adam Scott again took the honours when winning The Perthshire Handicap Chase with Rashiegrain, completing a quick double. This inaugural meeting did not pass without incident, however, with reports of several cases of welshing. One bookmaker was grabbed by a group of angry racegoers and it was only the local constabulary that saved him from being thrown in the river.

At the September meeting in 1921 Adam Scott, who was a private trainer, proved to be quite a favourite at Perth when over two days he trained eight winners, riding three of them himself. His winners were Lady Peasemore, Sirup, Perisheen and Hectic on the first day followed by Lady Peasemore, Command, White Swain and Hectic on the second. In the main event, the Perthshire Handicap Chase, riding Command he just failed by half a length to beat Awbeg, owned by Mr S Thomson.

Racing does not take place in the winter because of the heavy Perthshire soil and, until recently, fixtures were confined to the spring and the autumn, but with the introduction of summer jumping Perth hosted the opening fixture on 8 June 1995. The three-day festival in April is still the highlight of the season, and is very popular with southern trainers, especially Nigel Twiston-Davies, Philip Hobbs and Paul Nicholls.

Before the Second World War the stables were on the first floor above a garage and running at Perth could mean an 800-mile round trip for any southern raiders; so they must have been relieved when the stabling block was modernised. Conditions and amenities have all greatly improved, culminating in a new stand in 1992 opened by Sir John Sparrow, chairman of the Levy Board.

One visitor, on 26 September 1973 ,who may not have been impressed was Ginger McCain, trainer of Red Rum, who brought his 1973 Grand National hero to contest the Perthshire Challenge Cup. Red Rum passed the post in first place but was subsequently disqualified for squeezing on the run-in the second horse Proud Stone, trained by Gordon Richards and ridden by Ron Barry. Ginger, who was visiting Perth for the first time, was not best pleased with the stewards' decision and claimed that the two horses had barely touched. He later joked, 'Have you ever tried squeezing Ron Barry?'

Perth has gained a reputation of being a very laid-back and friendly course, with the motto – 'It's not the winning, it's the taking part'. Try telling that to Ginger McCain.

Runners make their way past Scone Palace in 2006.

189

Plumpton got off to a flying start in 1884, thanks to the Haywards Heath to Lewes railway (which had opened in October 1847) and a brand-new station in the new village of Plumpton Green. Racegoers from London and the south coast now had access to Plumpton racecourse, nestling in deepest Sussex, two miles from the village of Plumpton and five miles from racecourse neighbours Lewes. Flat racing had taken place at Lewes since 1727, but now Plumpton was to provide National Hunt sport for the folk of Sussex (now East Sussex).

The land on which the racecourse was built was owned by W F Wheatley and originally used for hare coursing. National Hunt racing took place at Plumpton for the first time on 11 February 1884. The first race was the Hunters Selling Hurdles Plate, won by the 7/2 shot Cowslip by 40 lengths. He was owned by the Clerk of the Course, Mr S Savage, and ridden by Harry Escott, who, later in the afternoon, completed a treble, including another win with Cowslip, but this time in a chase. Harry Escott became one of the top jockeys to ride at Plumpton, totalling 34 winners before his retirement, after which he took up training at Lewes. Among his successes were Lutteur III and Poethlyn in the Grand National (1909 and 1919 respectively).

During the remainder of the 19th century there were at least six meetings a year, plus an equal number of coursing meetings, but none was more strange than the Ovingdean Chase on 17 December 1892. Covert Side at 20/1 was the outsider in a three-horse race and was beginning to tail off, so his jockey, a Mr Thompson, called it a day and returned to the paddock. A spectator shouted at him to remount, as both his opponents (Arran and Sea Wall) had fallen. Mr Thompson took his mount back to the track and completed the course to win.

Hare coursing ceased in 1908 and racing fixtures gradually increased. The course was by now being managed by Pratt and Co under the title of Plumpton Racecourse Limited and one of the first improvements they made was to put in place a new grandstand, which was acquired from Northampton following its closure in 1904. However, whilst facilities were improving, the course was still subject to criticism. The downhill fences on the far side were very tricky, especially for novices, resulting in a high number of fallers. Trainer Toby Balding – despite a fair amount of success – once commented, 'I avoid Plumpton like the plague'. Improvements had to be made, and eventually the middle fence on the far side was repositioned on to level ground – but not before a tragic incident.

On 15 February 1941 Roman Chief was running in the Cuckfield Handicap Chase. Having negotiated the notorious fences successfully, the five-horse field encountered an unusual obstacle. As they reached the bend by the station they met a motor car crossing the course. Four of the runners managed to swerve round it but Roman Chief, ridden by Sean Magee, decided to jump over it. He sustained such serious injuries that he had to be destroyed.

Improvements to the course continued and, in 1962, a huge amount of earth was removed from the centre of the course, resulting in a perfect view for all spectators. But flooding was becoming a problem due to the clay soil, leading to many cancellations. In 1975 five consecutive meetings were lost.

Plumpton does not usually attract top-class chasers, and it would be unheard of to run at Plumpton a week before a big race at Cheltenham – unless the horse was owned by Dorothy Paget. Roman Hackle had already won the 1940 Cheltenham Gold Cup and was attempting to do the same in 1941. Having had a moderate season, he ran in the Ardingly Optional Selling Chase at Plumpton, his final prep race, in which he scrambled home by less than a length. Not surprisingly, he was unplaced in the Gold Cup.

The most prolific winner at Plumpton has to be Manhattan Boy, a gelding by Oats out of Into Harbour, trained by John Ffitch-Heyes at Lewes. During his career he won 14 times at Plumpton between 1986 and 1993, every one in a selling hurdle. In his first win he was ridden by the trainer's daughter Penny and in his final win by Adrian Maguire. He was a true course specialist, running a total of 64 times at Plumpton, and he won or was placed in 35 of them.

In contrast, one jockey who made just a single, but memorable, appearance at Plumpton was Prince Charles, making his racecourse debut on 4 March 1980 in the Madhatters Private Sweepstakes, a two-mile flat race.

Riding Long Wharf, the 13/8 favourite, he finished second to Classified, ridden by Derek Thompson. Prince Charles was very gallant in defeat and enjoyed the experience so much that he rode again four days later, making his debut in a steeplechase at Sandown. He was unplaced.

From the heir to the throne to the greatest National Hunt jockey of all time. Plumpton was proud to be part of history on 9 February 2009 when Tony McCoy rode his 3,000th winner there. On a very wet and dismal Monday, he partnered Restless D'Artaix, a seven-year-old gelding trained by Nicky Henderson, to victory in a novice chase.

The final mention belongs to an extraordinary race on 17 November 1954. It was the 5.00pm race, the Cuckfield Novices Chase, with seven runners, heavy going and rapidly fading light. Top Gem fell at the first, bringing down Maid of Valence. At the third, Dancing Warrior fell and there was carnage at the water jump when one of the loose horses brought down the favourite Green Flax, as well as Canon Flame and Magna Carta. This left Struell Well alone with one circuit remaining, but Magna Carta had been remounted, only to refuse three times at the next. Struell Well was far from happy and managed to scramble over several obstacles. Eventually, Struell Well fell at the fifth-last but his rider Alan Oughton managed to catch him and remount with four to jump. He nearly fell at the water and refused again at the third last, but jumped it at the second attempt. At the second last he refused again, dumping his rider on the other side of the fence, but Alan Oughton caught him again and took him into the infield before one last attempt. By this time it was getting very dark and many of the crowd had gone home. Horse and rider came back out on to the course but, after several more attempts, Struell Well had had enough, and they walked back to the paddock with the race declared void. It was rumoured on reaching the weighing room that the stewards had also left, but they did leave Mr Oughton a note – could he please lock up and turn off the lights?

PLUMPTON

The footbridge over the railway line at Plumpton is a good place for trainspotting as well as watching the races.

Pontefract racecourse lies in a park originally laid out by the Normans for hunting. Once a huge wooded area, it was gradually reduced in size and the first defined racecourse was laid out roughly within the boundary of the present course. There is evidence of a meeting taking place in March 1648, which is quite astonishing, given that this was during the English Civil War and one of the royalist's strongholds was Pontefract Castle.

The castle was built by Ilbert De Lacy, one of William the Conqueror's generals at the Battle of Hastings. During the Civil War, from 1642 to 1648, Pontefract Castle, defended by Charles I's followers, was repeatedly under siege from Oliver Cromwell and his Roundheads. Cromwell eventually took control, the Royalists were defeated and the castle was partly demolished. Remarkable though it was that Pontefract should stage a race meeting during this hostile period, it was short-lived and there were no more recorded meetings until 1738.

The first major race to be run was the Pontefract Gold Cup in 1802, won by the Earl of Darlington's Muley Moloch, who had been beaten by Quiz in the 1801 St Leger. Lord Darlington went on to win four more Gold Cups. In 1816, The Duchess won, before winning the St Leger that year; in 1823 the winner was Doctor Syntax, whose victory was his 20th Gold Cup, which included a remarkable record of seven consecutive Gold Cups at Preston. He won a total of 36 races and became a very successful stallion.

In 1821, a spring meeting was inaugurated for the benefit of the Badsworth Hunt, but by 1835 the course had gone into decline and it was nearly 20 years before racing resumed, although the Badsworth Hunt did host a few National Hunt meetings in the interim. When flat meetings got under way again they were very spasmodic and even when the local council acquired the land in 1906 they did nothing to improve racing or the amenities. After the First World War the council leased the land to the newly-formed Pontefract Park Racecourse Company. In 1919 they laid out the present finishing straight behind the old stands and built two new stands in 1922, which still exist today. One of the old stands still remains today, known affectionately as the 'pepper pot'. For many years it was used as a number board.

The course itself is a complete left-handed circuit of two miles and 125 yards and is the longest continuous flat circuit in Europe. Indeed it was even longer at one point,

Approaching the finish at Pontefract, the 'pepper pot' number board and the modern digital display in the background.

before two major modifications. In December 1849, the Monkhill to Castleford and Methley railway line was opened, taking a considerable slice off the circuit. In 1971 the shape altered again with the construction of the M62 motorway, with all starts from one mile and over having to be repositioned. However, the round course was not used between 1922 and 1983. During this period, the course had operated only from the one-and-a-half mile start to the winning post. It is believed that the full circuit had been used during the 19th century.

During the Second World War only five courses were allowed to race and Pontefract was selected, along with Stockton, to cover racing in the north. The Lincolnshire Handicap and the Manchester November Handicap were both run at Pontefract from 1942 to 1945. Among the substitute Lincoln winners was Captain Charles Elsey's Double Harness, who won in 1945 carrying 6st 10lbs at 33/1. Fred Armstrong won two Manchester November Handicaps with Kerry Piper (1944), ridden by Charlie

Spares, and Oatflake (1945), ridden by top northern jockey Edgar Britt. Both jockeys went on to win English classics a few years later.

Since the war, Pontefract has grown to be very popular with northern racegoers, even though top-class horses have not been in abundance. 1998 Derby winner High-Rise did make his three-year-old debut here, as did 1997 St Leger winner Silver Patriarch, but trainers generally regard the course to be very stiff for these lightly-raced classic hopes, with the last four furlongs against the collar. The popularity of racing at Pontefract is not only due to the competitive nature of the races, which has been a big attraction with the local community, but also the good foresight of the management in allowing racing to start at the unusual time of 2.45 pm. Being a large coal mining area, this was to allow miners coming off the morning shift time for a wash. Since the mining industry has now almost disappeared, more normal times have been resumed.

Punchestown is the most rural of Irish racecourses, situated near Naas in the rolling countryside of County Kildare, stretching out to the beautiful Wicklow Mountains.

The first recognised meeting took place on 2 April 1850, when it was predominantly a National Hunt racecourse. Racing took place under the title 'Kildare and National Hunt' meeting in those days, but in 1962 the name was changed to Punchestown. It was at this time that flat racing was introduced, but it has always been overshadowed and only recently it has been discontinued.

The course got off to a flying start in 1868 with a crowd estimated at around 150,000 for a visit by the Prince of Wales. This high attendance set a pattern and Punchestown has remained extremely popular, with its perfect location and top-class racing to match.

The highlight of the year is their National Hunt Festival at the end of April, which has become the Irish version of Cheltenham. It dates back as far as 1852, when

a two-day meeting was held. It was extended to three days in 1963, four in 1999 and now to five days, featuring a total of 12 Grade I races – more than any other European Festival.

One particularly special race is the La Touche Cup, run over the Banks course. It has been run since 1922 and was named after Percy La Touche who died the previous year having served as manager of Punchestown for nearly 30 years. While Cheltenham has recently introduced a cross-country course with banks, it does not compare with the La Touche course, now run over four miles one furlong and 32 obstacles – although the distance and number of obstacles tend to vary from year to year. It consists of a huge bank (which the runners meet from two different directions), hurdles, timber fences, bush fences, hedges, a stone wall and even a chicken coop.

One notable winner of this unique event was Risk of Thunder, owned by Sir Sean Connery and trained by cross-country specialist Enda Bolger, who won the La

Dawn Run and Tony Mullins on their way to victory in a match against Buck House at Punchestown in April 1986.

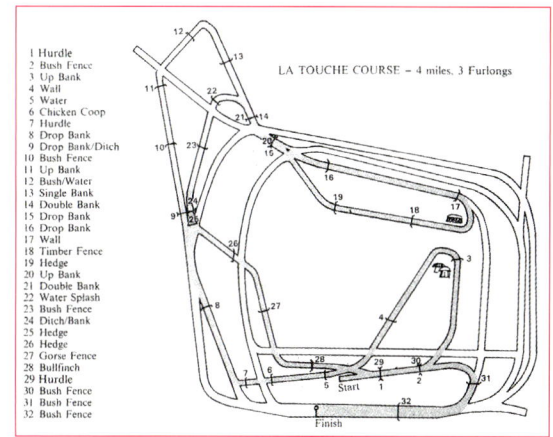

A diagram of the unique La Touche course in 1988.

Touche Cup seven times in a row (1995-2002, excluding 2001 when there was no race). A fence on the course has now been named after him.

Many equine superstars have won at Punchestown, including Ireland's two favourite horses, Arkle and the mare Dawn Run. Arkle won the John Jameson Gold Cup in 1963, while Dawn Run won here over hurdles and fences. Her final chase on Irish soil was a match against Buck House in 1986, which she won easily. Tragically, she was killed two months later in France, leaving the whole of Ireland in mourning.

Finally, back to Percy La Touche and the Prince of Wales. The Prince had been a frequent visitor to Punchestown, even after he was crowned King Edward VII in 1902. It was on a visit as King that he accidentally hit La Touche on the shoulder while gesturing with his walking stick. La Touche is reported to have said, 'Sir, I don't know if you've knighted me or broken my collar bone.'

La Touche never got his knighthood, but his memory lives on.

The field take the bank on the La Touche course in April 2013.

197

Redcar races began in the 19th century in a very humble way on the nearby sea shore. They were held on the local sands for many years with mixed events, the prizes for which were a saddle or a bridle, or just a few sovereigns. The run-in was roped, the judge gave his decisions from a bathing van and the stewards had as their stand a farm wagon. Hunters and ponies competed, and there was even one contest between foxhounds and racehorses to discover which were the faster. Unfortunately, the trail laid for the hounds was blown out to sea by the strong winds, the selected representatives of the Cleveland pack spread in all directions and the race proved a fiasco.

Many northern jockeys, including the popular John Osborne, preferred racing on the sand as opposed to dangerous courses like Durham, Richmond and Paisley. Even these days it is not uncommon for trainers to gallop their horses on the sands when their own gallops are frozen.

Eventually, the race committee decided to move from the sea shore and build a new course on the turf, whereby admission could be charged and more prize money could be offered to attract more horses. So the final meeting on the sands took place in 1870, when John Osborne won the Cleveland Hunt Cup worth £30 and a Mr Peacock won the Licensed Victuallers Stakes worth £315. That year the Jockey Club passed a new rule that no race should be run for a value of less than £50.

The first meeting on the new course (where it stands today) was held in August 1872. Admission to the grandstand enclosure cost 6/- and admission to the course 2d, while 5/- was charged for four-wheeled carriages and 2/6 for those with two wheels. At this inaugural meeting there were five races, the most important of which was the Redcar Handicap with £50 added. The opening event was the Zetland Welter Handicap, won by John Osborne's Wetherby.

At first a wooden stand was erected and dismantled for each meeting, but, by 1875, a permanent building had been constructed with the aid of the newly-formed Redcar and Coatham Grandstand Company. The cost was £2,650, a huge sum in those days that signified the importance with which Redcar was regarded, ranking among the best meetings in the North of England. That same year, with the help of the Marquess of Zetland, a straight mile course was built, later extended to nine furlongs – until the early 1970s it was the second-longest straight course in the country after Newmarket.

Left: the 3rd Marquess of Zetland, with John Sanderson and Major Leslie Petch, opens the new Tattersall's restaurant bar in 1977.

Bottom left: Kalahari King enjoying a roll on Redcar beach while trainer Ferdy Murphy's Middleham Stables are snowbound.

By 1877 it was decided to erect a stand for those in the second enclosure, it having been the policy of the Redcar executive to cater for the comfort of all their patrons on all parts of the course. The following year, plans were passed for the erection of stables on the course, thus bringing to an end the practice of using stabling in hotel yards and bringing horses to the course through all the traffic of a busy race day.

There were both steeplechase and hurdle races around this time but, by the October meeting in 1878, these were discontinued for lack of entries, after which a few hunter flat races remained for a short while. Just two flat meetings a year followed – a one-day fixture in June and a two-day fixture in August.

Following the First World War, Major Leslie Petch was appointed Managing Director, Clerk of the Course and Secretary at Redcar. Under his guidance the Redcar meetings increased in stature, reputation and popularity. He gave endless thought, time and energy to further the interests and prosperity of Redcar and in that spirit

the course has gone from strength to strength. He was instrumental in the addition of the Vaux Gold Tankard in 1959, which at the time was the richest handicap in Europe. Other big handicaps he introduced were the Zetland Gold Cup and the Andy Capp Handicap. The rich two-year-old race run in October, then known as the Racecall Gold Trophy and now as the Totepool Two-Year-Old Trophy, was also his brainchild.

It was the two-year-old Provideo which gave Redcar a special place in turf history. On 1 November 1984, he recorded his 16th victory, winning the Dinsdale Spa Stakes at odds of 1/8. Trained by Bill O'Gorman, Provideo was running in his 23rd race, having started the season by winning the Brocklesby Stakes at Doncaster in March. His victory equalled the all-time juvenile record of 16 wins set in 1885 by The Bard, who also started his career by winning the Brocklesby. This record still stands today, although Timeless Times, also trained by Bill O'Gorman, equalled the record at Pontefract six years later.

Another momentous occasion at Redcar came on 5 August 1986, when Princess Anne rode into the winners' enclosure after winning the Mommessin Stakes for Amateur Riders aboard Gulfland, a five-year-old gelding by Gulf Pearl and trained by Gavin Pritchard-Gordon. Starting at 5/1, Gulfland won by five lengths from the 4/6 favourite Positive, ridden by Mr T Thomson-Jones. Not only was it the Princess's first winner from 13 rides, but she was also the first member of the Royal Family to win a race since Charles II triumphed at the Newmarket Spring Meeting of 1674.

Ripon (known as the Garden Racecourse) is one of the most attractive and picturesque racecourses in Britain, with floral displays, well-kept lawns and a majestic line of trees in the paddock. The course itself is flat with very slight undulations in the straight, stretching for six furlongs. The round course enters the straight over five furlongs out, giving Ripon the longest final straight in Britain (Chester has the shortest).

The first meeting at Ripon on the present course was staged on 6 August 1900, although racing has taken place in Ripon for centuries. Including the present course, the ancient city of Ripon has had six different racecourses. Racing took place on Bondgate Green in 1664 and on Moncton Moor in 1675. In 1714 the Corporation decided to level off High Common for racing and it was here that a powerful local family by the name of Aislabie became Ripon's biggest supporters, often providing the prize money. In 1723 Ripon could boast the first-ever ladies' race, for which Mrs John Aislabie donated a plate to the winner.

The races declined in popularity after William Aislabie's death and the enclosure of High Common put a stop to racing at Ripon in 1826. However, ten years later a local publican held a modest race meeting in his own field beyond North Bridge by the river Ure, and this lasted until 1865 when it was superseded by a new course on Redbank, where it remained for nearly 40 years. The grandstand at

Redbank is now the Cathedral Choir School but it is said to be haunted by the ghost of a jockey who died on the course. In 1900 a new racecourse was established near Hewick Bridge and this is the present course.

The city of Ripon is steeped in history, reflected in some of the races. The Great St Wilfred Handicap is named after the Patron Saint of Ripon. The Hornblower Stakes commemorates the surviving tradition of a horn blower blowing a horn outside the Mayor's house at 9.00 pm each evening. The Ripon Rowels Handicap honours the local spur-making industry.

The Great St Wilfred Handicap has been one of the highlights of the Ripon calendar for many years. It is a very competitive six-furlong handicap, run on a Saturday in August and usually attracts a large field of good-class sprinters. The most notable winner was Soba in 1982, trained by David Chapman and ridden by David Nicholls. The 9/4 favourite carrying top weight of 9st 7lb won easily to record her ninth win of the season.

Another important race at Ripon is the Champion Two-Year-Old Trophy, held in the autumn. High Top, trained by Bernard van Cutsem, won the race in 1971 and went on to win the 2,000 Guineas the following year, while Provideo, a prolific winning two-year-old also triumphed at Ripon in 1984, winning for the 14th time. Provideo went on to win 16 times in one season, a record-breaking performance for a two-year-old.

With records indicating that Ripon may have hosted the first-ever ladies race, it seemed appropriate to hold the Ladies' Derby there as well. The first running took place on 6 June 1973.

The first running was won by Pee Mai at 2/1, ridden by Linda Goodwill, earning his owner, Mr C Barber-Lomax, a modest £522. On the same day, just 20 minutes earlier, Morston had won his owner £66,348 in the Epsom equivalent.

The Ripon Hornblower. Since the year 886, a Wakeman has kept watch over the city of Ripon at night. Every evening on the dot of 9 pm, the horn-blower has sounded his horn 4 times outside the mayor's house in the market square.

ROSCOMMON

Roscommon is steeped in National Hunt tradition. The first organised steeplechase to be run in Ireland was held at Roscommon on St Patrick's Day 1813, run over a six-mile course on Racroghan Plain. The idea came from an event held in England at Bedford in 1810, which had been restricted to horses that had 'been in at the death of three foxes in Leicestershire' and had a certificate from the Master to prove it.

The present racecourse in the County town of Roscommon, 85 miles west of Dublin, is known locally as Lenabane. The course is only a mile from the town, on rich pastoral land owned by the Ministry of Agriculture. The first ever recorded meeting took place in 1837 and was organised by the British military, which then had a base in the town. Racing proper began in 1885 and has continued ever since, with the exception of a twelve year period from 1936 to 1948.

In 1891 a young veterinary student named James Parkinson (1870–1948) rode his first winner at Roscommon. He later turned his attention to training and, in his heyday, trained the largest string in Europe and was champion trainer in Ireland on eight occasions. Although generally associated with moderate horses, Parkinson won the Irish Derby twice and the Irish Oaks four times, as well as winning all the major two-year-old races during his career.

The two-mile Kilbegnet Novice Chase is the biggest National Hunt race, run in October with a prize of €40,000. The 1996 Cheltenham Gold Cup winner Imperial Call had his first outing over fences in this race, finishing third. The biggest race on the Flat is the Lenebane Stakes, a Listed race over a mile-and-a-half, which is run in July. Over the past two years this race has attracted runners from English stables.

When racing was revived at Roscommon on 25 May 1948, Martin Molony, then at the height of his brilliant but brief career, rode a double, winning two steeplechases on Bamboozle and Lough Conn. The latter was famous for having finished second to Caughoo in the previous year's Grand National. In a controversial race run in dense fog, Lough Conn was partnered by Daniel McCann, who later alleged that 100/1 outsider Caughoo completed only one circuit. He claimed he hid somewhere near the Canal Turn. Caughoo had poor form, although he did win twice at Downpatrick and yet again at Liverpool in a field of 57 he won by 20 lengths, beating 21 finishers. The jury is still out.

Above: Roscommon has always attracted big crowds and runners from all over the country.

Below: The Silver Crown causes havoc as she jumps through the railings after unshipping Gary Carroll at the start during the Irish Stallion Farms European Breeders Fund Fillies Handicap in 2010.

SALISBURY

S alisbury is one of the oldest racecourses in the country – it is reported that a meeting was held there in 1584. One early visitor was Queen Elizabeth I in May 1588, on her way for a chat with Sir Francis Drake before the defeat of the Spanish Armada. The racecourse is high on a hill east of the city centre at Netherhampton, from where you can see Salisbury's magnificent 13th-century cathedral with its 400-foot spire, the tallest in the UK.

Racing was on a firm footing by 1722 and one of Salisbury's oldest races was inaugurated in 1765 – the City Bowl, which is still run today. The first winner was Mr Larkin's grey horse Cyclops, but two immortals of the turf were also early winners here, in Gimcrack (1768) and Eclipse (1769).

Salisbury was hosted by the Bibury Club in 1899, which is the oldest racing club in the world. First established in 1681 at Burford, it has since had other venues at Cheltenham and Stockbridge. With the closure of Stockbridge in 1898, the club moved to Salisbury, where for over 100 years the Bibury Cup has been run.

Another old race is the Champagne Stakes for two-years-olds. An early winner making his debut in 1912 was Aboyeur, who went on the following year to win the Derby at 100/1, albeit controversially (awarded the race following the disqualification of Craganour).

Several other future classic winners were seen in their early paces at Salisbury. Fred Darling, who trained at nearby Beckhampton, won here with Derby winners Cameronian, Pont L'Eveque and Owen Tudor, Fillies Triple Crown winner Sun Chariot, 2,000 Guineas winner Big Game and that fine sprinter Myrobella. Darling's successor at Beckhampton, Noel Murless, also won here with 1,000 Guineas heroine Queenpot (1948).

Another future champion to appear at Salisbury was the legendary Lester Piggott. On 7 April 1948 he had his first ride in public on the filly The Chase in an apprentice's race for his father, Keith Piggott. He finished unplaced, but four months later he rode his first winner on the same horse at Haydock.

Another jockey to make his debut at Salisbury was the American Steve Cauthen. This time it was a winning debut, when he steered home Marquee Universal for trainer Barry Hills on 7 April 1979. Steve later teamed up with Henry Cecil and his powerful Newmarket stable and was crowned champion jockey three times (1984, 1985, 1987). Also, on the same day in 1979, trainer David Elsworth saddled his first winner Raffia Set. He later became the trainer of the great Desert Orchid.

The finest Derby winner to triumph here was Mill Reef, who made his debut as a two-year-old in the 5f Salisbury Stakes on 13 May 1970. There were 11 runners in the field, including the mount of Lester Piggott, Fireside Chat, who had already won impressively at Newmarket on 2000 Guineas day. He was fully expected to win again and was a heavily backed 2/9 favourite.

Also among the opposition that day was an unraced colt by Never Bend called Mill Reef who was destined to become a champion of Europe. Owned and bred by the American philanthropist, Paul Mellon, ridden in all his races by Geoff Lewis and trained at Kingsclere by Ian Balding, Mill Reef was beaten only twice in a glittering career. In 1971, he won the Derby, the Eclipse Stakes, the King George VI and Queen Elizabeth Stakes and the Prix de l'Arc de Triomphe.

On that Wednesday afternoon in May 1970, Mill Reef made his racecourse debut. He made all the running, beating Fireside Chat by four lengths at odds of 8/1 (nearly 12/1 on the Tote). Oh, for a crystal ball!

The statue of Mill Reef at Rokeby Stables in Virginia bears this inscription on the other side:

Swift as a bird I flew down many a course.
Princes, Lords, Commoners all sang my praise.
In victory or defeat I played my part.
Remember me, all men who love the Horse,
If hearts and spirits flag in after days;
Though small, I gave my all. I gave my heart.

Sandown Park may well have had the distinction of changing the face of horse racing as we know it today. In 1875, Sandown Park became the first racecourse to be enclosed, with an admission fee of half a crown. In doing so it became known as the 'drawing room course' and other racecourses like Kempton, Hurst Park, Lingfield, Plumpton, Folkestone and Haydock would soon follow suit. Before 1875, courses were on open land and anybody could attend, which allowed them to become a meeting place for ruffians and other unsavoury characters. The Sandown Park innovation allowed ladies to attend meetings unescorted and without having to witness any bad behaviour, whereas before it would only have been proper to be escorted by a gentleman.

Sandown Park lies on the edge of the town of Esher in Surrey, less than 15 miles from the centre of London. The site of the racecourse was originally Sandown Farm, and long before was the home of the monks of the Augustine Priory of Sandon, built by Henry II in the 12th century (the monks were wiped out by the great plague of 1390

and the Priory was later demolished). The only remnant today is the pond, which is now famously part of the National Hunt course and known as the Pond fence, but one could imagine it was once a lovely fishing spot for those Augustine Monks. The site remained a farm until 1870, when the land came up for sale and was acquired by Sir Wilfred Brett, whose brother William became the first Viscount Esher, a celebrated lawyer (he became Master of the Rolls) and Conservative MP. With the support of Lt Colonel Hwfa Williams, a keen gambler and close friend of the Prince of Wales, plans were laid to develop Sandown Park racecourse. There was some opposition, as others thought the site more suitable for a model village or a lunatic asylum, but Sir Wilfred Brett and his consortium had their plans accepted. The first task was to build a fence enclosing the whole area (at a cost of £2,000) and a grandstand, in time for the inaugural meeting.

Unfortunately, bad weather marred the first meeting on 22 April 1875. It was a mixed card and attendance was poor, but Fred Archer lit up a gloomy afternoon by riding a winner. The first steeplechase at Sandown Park was the Household Brigade Cup, won by Lord Douglas Gordon riding Sandy. This race set the trend for the strong military flavour which persists today. The meeting lasted three days and on the second day the Military Steeplechase Cup was won by Highland Mary, ridden by Lord Marcus Beresford, another close friend of the Prince of Wales. Six years later this race was replaced by the Grand Military Gold Cup. Held at various venues until 1880 (with a break for the Crimean War), Sandown Park has remained host to this prestigious race up to the present day.

It was appropriate that the inaugural meeting should be a mixed card because Sandown Park has provided top-class sport under both codes ever since. The main race on the flat is the Group 1 Eclipse Stakes, run in July. Other group races include the Classic Trial in April, followed by the Gordon Richards Stakes, the Brigadier Gerard Stakes and the Henry II Stakes (in memory of the founder of the Augustine Priory and often a rehearsal for the Ascot Gold Cup). For two-year-olds, there is the National Breeders Produce Stakes, now known as the National Stakes, and in the autumn the Solario Stakes. The National Hunt showpiece is the bet365 Gold Cup, which brings down the curtain on the National Hunt season these days. In 1957, it was the first race ever to be sponsored when called the Whitbread Gold Cup, and is still affectionately known by its original title by many racegoers. Other big National Hunt races here include the Tingle Creek Chase and the Imperial Cup, a valuable handicap hurdle run just before the Cheltenham Festival.

Eclipse Stakes

The Eclipse Stakes was first run in 1886 and was won by Bendigo. It was worth a massive £10,000 – the richest race ever to be run, and worth far more than the Derby of that year. Bringing together the very best three-year-olds against older horses has provided many epic battles between generations. The finest example took place in

1903 when the five-runner field included the 1903 Derby winner Rock Sand (also Triple Crown winner), the 1902 Derby winner Ard Patrick and the four-year-old filly Sceptre, the winner of four classics in 1902. It was billed as the race of the century and so it proved, with Ard Patrick beating Sceptre by a neck and Rock Sand three lengths back in third. Sceptre was arguably an unlucky loser, as the filly was at a disadvantage in terms of fitness and was also ridden by a far less experienced jockey.

In 1968, the Eclipse produced an almost identical race with the clash of the 1967 Derby winner Royal Palace, the 1968 Derby winner Sir Ivor and the French colt Taj Dewan, who had come second to Royal Palace in the previous year's 2,000 Guineas. It lived up to all expectations, with all three colts in line with a furlong to run. Sir Ivor was the first beaten and the two four-year-olds fought a titanic battle, with Royal Palace winning by a short head. The judge took over 15 minutes to announce the result, much to the disbelief of Taj Dewan's connections, and some racegoers still to this day feel the judge made a mistake.

Until Sea the Stars won in 2009, the previous Derby victor to win the Eclipse was Nashwan in 1989, but to do so he had to beat the brilliant filly Indian Skimmer and Warning – another mouth-watering clash. Other Derby winners to succeed at the Eclipse in the same year were Flying Fox (1899), Diamond Jubilee (1900), Lemberg (dead heat 1910), Coronach (1926), Blue Peter (1939), Tulyar (1952) and Mill Reef (1971), while Derby winners to win as four-year-olds were Isinglass (1894), Persimmon (1897), Ard Patrick (1903), Windsor Lad (1935) and Royal Palace (1968). Other champions to win the race were Bayardo, Ballymoss, Brigadier Gerard, Pebbles (first filly ever to win), Dancing Brave, Giant's Causeway and dual winners Mtoto and Halling – all in all, quite a list.

It was poignant that Sir Gordon Richards' final ride was in this high-profile race. On 10 July 1954, he rode Landau for the Queen, but could finish only third to Willie

Stephenson's colt King of the Tudors. Half an hour later in the Star Stakes for two-year-old fillies, his intended mount Abergeldie unseated him in the paddock and rolled on top of him, fracturing his pelvis, and Richards' career in the saddle came to an abrupt end. The final winner of his career was Princely Gift at Sandown Park the previous afternoon.

It is fair to say the Eclipse Stakes has overshadowed the other Group races at Sandown Park, but in the early 1900s Sandown Park was witness to two astonishing performances by two-year-olds that were later to make their mark in racing history. The first was a filly called Pretty Polly, who made her racecourse debut on 27 June 1903 in the British Dominion Two-Year-Old Plate over five furlongs. Trained by Peter Gilpin at Clarehaven Stables in Newmarket, neither the trainer nor anybody else could believe the astonishing performance she put up, as she had appeared rather backward and had not done any serious work. She started at 6/1 and was ridden by an inexperienced jockey called Trigg. The favourite was John o'Gaunt, who had finished fourth in the Coventry Stakes at

Royal Ascot and was to finish second in the 2,000 Guineas and the Derby the following season. Pretty Polly flew out of the gate and, after two furlongs, was ten lengths in front. Most people in the stands thought there must have been a false start, but in fact the runners got away to an even break. She passed the post on a tight rein to the astonishment of Trigg and the other riders. Many racegoers regarded the win as a fluke but her second appearance, also at Sandown Park in the National Breeders Produce Stakes, this time starting 2/1 favourite, was equally impressive. She ran a total of nine times as a two-year-old and remained unbeaten. The following season she won the Fillies' Triple Crown and was beaten only twice from 24 starts; had she been entered in the Derby she almost certainly would have won that as well.

The National Breeders Produce Stakes of 1913 was the focus of attention for another remarkable performance. The Tetrarch, a colt trained by Atty Persse at Stockbridge, had already won the Woodcote Stakes at Epsom and the Coventry Stakes at Royal Ascot by ten lengths. Starting at odds of 8/100, The Tetrarch won by a neck. Fog had made it impossible to see the five-furlong start from the stands and many people at first doubted it was the performance of a wonder horse, but it was revealed that when the tapes went up The Tetrarch stumbled, came down on his knees and was left fully 20 lengths behind. Once recovered, he showed blistering speed to get up in the last few yards and keep his reputation intact. He remained unbeaten in seven starts that season but, sadly, through injury, never raced again; however, many of his progeny have kept the family flag flying.

The Tetrarch and Steve Donoghue, winners of the 1913 National Breeders Produce Stakes. Known as 'the Spotted Wonder' the stallion was unbeaten in seven starts and became an influential sire.

National Hunt racing

National Hunt racing at Sandown Park has been just as spectacular as the Flat. The flagship has been the Whitbread (now bet365) Gold Cup – the first race ever to be sponsored, as mentioned. Every year the race was preceded by the appearance of the magnificent shire horses employed by the Whitbread Brewery Company parading in front of the packed stands, pulling a dray cart. This three-mile-5 1/2-furlong handicap steeplechase has always been run at the end of April, often on a mixed card, and now closes the National Hunt season.

Twenty-four horses lined up for the inaugural running in 1957, and what a line-up it was. The reigning Cheltenham Gold Cup winner Linwell was there with the 1955 Gold Cup hero, Gay Donald. Sundew, who four weeks earlier had won the Grand National, was also among the runners, along with a youngster called Mandarin, who, in later years, became a brilliant chaser. Also in the field was the nine-year-old Much Obliged, trained by Neville Crump, and it was he who won, holding off the late challenge of Mandarin to scoop the £4,250 first prize.

Former Gold Cup winner Pas Seul triumphed in 1961, the first of many greats to land the race, but his performance and every other was eclipsed by what happened four years later. The Irish legend Arkle had just won his second Gold Cup and lined up for the Whitbread carrying the almost impossible burden of 12st 7lb. Despite having to concede 35lbs to his six rivals he started at 4/9 – such was his dominance. His five-length victory remains one of the greatest handicap performances of all time.

The race continued to attract the biggest names in racing. Mud-loving What a Myth won in 1966, and a year later the great Mill House returned for one last hurrah and secured an emotional victory.

The Sandown Park hill has witnessed a great many famous finishes, none more so than the amazing 1984 Whitbread Gold Cup. On very firm ground, dual winner Diamond Edge, Lettoch and Plundering took the last fence together, with the Queen Mother's Special Cargo four lengths behind. In a finish regularly voted the greatest in racing history, Kevin Mooney brought Special Cargo with a devastating run to pip Lettoch and Diamond Edge by two short heads. It was trainer Fulke Walwyn's seventh victory in the race – a feat that may never be equalled. Desert Orchid was another popular winner in 1988 and

The famous Whitbread shires open proceedings for the Whitbread Gold Cup, the first race ever sponsored, in 1957.

The legendary Arkle jumps the last fence at Sandown to win the 1965 Whitbread Gold Cup.

when Mr Frisk won in 1990, ridden by Marcus Armytage, he became the only horse in history to win the Grand National and the Whitbread in the same season.

One of the most thrilling rivalries of the 1960s was that between Arkle and Mill House. On 6 November 1965 in the Gallaher Gold Cup, they met for the fifth and final time. The score stood at 3-1 in the Irish horse's favour but this time Arkle, carrying his usual 12st 7lb, had to concede 16lb to Mill House, as well as Rondetto and The Rip. Many thought it was an opportunity for Mill House to turn the tables, especially when he jumped into the lead on the second circuit. However, Arkle, who was four lengths down at the final railway fence, began to turn on the power. At the Pond fence, Arkle took control with a magnificent leap and eventually beat Rondetto by 20 lengths, with an exhausted Mill House only third. Arkle that day proved, as if there had been any doubt, that he was the greatest steeplechaser of all time.

Another National Hunt race to whet the appetite is the Grade 1 Tingle Creek Chase. It is named after the exciting chaser trained by Harry Thomson-Jones, who won 23 of his 49 starts and was undoubtedly one of the fastest jumpers over two miles – his speed over the railway fences at Sandown Park often ensured victory. Top two-mile chasers to win this race were Desert Orchid, Viking Flagship, Moscow Flyer (twice) and Flagship Uberalles (three times). The Tingle Creek Chase is run in December and is probably the best two-mile chase outside the Cheltenham Festival.

The Imperial Cup, a handicap hurdle over two miles, is the most valuable hurdle race at Sandown Park and is run a week before the Cheltenham Festival, with a bonus added for any horse that can win the Imperial Cup plus any race at Cheltenham. Three horses have achieved this double – Olympian, Blowing Wind and Gaspara – but arguably the greatest winner in the history of the race was Lanzarote in

1973, carrying 12st 4lb. He went on to win the Champion Hurdle for trainer Fred Winter the following year.

Sandown Park used to host the Doug Barrott Novices Handicap Hurdle, commemorating the jockey who died on 3 May 1973 at the age of 26. Barrott died of multiple head injuries following a fall on French Colonist in the Whitbread Gold Cup five days earlier. He was riding for his boss Josh Gifford, for whom he had ridden over 60 winners in his short career. Among his winners at Sandown Park was the 1971 Imperial Cup winner Churchwood and the 1973 Stone's Ginger Wine Chase winner Avondhu.

There are two military meetings, the Royal Artillery Gold Cup Meeting in February, and the Grand Military Meeting in March, both dating from Sandown Park's inception. The Grand Military Gold Cup was first run at Northampton in 1841 and had many venues until it moved temporarily to Sandown Park in 1881. It was then staged at Rugby, Aylesbury and Aldershot before finally settling at Sandown Park in 1888 where it has remained (with breaks for the two World Wars). One of the conditions for the race is that owners and riders must be officers of Her Majesty's Armed Services, past or present, on full or half pay.

In 1970, the Queen Mother became Patron of the Grand Military Race Committee and would often present the trophy. Having won the race herself five times, notably with Special Cargo (1984, 1985, 1986), the honour was bestowed on another member of the committee. In 1990 (the 150th running), she won it again with The Argonaut and was presented with the cup by her daughter, HM The Queen.

The Royal Artillery Gold Cup has had a similar history. The inaugural meeting was in 1862 at Eltham and it first appeared at Sandown Park in 1878, but it was mostly hosted by Croydon, Bromley, Plumstead and, for longer periods, at Aldershot. It returned permanently to Sandown Park in 1921 but ten years were lost to the

Second World War, and it did not return until 1949 because of a shortage of riders, many of whom were still on active service.

The 1978 race was graced by the presence of the 1975 Cheltenham Gold Cup winner, Ten Up. Now enjoying a more sedate life in hunter chases, he proved that the old class was still there by landing the Cup (and winning it again in 1980 and 1982, plus the Grand Military Gold Cup in 1979). The 1980s were dominated by two horses, Quarrier and De Pluvinel. Quarrier, owned by Major Sir Kenneth Butt and ridden by Tim Thomson-Jones, won the race in 1984, 1986 and 1987, but the record of De Pluvinel was even more remarkable.

De Pluvinel ran in the Royal Artillery Gold Cup eight times from 1982 to 1990. Originally owned by Lt-Colonel J W Deacon and then by his former rider Guy Prest, he finished second on his first appearance in 1982, winning in 1983 and second again in 1984, 1987 and 1988 – and proved he was not ready to be written off when dramatically regaining the title in 1989. He was still not done, however, for he won a third time in 1990 at the age of 17, on which occasion the reception he received nearly lifted the roof off the new stand. Another loud cheer came in 1996 for the Queen Mother, when her Norman Conqueror was successful. Having presented the Gold Cup for well over 30 years it was fitting that she, with all the support she gave to National Hunt racing, got to receive the trophy for a change.

The Queen Mother may not have had a prouder moment than at the Grand Military meeting on 8 March 1980. In the Duke of Gloucester Memorial Trophy Chase for Amateur Riders, she wished good luck to the rider of Sea Swell, her grandson HRH Prince Charles who was having his first ride in a steeplechase. His mount, trained by Nick Gaselee, had four opponents including Coolishall and Ten Up, but finished a respectable fourth. Afterwards he drew praise from Fred Rimell: 'A good style for a new boy'.

SEDGEFIELD

Sedgefield will always be recognised as one of the 'gaff' courses but, nevertheless, National Hunt sport is very popular in this part of Durham, even if the quality of racing is not the highest. There was once a wonderfully-named race here called the Plodders Handicap Chase, but this was discontinued. (A proud owner probably complained on the grounds of discrimination).

Racing began here in 1846 in the grounds of the Sands Hall estate, the home of the Ord family. The early meetings were hosted by the Lambton Hunt, a club that had been formed in 1804 at a local hostelry, The Hardwicke Arms, by Ralph Lambton who was an ancestor of the Earls of Durham. Before making Sedgefield their headquarters they had raced on land made available by the Earl of Darlington.

The feature race at Sedgefield is the Durham National, but just two winners have gone on to glory at Aintree. Red Alligator, trained locally by Denys Smith, won both but in different years. Ridden by Brian Fletcher (who later

partnered Red Rum in two of his famous Grand National victories), Red Alligator won at Sedgefield in 1967 before finishing third in that dramatic race behind Foinavon and then went on to victory himself at Aintree the following year. Rubstic won the Grand National in 1979 and created a piece of Sedgefield history by winning the Durham National in three consecutive years (1978, 1979, 1980), and completed the double in the same year on the second occasion. Trained by John Leadbetter at Hawick and ridden by Maurice Barnes, he became the first horse trained in Scotland to win the Grand National. His victory was quite remarkable in that two years previously he had been seriously ill, nearly dying of dehydration.

Sedgefield was famous for many years for having one of the longest run-ins from the last fence and being unique in that it was the only track where the open ditch was the last fence. The reason for this was that the water jump was situated at the bottom of the home straight and had to

Sedgefield in 1985, from the centre of the course.

be avoided on the final circuit. However, when the rules regarding the inclusion of water jumps on racecourses was relaxed, consultation was held with the jockeys, trainers and other interested parties as to whether the Sedgefield course could be improved by the omission of the water jump and the introduction of a further fence. The jockeys were worried that a further fence might be a hazard if it were situated at the bottom of the hill where horses would be gaining speed just before the winning post. It was eventually agreed that a portable fence be purchased and positioned by the furlong marker, and the water jump be removed and filled in. The work was carried out in 1992 and this layout has been used ever since. It seemed to be generally agreed that this improved steeplechasing at Sedgefield and made it a fairer test for horses, as well as a better spectacle for the spectators.

An amusing story emerged surrounding an amateur riders' chase over a hundred years ago and that final open ditch. There were seven runners, of which five had either fallen or pulled up. The leader was a fence clear of his solitary opponent when he fell at the final fence. The unfortunate beast lay on the ground, clearly winded, while his rider, Captain J E Rogerson, tried to urge his mount to his feet. By the fence stood some lads from the local coal mine, who were watching the race on their way home from the pit.

'Hey lads,' shouted the Captain. 'Give us a hand to get this horse up.'

'Nay, guv'nor,' they replied.

'Why ever not?' growled the Captain.

''Cause we've backed t'other one.'

SLIGO

The town of Sligo is in the heart of Yeats country. William Butler Yeats was captivated by the sheer beauty of the area and may well have regarded Sligo as the 'Land of Heart's Desire'. The whole area is immortalised in his poetry and the paintings of his brother Jack. The beautiful surroundings of the present racecourse at Cleveragh would be a fine example, nestling in the shadows of Mount Benbulbin, making it one of the most scenic in the country.

Racing began here in September 1781 at Bowmore, Rosses Point, where there now stands a championship golf course which stages the West of Ireland Amateur Open tournament every year. In 1873, Sligo races moved to Hazelwood, an attractive course on the banks of picturesque Lough Gill, but in 1942 the land was claimed by the Land Registry.

An alternative course was sought and for a while the fixture was continued at Mullingar, but this did not suit the locals. Eventually, the present course was leased from Sligo Corporation. Work commenced on building a new racecourse. Everything was ready for a grand opening in 1954 but, because of persistent bad weather, this had to be postponed for 12 months to protect the newly-seeded course.

The new date was 24 August 1955 and it brought beautiful weather and a huge crowd of 8,000. Sligo became Ireland's youngest racecourse (a title it held until 2001 when the new Limerick course opened). The meeting was a huge success after a lapse of 13 years, and the call of, 'They're off!' for the first race was met with a resounding cheer. The honour of winning the opening race, the Cleveragh Hurdle, went to Soloe, owned and trained by D L Moore in the hands of Pat Doyle.

W B Yeats died in 1939 and is buried at Drumcliff, less than five miles from Sligo racecourse. If he had been looking down that day he would have approved.

Nowadays Southwell is more renowned for all-weather racing, having been one of its pioneers in 1989, but it used to be a strictly National Hunt course dating back to 1898.

Racing had begun just outside the town in 1886 but that course was deemed unsafe and the National Hunt Committee refused to renew its licence after the meeting on 17 October 1897. The newly-appointed racecourse committee took a lease on the land at Rolleston, between Southwell and Newark, where the present course now stands. The first meeting took place on 16 May 1898.

All-weather racing has certainly put Southwell on the map, with currently over 60 meetings a year compared to a handful of National Hunt fixtures. The first all-weather meeting, on 1 November 1989, was ironically a National Hunt fixture but it did not meet the safety regulations and was soon abolished. The first all-weather flat meeting took place a week later and its growing popularity led to flat meetings at Southwell being extended to a few turf fixtures in 1991. It was at this time that a new grandstand was built, along with a new weighing room plus a new paddock location.

The most prolific winner on the all-weather track was the impeccably-bred Tempering. Foaled in 1986, he was a colt by Kris out of a Nijinsky mare, Mixed Applause, and was owned and bred by Lord Howard de Walden. He first saw a racecourse as a three-year-old when trained by Henry Cecil, winning just one small race at Redcar. He moved to the stables of William Jarvis without success, and in 1990 he was sent to the Newmarket September Sales, where he fetched 9,200 guineas. The buyer was Yorkshire trainer David Chapman on behalf of one of his owners, Michael Hill.

After a couple of races on the turf David Chapman campaigned Tempering on all-weather tracks, almost exclusively at Southwell. He won for the first time on this surface on 5 December 1990, an 11-furlong handicap. Chapman kept him to middle distances and over the next six years ran him 82 times at the Rolleston track. He won a total of 22 races here, half of which were claimers. His best season was 1993, when he won eight times – more than any other horse in Britain that year.

Keeping Tempering sound and interested was down to the skill of David Chapman, a past master of finding the right opportunities for this type of horse; Tempering loved Southwell and they loved him.

Sonny Somers aged 18 in 1980, the year he became the joint-oldest horse to win a race in Britain.

National Hunt racing at Southwell has always been low-key, but two pieces of racing history were made here. On 14 February 1980 the Star and Garter Handicap Chase over three miles was won by the Fred Winter-trained Sonny Somers, ridden by Ben de Haan. He finished eight lengths and 15 lengths ahead of two nine-year-olds, Trojan Walk and the favourite Lord Brae. The amazing thing was that Sonny Somers was 18 years old and had equalled the record for the oldest horse ever to win a race in Britain. What is more, he went on to win again at Lingfield two weeks later. His final record showed that he won 26 races from 123 starts in 14 years, comprising one bumper (in Ireland), nine over hurdles and 16 over fences. He was second in the 1971 Cathcart Chase and became one of the nation's favourite horses. Fred Winter was quoted as saying, 'This old horse has given me more pleasure than you can imagine'.

On 3 September 1986, the jockey Phil Tuck also entered the history books at Southwell by winning the Racing Post Handicap Hurdle on Doronicum, equalling Johnny Gilbert's record of riding ten consecutive National Hunt winners, which had stood for 27 years. Between 23 August and 3 September he won on Norval, Doronicum, Easter Brig, St Colme and Atkinsons at Cartmel; Golden Fancy, Norval, Master Lamb and Atkinsons at Perth; and finally Doronicum at Southwell. Had Easter Brig won later in the afternoon, Phil could have claimed the record outright, but the odds-on favourite could finish only fifth.

From two special moments to a tragedy. In July 1996, the racing world mourned the death of jockey Richard Davis who died of his injuries following a fall at Southwell (a race is held in his honour at Worcester). The highs and lows of National Hunt racing are clearly illustrated when such a terrible tragedy happens. The risks taken by both human and equine, for the love of the sport, can never be sufficiently appreciated.

Finally, a heart-warming example of courage. A six-year-old gelding called Harry Potter, trained in Wales by Evan Williams, won the Ladbrokegames.com Selling Hurdle at Southwell in August 2005. Four months earlier he had been hit by a car and sustained two fractures to one hind leg and a break in the other. The injuries were near his hock and his fetlock, and his life was very much in the balance. The car had pushed him through a five-bar gate, so his mental recovery would have been just as difficult as the physical. The skill of Evan Williams and the courage of Harry Potter will never be forgotten.

Southwell may not be the most glamorous of courses, but the all-weather Fibresand track is a godsend to riders and trainers when icy conditions grip the country. Here a few hardy souls turn out to watch Linroyale Boy and Robert Winston win in March 2013.

Anne Hathaway's cottage is one of the biggest tourist attractions in the perfect old English town of Stratford-on-Avon. Just a stone's throw from the beautiful thatched cottage lies Stratford racecourse, on a piece of land known as Shottery Meadow. Anne Hathaway married William Shakespeare in 1582, and it is quite possible that the young couple may have spent time courting here.

Many years later – 173 to be precise – the meadow became the venue for the first race meeting at Stratford and, on 22 September 1755, Forrester won the opening race for his owner, a Mr Campbell. In 1769 David Garrick, a theatrical legend of the era and at the time playing the leading role in Shakespeare's *Richard III* at Drury Lane, instigated a three-day festival in September. The main race was a Jubilee Cup, for which the winner received a piece of plate inscribed with Shakespeare's falcon-dominated arms. David Garrick presented this handsome

prize to Mr Pratt, the owner of Whirligig, who beat just four opponents after three three-mile heats on a course flooded in some places to a depth of two feet.

Racing came to a sudden halt in 1778, when protesters, led by local farmer Jim Reade, put a stop to further meetings because of the damage being caused to crops and fences. Stratford remained closed for 58 years. One of the early attractions of the revived meetings was the appearance in 1839 of Lottery following his Grand National success at Aintree, and he duly obliged at odds of 1/2, ridden by his usual jockey Jem Mason. Stratford failed to attract horses of such calibre very often and racing gradually went into decline, becoming little more than a Hunt meeting.

It was not until 1949 that Stratford turned the corner, with the appointment of Gay Shepherd as Clerk of the Course. He introduced the Horse and Hound Cup, a hunter chase final run at the end of May, a meeting that used to bring down the curtain on the National Hunt season. First run in 1959 (won by Speylove), it always attracts Stratford's biggest crowd of the season. Some fine hunter chasers have won this prestigious event, with pride of place going to Credit Call and Baulking Green. Credit Call (1971, 1972, 1973, 1975), trained by Arthur Stephenson, won a total of 37 races in his career, while Baulking Green (1962, 1963, 1965), trained latterly by Tim Forster, won a total of 22 races. No other winners can match their records, but dual winners include Bantry Bay, Otter Way, Rolls Rambler, Three Counties and Mystic Music. Otter Way's two victories spanned seven years (1976 and 1983) at the age of eight and 15, and he lost only by a short head in 1982 to Loyal Partner.

Another popular winner of the Horse and Hound Cup was Spartan Missile (1979), ridden by his owner/trainer John Thorne. Regarded by many as the finest amateur rider to grace the National Hunt sport, he tragically died in 1982 from a fall in a point-to-point meeting at Bicester.

His career spanned 33 years, but nothing would have given him more pleasure than when, at Stratford on 7 February 1976, he finished second on one of his own horses, Air General, in the Nimrod Hunter Chase – because he was beaten by another of his horses, Ben Ruler, ridden by his daughter Diana, who created history by becoming the first lady rider ever to win a race under National Hunt rules – a memorable family occasion.

Two other jockeys will also have fond memories of Stratford, even though they might not compare with Diana's historic day. Three-time champion jockey Stan Mellor (the first National Hunt jockey to ride 1,000 winners) rode his last winner, Arne Folly, here on 2 June 1972 for Lambourn trainer Major Edward Champneys, while A P McCoy had his first-ever ride in England at Stratford on 13 August 1994, finishing second on Arctic Life in a novice hurdle for trainer John Jenkins. Diana, you can't keep much better company than that.

Left: Credit Call.

Below: Sisters Diana and Jane Thorne in their early days.

For over 80 years Taunton was Britain's youngest racecourse until Great Leighs in Essex opened in 2008. (Pershore would have held the title, having opened a new course in 1935, but it closed four years later with the outbreak of the Second World War and never reopened).

There had been flat racing in Taunton in 1802 on a course closer to the town, but this was discontinued after ten years. Nearby Bridgwater took the opportunity to establish a new racecourse in 1813 and their venture lasted a little longer before it, too, fell by the wayside. There was then quite a hiatus before the Portman family came to the rescue, prompted by the opening of a new course at Chepstow in 1926.

The present course at Taunton was laid out by the 5th Viscount Portman on Orchard Great Field immediately north of Orchard House, a vast Tudor mansion and seat of the Portman family which was demolished in 1843. Eventually Taunton opened for National Hunt racing on 21 September 1927

The course has been transformed and extended over the years. It has been widened, and the back straight and bends built up and extended, while the Somerset clay soil has been well drained to provide the best possible going throughout the season. Facilities for spectators have been vastly improved since the early days, when viewing was from a small wooden stand, often surrounded by a sea of mud. A members' stand bearing the Portman name was completed in 1968 and a new stand, which includes the Orchard Restaurant, was opened in 1989. Orchard and Portman's important local historical connections are thus kept alive on the course and provide a link with the Portman family home which stood on ground now part of the back straight.

Taunton has rarely attracted top-class National Hunt horses but it certainly helped to launch the career of a top-class trainer. On 9 May 1975, local trainer Martin Pipe sent out his first winner to start what would become a magnificent career. It was a humble beginning, as the race was the Division 2 Motorway Selling Hurdle over two miles and his winner, Hit Parade, made all under jockey Len Lungo to get the show on the road. Martin also owned the horse, a gelding by Sing Sing, who was bought in for 600 guineas.

If it hadn't been for Hit Parade, who knows what would have happened next, but the rest, as they say, is history. Martin Pipe became champion trainer 15 times and trained 4,191 winners before his retirement in 2006.

To Martin Pipe, Taunton will always be special.

Martin Pipe and his 10 jockeys for a handicap hurdle at Taunton in 2005.

The jockeys from left to right are Noel Kavanagh, Rodi Green, Seamus McHugh, Paul Flynn, Gerry Supple, Richard Johnson, Jamie Moore, David Howard, Liam Cummins and Tony McCoy.

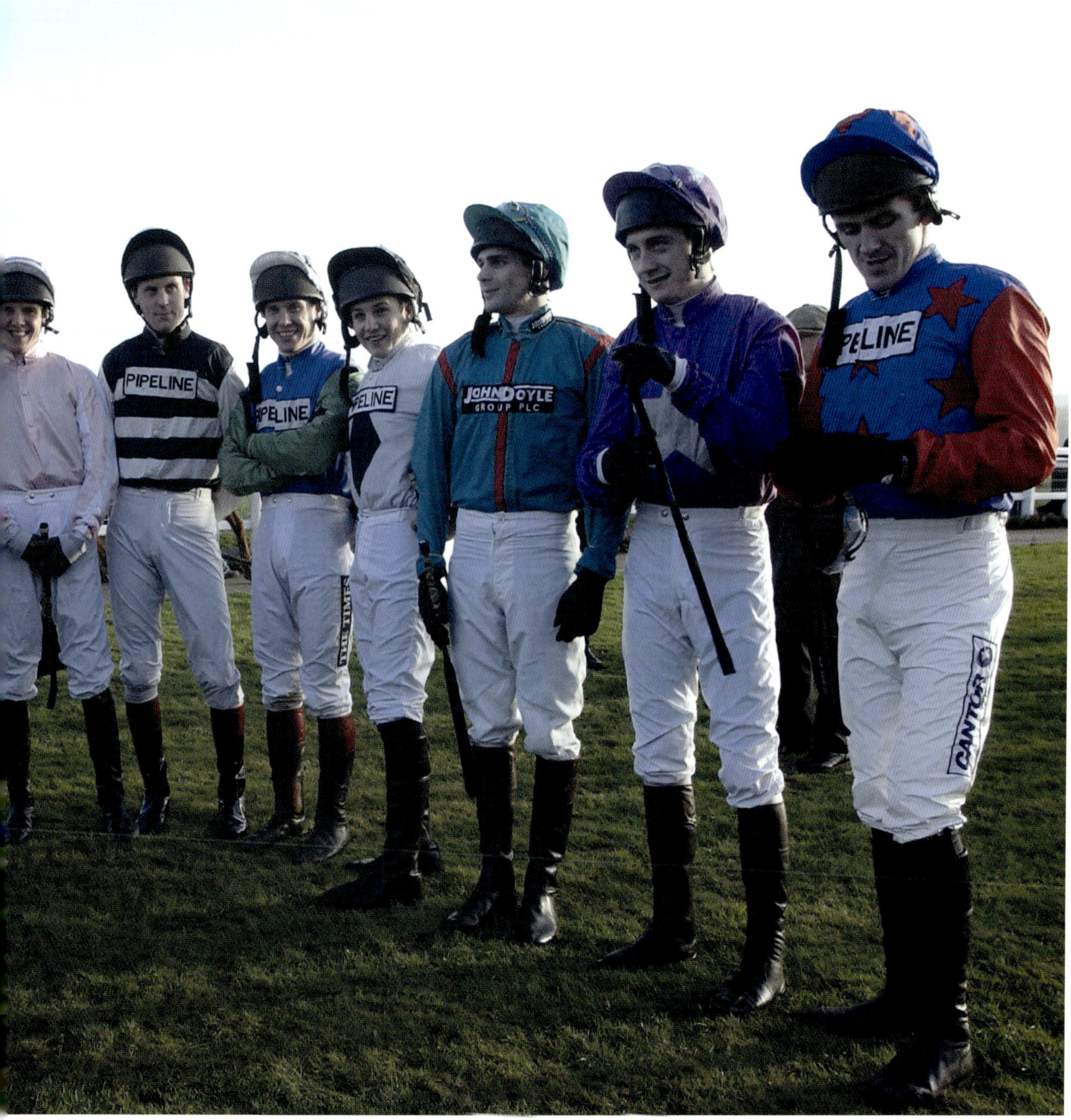
PIPELINE
PIPELINE
PELINE
JOHN DOYLE
GROUP PLC
PELINE
THE TIMES
CANTOR

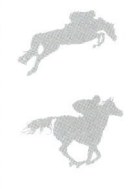

THIRSK

Thirsk is a traditional North Yorkshire market town with a cobbled market square and numerous coaching inns. It nestles between the Yorkshire Dales and the North Yorkshire Moors, just eight miles away from where Hambleton racecourse once stood, dating from 1612. Hambleton had become established as the headquarters of Northern racing and, together with the training facilities on the fine turf of the Hambleton Hills, the whole area would have been the equivalent of Newmarket today. Hambleton racecourse closed in 1776, although Hambleton remains an important centre for training to this day. Decades later, Squire Frederick Bell of Thirsk Hall decided to start a race meeting on his estate and, after some discussions with a few of his chums in the comfort of the Golden Fleece Hotel, on 15 March 1855 the first meeting took place where the course stands today.

A former schoolmaster, George Nicholson, was appointed Clerk of the Course but 20 years later he died of a heart attack – which coincided with him successfully landing a large bet on the outcome of the autumn double. His successor in 1875 was Thomas Dawson, who came from a racing family and had far more experience. He once trained at Hambleton but his father, Tom Dawson Sr, was better known for having trained Derby winners Ellington (1856) and Pretender (1869) from his stables in Middleham. His younger brother, Mathew, trained no

Ellington, trained by Tom Dawson and ridden by Thomas Aldcroft, winning the 1856 Derby. (From The Illustrated London News.)

fewer than 28 Classic winners and, having given him his first apprenticeship, retained Fred Archer as stable jockey in 1874.

Thanks to Thomas Dawson Jr, Thirsk grew in popularity. He increased the prize money, which attracted owners and trainers from north and south with the aid of the railways – Thirsk was ideally situated on the main line from London to Scotland. During the First World War the course closed, and did not reopen until 1924, during which time a new grandstand was built, along with other course improvements.

Thirsk hosted the 1940 St Leger, relocated from Doncaster due to the Second World War. It attracted a large crowd on 23 November (very late in the year but dictated by the constraints of war), who witnessed Gordon Richards winning on the Aga Khan's Turkhan, trained by Frank Butters, beating his better-fancied stable companion, Stardust.

The feature races at Thirsk are the inherited Hambleton Cup, once a two-mile Cesarewitch trial but nowadays reduced to a mile-and-a-half, the Thirsk Hunt Cup and the prestigious Thirsk Classic Trial, which was first run in 1948. It was run in April for classic hopes for the coming year. Nimbus (1949) was the only Derby winner to emerge from the race, while Alycidon (1950), Sweet Solera (1961) and Tap on Wood (1979) were other winners to taste classic glory.

In 1972, the Classic Trial produced two classic winners when High Top beat the filly Waterloo, and they both went on to Newmarket to win the 2,000 Guineas and 1,000 Guineas respectively. Sadly, the race gradually fell into decline and, after various sponsorships, has now been lost forever.

In Thirsk's early days, Fred Archer was often seen riding winners for the local gentry. On 16 April 1988, another champion jockey, young Irishman Keiren Fallon, made his English debut in the Thirsk Hall EBF Stakes.

The legendary Fred Archer. A tall man, Archer had to diet drastically and the effects of this on his health, as well as the death of his wife, led to his suicide at the age of only 29 in 1886.

Riding Evichstar for Jimmy Fitzgerald, he won by one-and-a-half lengths, having been backed from 14/1 to 11/2.

Finally, back to Tom Dawson Sr. When his horse Ellington won the 1856 Derby, he collected £25,000. On receiving his winnings in cash, he put the money in a hat-box and boarded a train home. He fell asleep and had to scramble to change trains at Northallaton, leaving the hat-box in the luggage rack. The train was bound for Aberdeen, so he quickly sent a telegram to the station master. The hat-box and its contents were duly returned.

Thurles is the largest town in rural County Tipperary, with a population of nearly 10,000. The racecourse is situated just outside the town, on the road that leads to the wonderfully-named Devil's Bit Mountain.

The course is quite ancient, with the earliest records showing a three-day meeting in June 1732, but by October 1760 there was a six-day meeting, with one race confined to horses owned by Freemasons. Thurles is principally a jumping course, although a small number of flat races were run there every year, which have now been discontinued.

The venue is associated with the Molony family, who own the property. Pierce Molony is the man in charge at the present time. He and his wife Riona have been running Thurles since 1974 and, although it has sometimes been a struggle, the racecourse is in their blood and their endeavours have ultimately been rewarded. His father – also Pierce – was a very influential figure in Irish racing and was elected a member of the Turf Club in 1943. Molony's grandfather (also called Pierce!) took over the running of the course in 1911 and, to date, three generations of the family have been involved in its upkeep – four if you include the present owner's four daughters, who also help out occasionally.

It was in 1907 that the Turf Club first appointed an Inspector of Courses and Thurles was among several others that were in urgent need of improvement. While Cork Park, Fethard, Cashel and Nenagh all eventually fell by the wayside, Thurles brought its facilities up to date and its ability and willingness to take winter fixtures ensured its survival.

Pierce Molony (right) walks the course with Lorcan Wyer, Thurles' Clerk of the Course.

The parade ring on a winter's day.

Among the jockeys who rode their first winners at Thurles are Bill McLernon, the three-time Irish Amateur Champion, Gerry Newman, who emulated his father by winning the Irish Grand National and rode Captain Christy to victory in the King George VI Chase at Kempton Park, and A P McCoy. On the 26 March 1992, McCoy rode Legal Steps to win a flat race at Thurles. It was the first rung on a small ladder – four years later he was champion.

Thurles runs two good Cheltenham trials in February, the Kinloch Brae Chase over two-and-a-half miles (formally known as the PZ Mower Chase) and the Michael Purcell Memorial Novice Hurdle, both being Grade 2 events. The outstanding winner of the former race was Native Upmanship, who won it three times in succession (2002 to 2004), and also won the Melling Chase, a Grade 1 race run at Aintree, twice. However, the outstanding racehorse to run at Thurles was Vintage Crop, the Melbourne Cup winner, who won his first race here. Another racing hero, Buck House, who also won the PZ Mower Chase (1986) and the Queen Mother Champion Chase the following month, is believed to be buried within the enclosures. What a perfect resting place.

TIPPERARY

The popular song 'It's a long way to Tipperary' must also apply to Limerick Junction, as it was by this name that the racecourse was known until 1986. Racing began here in September 1916 thanks to T Gardner-Wallis, who secured an option on the 190-acre site. The major incentive to open as 'Limerick Junction' was the promise of a special railway siding from the Great Southern and Western Railway Company.

The first recorded meeting in the area was at nearby Barronstown on 27 March 1848. In 1871–72 the races were abandoned due to smallpox, but were revived in 1881. In those early days at Barronstown there was only one bookmaker, who also had a roulette table.

Two great champions appeared here in the early stages of their careers – Cottage Rake and Istabraq. Triple Cheltenham Gold Cup hero Cottage Rake made a winning debut here in a two-mile maiden hurdle on 27 December 1945. Owned and bred by Dr 'Otto' Vaughan, he had sent his six-year-old to a young trainer in only his third season – Vincent O'Brien. Dr Vaughan had tried to

Cottage Rake with Aubrey Brabazon, winning his third Cheltenham Gold Cup in 1950.

sell him before he sent him to Vincent, but he failed to get a satisfactory veterinary report. In order to keep the owner happy, Vincent ran him at Limerick Junction completely unfancied; he won, at 10/1, in the hands of Danny O'Sullivan, one of Vincent's best schooling jockeys. He proved this was no fluke by then winning a bumper by ten lengths at Leopardstown.

Dr Vaughan eventually sold Cottage Rake to Frank Vickerman for £3,500, which he must have lived to regret. 'The Rake' proved himself to be a very versatile horse when having the speed to win two high-class races on the flat, the Naas November Handicap and the Irish Cesarewitch at the Curragh, before his three Cheltenham Gold Cups – the first of which, on 4 March 1948, was Vincent O'Brien's first ever runner in England.

The John James McManus Memorial Hurdle was first run in October 1997 – established by J P McManus in honour of his late father. It was highly appropriate that his triple Champion Hurdle winner Istabraq should win the first three runnings, and he was particularly impressive in 1999 when beating the high-class Limestone Lad. Each year he went on to win the Champion Hurdle the following March, only to be cruelly denied a record four-timer in 2001 by the outbreak of a foot-and-mouth epidemic. Nevertheless, Istabraq and Tipperary will remain very special to J P McManus.

In May 2013 the redevelopment of Tipperary, which includes the new entrance building, was opened by Lester Piggott. On his left is Tim Hyde, Chairman of Tipperary Racecourse and on his right is Joe Keeling, Chairman of Horse Racing Ireland.

TOWCESTER

Towcester Racecourse is set in beautiful countryside on Lord Hesketh's estate at Easton Neston. Racing began here in 1876, when Empress Elisabeth of Austria, an Easter guest of Sir Thomas Henry Fermor-Hesketh, 6th Baronet, sought to amuse her during her stay. Some racing was arranged for her and from then on a one-day fixture was held every Easter. (Poor Sir Thomas died some weeks later – whether the excitement of the race or the Empress's visit contributed to this, who knows?)

In those days, racing in the area was concentrated at nearby Northampton but when that course closed on 31 March 1904, Towcester became more established. It soon became the venue for the Grafton Hunt and continued under this heading until 1928 when their lease expired. At the final meeting of the Grafton Hunt on 9 April that year, a crowd of 35,000 watched Rathowen, a 3/1 chance, win the big race – the three-mile Towcester Handicap Chase – from the 7/4 favourite Carfax. The final race of the afternoon was the Wicken Park Chase, won by the evens favourite Muster, ridden by M B Ancil.

Sir Thomas Hesketh, 8th Baronet, then formed the Towcester Racecourse Company and immediately began to transform the racecourse. He employed 30 men to work night and day, including Sundays, to relay a new right-handed course to replace the old left-handed one. Sweeping improvements were made, including a new stand whose main feature was a roof made of Norfolk reed thatch; the makers guaranteed it would last for 80 years.

The plans for the new course were provided by Messrs Smithson and Rainger of Cheltenham, who had been responsible for the work at Cheltenham and at Fontwell for their opening in 1924. The course at Towcester was to be over one-and-a-half miles round and 84 feet wide, and hurdle races would be introduced, along with a flat race and plans for two meetings a season.

So, thanks to the efforts of a great number of people, Towcester (as it was now officially called) was open in time for Easter Monday, 1 April 1929. The first race under the new banner was the Hulcote Selling Handicap Hurdle over two miles and was won by a Mr Cooper's bay gelding Monsieur Bacon at 6/1, ridden by J Norris and trained by the owner. The big race, the Towcester Handicap Chase,

Above is the original stand, which was built in 1928, and was replaced in 2005 by the award-winning Empress stand shown on the left. The impressive grand archway entrance remains.

Towcester played host to a remarkable achievement on 27 April 1989 when Peter Scudamore became the first National Hunt jockey to ride 200 winners in a season. Riding for the powerful Martin Pipe stable, he had already reached 1,000 career winners at Newton Abbot in February and had also passed Jonjo O'Neill's 1977/1978 record of 149 winners in a season, so it was no surprise to the racing world that the double-century milestone would soon be achieved.

It was at an evening meeting that history was made. Scudamore had begun the day on 197 and, in the afternoon, had drawn a blank from four rides at Hereford. Moving swiftly on to Towcester, he did it in style, completing a four-timer on Old Kilpatrick (13/8F), Canford Palm (4/1), 200th winner Gay Moore (10/1) and finally Market Forces (7/2). The winning distances were 12 lengths, 20 lengths, 12 lengths and seven lengths respectively, making an aggregate of 51 lengths! Scudamore completed that season with an astonishing total of 221 winners, a figure most people at the time thought would never be beaten.

But just when you thought it couldn't get any bettter, on 7 November 2013 it did. Tony McCoy rode Mountain Tunes, a bay gelding by Mountain High, into the winners' enclosure to record his 4,000th winner. Towcester was again honoured to host another historic moment.

Finally to return to 1928, the year Towcester was transformed. Soon after the Grafton Hunt had held their final meeting in April, an advertisement appeared in *The Northampton Mercury*. As the Grafton Hunt committee ceased to be, their effects were to be sold by public auction, comprising Starters Box 5/-, Number Board 6/-, Judges' Box and Pay Boxes £3 to £3/15/-, Iron Hurdles 7/6 to 10/6 and an Iron Gate and Post for £6/15/-. What bargains.

was won by Viscount Ednam's Glanmore at 7/2, ridden by M Keogh, while the Hunters Steeplechase was won by Muster, the 5/4 favourite owned and trained by B Ancil. By a strange coincidence, Muster had also won the final race under the Grafton Hunt regime the previous year.

These days, Towcester can boast 16 meetings a year. Most notable races are run at the Easter meeting, including the Empress of Austria Hunter Chase (two miles six furlongs), the Schlizzi 1906 Commemorative Challenge Cup Chase (two miles six furlongs) and the Schlizzi Challenge Bowl Chase (two miles). The inaugural running of the last two events took place on 9 April 1966, with two handsome cups presented to the winning owners by John Schlizzi to celebrate his 60 years of racing at Towcester. The Challenge Bowl Chase in this first year was won by Stalbridge Colonist, whose claim to fame was to beat Arkle in the Hennessey Gold Cup later that year, albeit receiving 35 lbs.

The finish at Towcester is probably the stiffest in the country, with the last six furlongs uphill. When the ground is heavy a two-mile race can seem more like three and because of this Towcester rarely seems to attract top-class horses.

Below: England rugby international players hooker Dylan Hartley and right wing Chris Ashton lift Choc Thornton on their shoulders to celebrate the jockey's 1,000th UK winner in March 2011.

Right: During an interview with Luke Harvey on 7 November 2013, Tony McCoy is sprayed by his colleagues after winning his 4,000th race on Mountain Tunes.

Racing was recorded in Tralee, County Kerry, as far back as 1767, when a week-long meeting was held. Various venues in the locality were used until the present site in Ballybeggan Park was opened to racing in 1898. The park was formerly a deer park and the stone for the surrounding limestone wall was quarried out of the land in the course's infield. The estate was formerly the property of famous Irish political figure, Daniel O'Connell, known as 'The Liberator', in whose honour the Liberator Handicap was run annually.

Tralee was the westernmost racecourse in Europe, overlooked by the Slieve Mish Mountains. The course was half a mile outside the town, which is a popular tourist resort and known as the gateway to the famous Dingle peninsula. The town played a big part in Tralee's main six-day festival in August, which was the highlight of the

year at the course. It coincided with the Rose of Tralee contest, a beauty competition where the elected young lady traditionally paraded at the races.

The most famous horse to run here was the mare Dawn Run, who remains the only horse to win both the Champion Hurdle and the Cheltenham Gold Cup. In only her third race she won, at 5/1, the Castlemaine Flat Race for amateur riders on 23 June 1982, in the hands of her 62-year-old owner Mrs Charmian Hill. It was the first of her 21 career victories but the last ride in public for her owner, whose licence was revoked immediately afterwards on the grounds of her age and various earlier injuries.

Another special horse to appear here was Vintage Crop. Trained by Dermot Weld, who enjoyed many winners here, he won the 1992 Carling Gold Cup, a handicap, carrying 9st 10lb under Mick Kinane, before winning the Irish St Leger twice (1993, 1994) and a magnificent win in the Melbourne Cup. Three other classic winners to win their maidens here were Desert King, Vintage Tipple and Alexandrova. Desert King will always be remembered, especially as he was the first classic winner for Aidan O'Brien, winning the 1997 Irish 2,000 Guineas and Irish Derby.

Aidan O'Brien will also have a soft spot for Tralee as it was here, on 7 June 1993, that he saddled his first winner. He took over the licence at Ballydoyle, which until then had been held by his wife Anne-Marie. The horse that set the ball rolling was Wandering Thoughts, ridden by Pat Gilson, who later that year went on to win the Irish Cambridgeshire.

Pat Crean, for 30 years secretary manager of the course recalls a story in which a race at Tralee was won by a dead horse! Apparently, as the horses passed the winning post, the second-placed horse dropped dead. After a stewards' inquiry and a referral to the Turf Club, the placings were reversed and the dead horse awarded the race.

During the 1930s, economic circumstances had seen the Tralee Race Company forced into liquidation, but the track reopened in 1946. In September 2003 they survived closure at the eleventh hour. Five years later, due to considerable ongoing financial losses, the majority of shareholders were willing to sell the property to developers and the final day's racing took place on 23 August 2008.

Could there be another revival?

Dawn Run, owned and ridden by 62-year-old Mrs Charmian Hill – the 'galloping granny' – and trained by Paddy Mullins, winning her first race at Tralee on 23 June 1982.

233

TRAMORE

Tramore is a major seaside holiday resort eight miles south of the City of Waterford and racing here is run under the title of Waterford and Tramore.

Racing first took place on the strand in 1785, the brainchild of Bartholomew Rivers, who realised that popularity of this lively seaside town could only be enhanced by a bit of horse racing. Although at first only held annually, it was an instant success and to honour its founder part of Tramore was named after him – Riverstown.

By 1807 a six-day festival was staged, and Hurdle races were introduced in 1840, but did not last. Because of its unusual location, racing was not free from hazards and some meetings were put in jeopardy. In 1855, a tide flooded part of the course, and a new course was located further along the strand. Nevertheless, in April 1911 a high tide broke the embankments and swept away the racecourse's fencing and hoardings. For any further meetings to take place, another location had to be found, on higher ground.

Local businessman and MP Martin J Murphy abandoned racing on the strand and moved the races on to his own property, known locally as Graun Hill, where racing takes place today. The new racecourse opened on 13 August 1912 with a three-day festival. The opening race, the Corinthian Plate, was won by L.A.P., ridden by Tommy Morgan and trained locally by J Fleming. The following day the first steeplechase was run, the Tramore Plate. Victory went to May Park, owned and trained by Mr W Murphy. In 1927 the festival was extended to four days and is still held every August.

That Tramore recently celebrated its centenary is remarkable, considering its humble beginnings. Its survival has not been without criticism, with the main problem being the small tight circuit measuring only seven furlongs round (it is the smallest racecourse in the British Isles). It is also very undulating and not entirely suitable for flat racing, with falls quite common. Houses surround the course so expansion is not possible, and even a move back nearer the sea was once being considered instead. But why change anything – one hundred years of racing at Graun Hill speaks for itself.

One of Tramore's most popular races is the Waterford Glass Trophy, first run in 1957. For many years the winning owners received an 88-piece set of Waterford Crystal, which made it a race well worth winning. The legendary trainer Paddy Mullins won it six times for his patrons.

Right side captions:

Left: a page the 2012 centenary racecard.

Below: the tight turn and undulating ground at Tramore makes for frequent stumbles and falls.

Within image 2:

Down Memory Lane

The opening of the new track in 1997 with jockeys Michael Kinane and Charlie Swan in centre.

The Baron Fleming and Mr JJ Murphy to the rear founders of Tramore Racecourse with Senator Parkinson. Photo taken at the Ballsbridge Bloodstock Sales.

Mary & Max Fleming

WATERFORD & TRAMORE RACES.
GLORIOUS TRAMORE.

August 11th, 12th, 13th and 15th, 1927.
The Greatest Racing Carnival of the Season.

440 Entries for Steeplechases, Hurdle and Flat Races.

Stabling has been booked for a large number of Horses, including several from England, and the best of Racing is assured.

On August 15th a Special Train will leave Waterford for New Ross at 8.30 p.m.

Special Cheap Fares from all parts, and greatly Reduced prices of Admission.

Martin Molony Rides Four Tramore Winners

BY OUR TRAVELLING CORRESPONDENT

WELCOME TO UTTOXETER

	1	D CROSSE ( )	7	P Aspell ( )	13
FIRST RACE	2	J E Moore	8	T J Malone (3)	14
GOING	3	F. KING (3)	9	T Burrows 10	15
GOOD TO FIRM	4	RP McNally ( )	10		16
	5	R Mackenzie (8)	11		17
	6	A O'keeffe ( )	12		18

NEXT MEETING   Sunday 19th September

UTTOXETER

The present racecourse at Uttoxeter was built and opened in 1907 by a company formed to take over the interests and licence of Keele Park Racecourse, which had ceased to operate the previous year. Keele Park was over 15 miles east of Uttoxeter and stood on a site now occupied by the M6 motorway – Keele Services now stands in place of the old grandstand. Keele Park opened in 1895 but, after only 11 years, ran into financial difficulties and, despite five fixtures being arranged for 1907, these were all eventually transferred to the new course at Uttoxeter. Keele Park had been much closer to the popular Shropshire course at Woore but for reasons not known they failed to reap the benefit of Keele Park's demise.

Uttoxeter became a popular substitute almost at once, partly due to the close proximity of the railway station adjoining the course. Special trains were laid on for the opening from Birmingham, Manchester, Derby and other Midlands towns and this proved to be the first rung to success. Before the present course opened, there had been racing in the area from the early 18th century. They were run at different venues, wherever available. Netherwood was one of the earliest and in the 19th century places such as Lamberts Park Farm, Rocester, Byrds Lane and Bramshall followed suit, but unpleasant events led to their closures.

The inaugural two-day meeting at Uttoxeter was held on 3 May 1907. According to advertisements, admission to the course cost one shilling, and to the ring, covered stand and paddock an additional five shillings for gentlemen and three shillings for ladies. For the very well off, membership to the club cost £3.3s. per annum, which entitled you to introduce two ladies. The opening race was the Brook Furlong Maiden Hurdle in which the 1/5 favourite Rose Point failed to beat Bombay, a 5/1 chance ridden by his owner Mr J Tomlinson (was this a sign of things to come?). The next day Mr Tomlinson elected to run Bombay again, this time in a chase, winning again at a generous 4/1.

The feature race of the meeting was the Osmaston Steeplechase, which went to Mr G Reed's bay gelding Royal Guide at 10/1, ridden by T Savage.

Uttoxeter closed during the First World War and reopened in 1921. During the Second World War, the course was again closed and was requisitioned by the War Office, but this time the course remained closed for 12 years. Before the war, the racecourse company owned all of the land bar 140 yards, which they leased from a local farmer. After the war, he refused to lease or sell on acceptable terms, and the future of Uttoxeter was put in jeopardy. Uttoxeter Urban Council stepped in and bought the land under a Compulsory Purchase Order and the course eventually reopened on 12 June 1952.

With the help of the Horserace Betting Levy Board, a new £167,000 grandstand was built in 1968 and opened by its new chairman, Lord Wigg. This resulted in a record attendance of 26,000 on Easter Monday 1969. Uttoxeter has continued to prosper to this day, with huge attendances. The new owner, Sir Stanley Clarke, must take much of the credit with his innovations and improvements to facilities.

He took up the post in 1988, and one of his brainwaves has been the promotion of the Midlands Grand National, which now takes place on the Saturday in March following the Cheltenham Festival rather than at the beginning of May as before. This gruelling four-and-a-quarter mile rehearsal for the big one at Aintree is by far Uttoxeter's finest day. Rag Trade (owned by the flamboyant hairdresser Teasy Weasy) is the only horse to achieve the double, winning the Midlands version in 1975 and then beating Red Rum at Aintree in 1976 for good measure. With the rescheduling of the Midlands race, from 1991 it has become easier to win both races in the same year, with Stan Clarke's own Lord Gyllene (1997) coming closest when he finished second at Uttoxeter before winning Aintree's Monday National a few weeks later.

The Midland Grand National was first run in 1969, when it was won by Happy Spring, trained by Stan Wright and owned by his wife. Ridden by Ken White, he had won the Welsh Grand National in 1967 and, in a distinguished career, won ten chases. His claim to fame was to be one of the very few horses to beat Arkle when, in the 1963 Hennessy Gold Cup, he finished second behind Mill House with the great horse third – what a CV.

Once upon a time Uttoxeter used to bring down the curtain on the National Hunt season, and in so doing the jockeys' championship was often decided on the final day. The most memorable was the finale of the 1966-67 season, when Josh Gifford – riding at Uttoxeter's evening meeting on 15 June 1967 – needed three winners to beat Fred Winter's 1952-53 record of 121. In front of a huge crowd, Josh rode the first winner, Stealthy Approach, trained by Earl Jones at Hednesford, and was unplaced in the second. He then equalled the record, riding Jolly Signal, again for Earl Jones. Needing just one more, Josh did something that would not be allowed today – he switched mounts. In that morning's papers he had been listed to ride Peace Prize, but he elected to ride the Frank Gilman-trained Red Flush – which won in a canter. He returned to the winner's enclosure to a tremendous reception.

Fifteen years later, on 1 June 1982, Uttoxeter was again the decisive venue when John Francome, on John Edwards' Buckmaster, rode his 800th overall winner to share the jump jockeys' title with Peter Scudamore, each riding 120 winners. Peter had been sidelined for the previous five weeks following a heavy fall at Southwell, but John had sportingly pledged that once he drew level with Peter he would retire for the season.

Champion trainer Michael Dickinson, who will always be remembered for training the first five home in the 1983 Cheltenham Gold Cup, can also add his own little piece of history at Uttoxeter – not for training winners there, but saddling his last runner in Britain before leaving to train in the United States. In May 1989, his runner Half Decent could, unfortunately, finish only fifth, but at Uttoxeter it is not always the winning, it's the taking part.

WARWICK

Beneath the turrets of the magnificent Warwick Castle lies one of the oldest racecourses in the country. Warwick opened in 1707 when Lord Brooke of Warwick Castle donated £15 'towards the making of a horse race'. Racing began with only two days a year, with one race each day being run in several heats.

In 1789, the Crown contributed 100 guineas in prize money for a Royal Plate to be run at Warwick over four miles, to please the subjects of King George III.

A grandstand was erected in 1809 and crowds soon began to gather. At a Flat meeting in 1825, there was an estimated crowd of 50,000. Warwick may also have been the first recognised racecourse to hold a race over obstacles, with a hurdle race in 1831.

With National Hunt racing gathering momentum during the 1840s, Warwick became even more popular in 1847 with the appearance of Chandler. In the Leamington Hunt Club Steeplechase, he leapt 39 feet to clear a brook and four fallen horses en route to victory. He deservedly won the Grand National the following year and a fence at

Warwick now bears his name.

National Hunt racing continued to outshine flat meetings and, in 1902, Warwick was honoured by hosting the National Hunt Chase for amateur riders, which is now a feature at Cheltenham. The race was first run at Market Harborough in 1860 over four miles and has since had many venues. Warwick played host seven times between 1902 and 1910; during this period the victors were Marpessa (1902), Comfit (1903), Count Rufus (1906), Red Hall (1907), Rory O'Moore (1908), Wychwood (1909) and Nimble Kate (1910). Since 1911 the race has become a permanent feature at the Cheltenham Festival, and remains a highlight of the amateur riders' calendar.

Warwick hosted the Brooke Bond Oxo National for a few years but now their highest profile race is the Classic Chase. Another notable race is the Crudwell Cup, run in March, celebrating that prolific chaser of Frank Cundell's who won a total of 50 races between 1949 and 1960, a feat that will probably never be equalled.

Crudwell, who was named after a Wiltshire village where his breeder Mr A Large resided, ran in 108 races, winning seven on the flat, four over hurdles and thirty-nine steeplechases. Altogether he won 11 times at Warwick, comprising four amateur riders' handicaps on the flat, partnered each time by Atty Corbett, and seven steeplechases including three successive runnings of the Honington Chase (1957–59). To commemorate Crudwell, the Warwickshire Handicap Chase, run over three miles four furlongs, was renamed the Crudwell

Challenge Cup. The inaugural running, on 4 March 1961, was won by Reprieved, ridden by Dave Dick. (A longer tribute to Crudwell appears in the Wincanton entry.)

A unique piece of National Hunt history occurred at Warwick on 15 January 1994 when, for the first time, a race was transferred from another course overnight. Due to Ascot being abandoned, the Victor Chandler Chase was run at Warwick and was won by that popular two-mile champion chaser Viking Flagship, ridden by Richard Dunwoody and trained by the late David Nicholson. Another ever-popular chaser to appear at Warwick was Dublin Flyer, trained by Tim Forster. On 21 February 1998 he won on his final appearance, receiving a huge reception from the crowd, worthy of a Gold Cup winner. His final tally was 14 wins and ten places from 34 races.

Flat racing never reached those dizzy heights, with the Warwick Oaks run at the end of June probably the only race worth a mention. An invitation flat race between Lester Piggott and John Francome did attract a crowd of over 7,000 on a wet Saturday evening in May 1985. Lester, riding The Liquidator, beat John's mount Shangoseer to thrill the record crowd. John Francome declared before the race, 'Whatever beats me will win.'*

Two champion National Hunt jockeys made history at Warwick that, 50 years ago, would not have seemed possible. Jonjo O'Neill's record of riding 149 winners in a season had stood since 1978, but on 7 February 1989 Peter Scudamore passed his total, riding Anti Matter for his boss Martin Pipe, and went on to ride 221 winners that season. This was a phenomenal achievement, which most racing folk thought would never be beaten – but nobody had heard of a young jockey from Northern Ireland called A P McCoy. He didn't ride in a National Hunt race until 1994 but by 1998, still in only his fifth season, he had passed

*After over 300 years, Warwick discontinued Flat racing on 25 August, 2014.

Peter Scudamore's record. He then set his sights on Gordon Richards' flat record of 269 winners, set in 1947, and on 2 April 2002 at Warwick, he made history again. Riding Valfonic for Martin Pipe in the last leg of a treble following Shampooed and Shepherds Rest, the 55-year-old record was broken. McCoy finished that season on 289 and has become the greatest National Hunt jockey of all time.

Finally, spare a thought for a jockey who holds his own proud record at Warwick – so special that even Messrs Scudamore and McCoy cannot equal it. On 16 October 1973 Victor Morley Lawson, a 67-year-old retired solicitor from Epsom, became the oldest jockey ever to win a race – and it was his first winner in 25 years' riding! He rode Ocean King at 4/1 to win the Corinthian Amateur Riders Maiden Stakes for trainer Arthur Pitt. Ocean King, a seven-year-old plagued by spinal trouble, was passed over a furlong out but fought back bravely to win by three-quarters of a length. This completed a lifetime ambition for Victor Morley Lawson of owning, breeding and training a winner, all of which he had accomplished with his horse Miss Popsi Wopsi and then, finally, riding a winner on Ocean King.

Ocean King and his friend Josser.

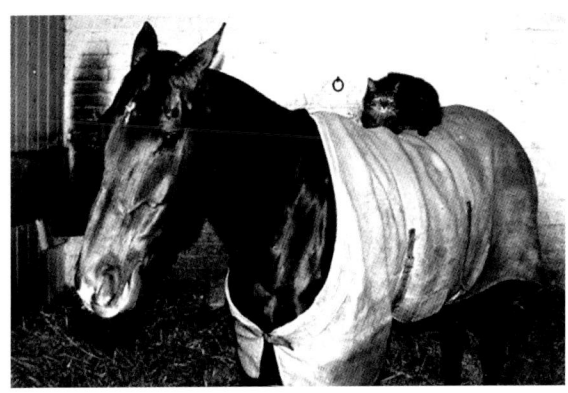

The course at Wetherby in West Yorkshire is regarded by many as the finest steeplechase course in the north of England. The fences are very stiff and probably only the Grand National fences at Aintree present a bigger challenge. Trainers from all over the country don't shy at sending their best chasers here and many Cheltenham and Aintree heroes have run at Wetherby.

It is believed the Romans used to race Arabian horses just a few miles away, on a site at Netherby, but racing properly began on the present course on Easter Bank Holiday 1891. From 1842 until then, Wetherby races had been held at Linton Springs on the banks of the River Wharfe, a few miles east of the present course. For nearly 50 years the Wetherby Steeplechase Committee had rented the land from local farmers, but the rent rose once too often and the committee decided enough was enough.

One of the committee members was local landowner Henry Crossley, who agreed to sell his land, and this is where Wetherby racecourse stands today.

One of the highlights of the old course was the National Hunt Steeplechase in 1865. Playing host for the one and only time, the race was won by Mr H Chaplin's Emperor, ridden by the fully-bearded amateur, Alex Goodman, whose claim to fame was to partner two Grand National winners in Miss Mowbray (1852) and Salamander (1866).

The new course alongside the Great North Road (now the A1) was laid out in just five weeks for that inaugural Easter meeting. With its rather primitive facilities, it took a few years to capture the general public's attention, but gradually the Yorkshire crowd began to warm to its new location, especially when jockeys Bob Harper and

George Gunter were riding. Bob Harper rode more than 40 winners in 1902, and George Gunter rode 11 winners in three meetings at Wetherby in 1911 before becoming a successful trainer.

In 1920 the course was bought by Captain F J Osbaldeston Montagu, a Coldstream Guards officer who had won the Military Cross in the First World War, and a new committee was formed, including its previous owner, Henry Crossley. One new appointment which was to change the face of Wetherby was that of Rowland Francis Meyrick as Clerk of the Course. Under his guidance many improvements were made, including new stands and a stabling complex. He also doubled the prize money, which put Wetherby on the map as a leading racecourse of the North and, thanks to him, this high standard has been maintained. It was not until 1947 that he retired, at the ripe old age of 80 but, sadly, he died five years later. In his honour, the Rowland Meyrick Handicap Chase was inaugurated in 1957 and is run at Wetherby's Boxing Day meeting.

The first household name to win the Rowland Meyrick was Merryman II (1960). Trained by Captain Neville Crump, the nine-year-old had won the Grand National eight months earlier and, carrying 12st 6lbs and ridden by Gerry Scott, he won at Wetherby in great style. He then went to Aintree again the following year, carrying top weight and conceding 25lbs, to be runner-up to the grey Nicolaus Silver. Merryman II's victory in the Rowland Meyrick was the first of a record seven wins for trainer Neville Crump. During the 1980s, there were wins for Forgive'N'Forget (1984) and The Thinker (1986), both of whom went on to win the Cheltenham Gold Cup, and also Yahoo (1987), who came so close to spoiling the party for Desert Orchid in the 1989 Gold Cup. More recent winners include the high-class six-year-old Behrajan (2001), who won by 13 lengths, and Truckers Tavern (2004), who had been a gallant runner-up to Best Mate at Cheltenham.

Another big race at Wetherby to whet the appetite is the two-mile Castleford Chase, also run at the Christmas meeting. Past winners include Tingle Creek, Rathgorman, Badsworth Boy, Pearlyman, Waterloo Boy and Viking Flagship.

The biggest race in Wetherby's history is the Grade 2 Charlie Hall Chase, first run in 1978. Run in October, it is the first big chase of the National Hunt season and it more than compensates for the loss of two fairly high-profile races introduced in the 1960s – the Emblem Chase and the Wetherby Pattern Chase. The Emblem Chase was inherited from Manchester following their demise in 1963 but disappeared from Wetherby's calendar ten years later, while the Wetherby Pattern Chase, first run in 1969, was replaced by the Charlie Hall Chase – although they did share the title for the first four years as the rather lengthy Charlie Hall Memorial Wetherby Pattern Chase.

The Charlie Hall Chase (then on its own) became Wetherby's flagship and the Yorkshire crowd have been treated to many steeplechasers of the highest quality. Five horses have won the race twice – Wayward Lad (1983, 1985), Celtic Shot (1990, 1991), Barton Bank (1993, 1995), One Man (1996, 1997) – whose trainer Gordon Richards won the race four times – and See More Business (1999, 2000). Other high-class chasers to win the race were Burrough Hill Lad (1984), Durham Edition (1989), Marlborough (2002) and Grey Abbey (2004).

The race was named after W A Charlie Hall, who trained locally at Tadcaster. Born in 1903, he was one of three brothers, along with Tom and Sam, all of whom were to become successful trainers. He started training in 1945 and his first winner, in November that year, was Culworth – at Wetherby, of course. The honour of having a race named after him was for his outstanding record at Wetherby, where he trained 169 winners, including Clear Cut ten times. In all, he trained 584 winners under National Hunt rules, plus some 100 winners on the flat.

Above: Wayward Lad takes one of the challenging fences at Wetherby.

Below: Trainer Jenny Pitman with Borough Hill Lad after his victory over Wayward Lad in the Charlie Hall Chase in 1984.

His biggest win was landing the 1956 Champion Hurdle with Clifford Nicholson's Doorknocker, and he went on to be champion trainer of that season with 40 winners. He retired in 1975, handing over the reins to his stepson Maurice Camacho, but sadly his retirement was brief and he died two years later.

One record Charlie Hall did not achieve was that of Peter Easterby, who saddled five winners at Wetherby on 15 October 1980: Alick 10/1, Clayside 3/1, Davidoff 4/1, Selby 3/1 and Wink the Cop 9/4, and the first four were all ridden by Jonjo O'Neill. At the time this was a record held jointly by eight trainers, but in January 2006 Paul Nicholls went one better, saddling six winners at Wincanton on a seven-race card.

Finally, a day to remember – as related by Jenny Pitman in her autobiography. She had decided to send Burrough Hill Lad to Wetherby for the 1984 Charlie Hall Chase, where he would meet Wayward Lad, the previous year's winner and the best horse in the country north of the Trent, trained locally by Monica Dickinson. Jenny received a phone call from Michael Seely, a well-known racing journalist, a few days before the race telling her that she was mad to take on Wayward Lad. She enquired if he had ever trained a horse. When he replied 'No,' she retorted, 'Well, stick to writing newspapers'. On the morning of the race she received a phone call to say that her son Mark had been involved in a car accident and had been admitted to Warwick Hospital. She was devastated but, after ringing the hospital, made her way to Wetherby. On arriving, she was approached by brothers Mick and Peter Easterby, who both told her that she had no chance of beating Wayward Lad, as he was a 10lb better horse at Wetherby. She tried to smile but her confidence was fading. What else could go wrong?

Result. Burrough Hill Lad won easily by ten lengths. Tears of joy all round – and probably even Charlie Hall was smiling.

WEXFORD

Wexford is steeped in tradition, deriving its name from its Viking heritage. It has always been foremost in the breeding of horses in Ireland and, in particular, National Hunt horses.

The earliest recorded racing here took place on an area of the Wexford Sloblands in the 1870s. (The Sloblands are 1,000 hectares of polder – low-lying flat land reclaimed from the sea – situated on the north side of Wexford Harbour.) By 1902, however, this had ceased and racing did not start again for nearly 50 years; the present course at Bettyville opened on 15 October 1951. Between 20,000 and 25,000 people attended the opening meeting as Wexford was the first new course in Ireland in over 25 years. (Their position as the youngest course in the British Isles lasted only four years, as Sligo's new course opened in 1955). Paddy Mullins trained two winners at the first meeting, as well as riding in one race.

The racing may be of a moderate class here but it became very popular in an area surrounded by horse breeding, so much so that two new stands were built and opened for the meeting on 31 May 1996. The official opening ceremony was conducted by the Irish Minister for Agriculture, Ivan Yates TC. Improvements continue to be made to the course, and two furlongs have been added to the track, all of which has resulted in bigger fields and better racing results.

Racing has taken place in Wincanton since the 18th century but the original site was at Hatherleigh Farm, south west of the town. The present company, Wincanton Races Co Ltd, was formed in 1913 and when the lease of Hatherleigh Farm expired in 1925 they purchased Kingwell Farm, the present site. The chairman of the new company was Lord Stalbridge, without whom Wincanton might have faced extinction. He himself was a National Hunt trainer of some repute but still managed to find time to put Wincanton firmly back on the map and this superb course in Somerset has thrived thanks largely to his efforts.

Six weeks before the opening meeting, Lord Stalbridge won the 1927 Cheltenham Gold Cup with Thrown In (10/1), which he owned and trained himself. The horse was ridden by his son and heir, the amateur the Rt Hon Hugh Grosvenor, who had only previously ridden in eight steeplechases. Nevertheless, he beat Tom Coulthwaite's younger horse Grakle, who went on to win the Grand National four years later.

It was, therefore, a great time for the family, with the opening of Wincanton on Easter Monday 1927, although it was a quiet beginning. The opening race, the Wincanton Handicap Hurdle, was won by 4/1 chance Pommel, trained by Herbert Smyth Snr and ridden by his son, and later in the afternoon the feature race, the Wincanton Foxhunter Chase, was won by Mona Bridge, trained by Charles Piggott and ridden by Mr W Morgan.

In the meantime, Hugh Grosvenor had become ADC to the Governor-General of South Australia, but in January 1930 he was killed in a flying-boat crash in Melbourne. The devastating news for his family led Lord Stalbridge to sell Thrown In and the horse was never seen again. Lord Stalbridge in later years also owned and trained the 1940 Grand National winner Bogskar, the last National before the war, and the 1945 Cheltenham Gold Cup winner Red Rower.

There had been no racing at Wincanton during the war years, the land having been requisitioned by the War Office. In 1945, Lord Stalbridge fell ill and was no longer able to play an active part, and for a while it seemed that the course would not survive. He died in 1949, but a race is now run in his honour, the Lord Stalbridge Memorial Handicap Chase, for which his widow donated the cup

Lord Stalbridge with Bogskar and jockey Mervyn Jones after their victory in the 1940 Grand National.

that was presented to her husband after Bogskar won the Grand National.

In the meantime, ten local businessmen purchased the farm and course and managed to restore the stands, building and course itself with their own hands – very necessary after six years of military occupation – and racing resumed. In 1966, the company sold out to Racecourse Holdings Trust.

These days, Wincanton attracts the best steeplechasers and hurdlers in the country. The Jim Ford Chase and the Kingwell Hurdle at the February meeting are first-class trials for the Gold Cup and Champion Hurdle at Cheltenham. The Jim Ford Chase was first run in 1971 and was won by Kinloch Brae (11/10 fav), trained by Toby Balding and ridden by Eddie Harty. In 1984 Burrough Hill Lad, trained by Jenny Pitman, won the Jim Ford Chase and the Cheltenham Gold Cup. Others who won both races, but in different years, were Silver Buck 1981 (1982 Gold Cup), Desert Orchid 1987 (1989 Gold Cup), Cool Ground 1991 (1992 Gold Cup) and See More Business 2002 (1999 Gold Cup). Sadly, since the race in 2002 the Jim Ford Chase is no longer run.

The Kingwell Hurdle was first run in 1961 and the inaugural race attracted four Champion Hurdle prospects

running for a £272 prize, but they were all beaten by The Finn at 7/2, trained by Bob Turnell and ridden by Jeff King. Eborneezer finished unplaced but went on to win the Champion Hurdle at 4/1, trained by Ryan Price and ridden by Fred Winter. The Kingwell Hurdle has often been won by Champion Hurdle winners, none better than Bula, trained by Fred Winter. In 1971, Bula came to the Kingwell Hurdle unbeaten in his last ten outings, ridden by sub Richard Pitman as his regular rider, Paul Kellaway, had broken his collarbone at Windsor the previous week. Bula duly won, beating Flower Picker and Right Proud, with Persian War, the triple champion, only fourth beaten ten lengths. He went on to win the Champion Hurdle, extending his winning sequence to 12. In 1972, Bula again completed the Kingwell Hurdle–Champion Hurdle double, but in 1973, after completing the hat-trick at Wincanton, failed at Cheltenham behind Comedy of Errors.

In 1974, Fred Winter produced another star in Lanzarote, who won three consecutive Kingwell Hurdles, giving his trainer a remarkable six-timer. Lanzarote managed only one Champion Hurdle before he also became a victim of Comedy of Errors. Other Kingwell Hurdle winners, who later became stars, were Dramatist, Floyd, Desert Orchid, Kribensis and Alderbrook. The latter pair went on to win the Champion Hurdle in 1990 and 1995 respectively, while Desert Orchid's finest hour came in the Cheltenham Gold Cup in 1989.

Desert Orchid won, altogether, six times at Wincanton – the Kingwell Hurdle 1974, Jim Ford Chase 1987, Terry Biddlecombe Chase 1987 and 1988, Silver Buck Handicap Chase 1989 and Racing in Wessex Chase in 1990 – and, deservedly, now has the Desert Orchid South Western Pattern Chase run in his honour. The first winner of the Lord Stalbridge Memorial Handicap Chase in 1951 was 14-year-old Red April (a half-brother to Red Rower), who ran in the colours of Lady Stalbridge, trained by Vernon

Lester Piggott rides out on 'Dessie' at the start of the Desert Orchid South Western Pattern Chase on 22 October 2000.

Clare Balding celebrates after wining the KJ Pike & Sons Celebrity Charity Flat Race at Wincanton in October 1997 on Pay Homage, owned and trained by her father Ian Balding.

Cross; in 1988 the winner was Seagram, who went on to win the Grand National (1991), while another Aintree hero to win at Wincanton was Highland Wedding (1969), who in 1966 won the Badger Beer Chase.

Many equine superstars have graced the turf at Wincanton over the last 50 years but pride of place must go to Crudwell, a 14-year-old who contested the three-mile Somerset Steeplechase on 15 September 1960. On a dreary Thursday afternoon the most amazing piece of National Hunt history was achieved when Crudwell won by two lengths, beating Gala Dance (Terry Biddlecombe) and Domino's Serenade (Gay Kindersley) to record the 50th win of his career. He was owned by Mrs D M 'Bunny' Cooper, trained by Frank Cundell and ridden by Michael Scudamore. Foaled in 1946, he ran between 1949 and 1960 in 108 races, winning seven times on the flat, four hurdles and 39 steeplechases. No other horse in the last 100 years has achieved this feat and only four before that in the history of horseracing. He was not top-drawer – he only ran in the Cheltenham Gold Cup once, in 1955, although he did win the Welsh National and the Henry VIII Chase in his younger days; but he was superbly placed by his trainer Frank Cundell, who maintained he was a much better horse in small fields. He was a sound jumper who was able to produce an electrifying burst of speed on the run-in – a wonderful and popular chaser, as was his great rival, Lochroe, trained by Peter Cazalet, who himself won 32 races. They don't make them like that anymore.

No trainer in the history of horseracing has ever gone through the card (i.e. trained every winner at one meeting). At least eight trainers have recorded five winners at one meeting, including Tom Coulthwaite, Arthur Yates,

Magnificent Seven: Paul Nicholls' seven Grand National jockeys jump over a Wincanton fence at the launch of The Betting Site Video Form. Left to right: J P Macnamara, Jamie Moore, Liam Heard, Joe Tizzard, Paddy Brennan, Christian Williams and Sam Thomas.

Fulke Walwyn, Ken Oliver, Arthur Stephenson, Gordon Richards, Peter Easterby and Martin Pipe.

On 21 January 2006 at Wincanton, local trainer Paul Nicholls broke the record that had stood for over 100 years when he saddled six winners. Alas, it was on a seven-race card, but it was nevertheless a magnificent achievement. The day began with Raffaello (Ruby Walsh) in the opener but any chance of going through the card was quickly dispelled in the second race, the Novice Chase, when Ballez pulled up. The rest of the afternoon belonged to Nicholls, with wins for East Lawyer, The Luder, Almost Broke, Nippy des Mottes and Bold Fire. Ruby Walsh partnered five of the six winners, the exception being Nippy des Mottes who won in the hands of Liam Heard.

At the time of writing, still no trainer has actually gone through the card and it has become more difficult with so many meetings containing seven and eight races – but not impossible. One world record that might be impossible to break is that of Michael Dickinson who, on 27 December 1982, saddled 12 winners in one day, but spread over six meetings.

Finally, on Boxing Day 1953, one young jockey rode his first winner over hurdles at Wincanton, in the Dartmouth Handicap Hurdle on the favourite Eldoret for trainer Bill Payne. His name was Lester Piggott. Having already ridden plenty of winners on the flat, would he be tempted to switch codes? His father, Keith, knew the hazards of the jumping game and would have given him some sound advice. Lester could be arrogant and ruthless, but he was no fool. Although he went on to ride 20 winners over hurdles during the next three years, he stuck to the flat. A wise decision.

Once upon a time, to visit Windsor racecourse cars had to cross a Bailey Bridge, since Windsor is on an island bounded by the River Thames and the Clewer mill stream. The island is called Rays Meadow, also known as Clewer Meads. A permanent bridge has now been built. Alternatively, you can travel to the course by river from the town centre, alighting on a small jetty adjacent to the enclosures – another unique addition to the charm of Windsor Racecourse.

Because of its close proximity to Windsor Castle, the island was chosen as a replacement venue after the course at nearby Datchet closed on 11 March 1865. The date of the opening of the new course, 5 June 1866, was specially chosen as it was the day after Founder's Day at Eton. The course is now often referred to as Royal Windsor.

The course itself is very sharp and is one of only two figure-of-eight courses in the UK, the other being Fontwell.

Being so close to the river, the ground is invariably soft, which often encourages large fields. Since its inauguration, Windsor has enjoyed racing under both codes. Racing even continued here during the Second World War (in the south, only Newmarket and Salisbury did likewise), but National Hunt racing suffered badly because of the river. Waterlogged ground was a concern during the winter, with meetings often cancelled. In the bitter winter of 1947, there was severe flooding to a depth of three feet in the grandstand, the damage costing £10,000. Thanks to the efforts of the Thames Conservancy, the course is no longer prone to such serious problems.

However, despite the vast improvements for National Hunt sport, it was eventually decided that after each winter the ground was not recovering in time for the flat meetings and jumping at Windsor was discontinued. The last National Hunt fixture took place on 3 December

The extreme weather of February 2014 saw the River Thames rise to record levels, and Windsor suffered again from flooding.

1998, a sad day for Windsor after 130 years. The honour of saddling the last winner went to Karl Burke, when Charlie Banker won the Norwegian Blue Handicap Hurdle by 12 lengths, ridden by Norman Williamson.*

Most notable in Windsor's racing history was a triple dead-heat on 21 September 1923. It happened in the Royal Borough Handicap for three-year-olds and was between Dumas (2/1 fav), ridden by E Gardner, Dinkie (6/1), ridden by Henri Jelliss and Marvex (8/1), ridden by Vic Smyth. Strangely, a triple dead-heat had happened eight years earlier at Sandown and had also involved Mr Gardner. In those days before photo finish cameras, all three jockeys claimed the win, and the three owners were glad to settle for a share of the £492 prize money.

Another piece of history unique to Windsor was the bookmakers' strike in 1926. Under Stanley Baldwin's Conservative government, the Chancellor of the Exchequer, Winston Churchill, imposed in his April budget a 5% betting tax to take effect at the beginning of November. Racing took place at Birmingham and Wye

* In December 2005, a final National Hunt meeting was held at Windsor, having been transferred from Ascot.

on 1 November 1926 without incident, but three days later Windsor bookmakers refused to chalk up any prices throughout their two-day meeting by way of a protest and the races were run in an eerie silence. Newport raced on the same two days but their bookmakers traded normally. The Windsor bookmakers resumed betting at Newbury later that week and the tax was soon abolished.

Gordon Richards rode many winners at Windsor but he will have special memories of 9 May 1955 when he saddled his first winner there as a trainer. Indeed, it was also his first runner and the horse to get him off to a flying start was The Saint, a recent purchase from Ireland by Dorothy Paget. The Saint, an even-money favourite ridden by Jock Wilson, won the Frogmore Plate by four lengths but, sadly, the great jockey's career as a trainer never reached the same heights as when he was in the saddle.

With flat meetings now taking centre stage, Windsor is hugely popular, with Monday evening fixtures first introduced in 1964. The best flat race is the Winter Hill Stakes, recently achieving group status, but there were two far more prestigious National Hunt races on the Berkshire course – the New Year's Day Hurdle and the Fairlawne Chase, run in February. Top-class hurdlers and chasers were often seen in these two events, with the winners invariably Cheltenham-bound.

The best New Year's Day Hurdle without doubt came in 1976, with Sea Pigeon and Comedy of Errors in opposition. In a thrilling finish, Comedy of Errors, in the hands of Ken White, won by a head. Trained by Fred Rimell, he had already won two Champion Hurdles, while Sea Pigeon had to wait four more years before his Cheltenham triumphs.

The Fairlawne Chase has seen many fine chasers over the years. One notable regular was The Laird, trained by Bob Turnell, but his fortunes were somewhat irregular. In 1968, he managed to fall at the last when disputing the lead. He won the race in 1969, finished third in 1970 to Specify (who won the Grand National the following year) and in 1972 won again, only to be disqualified. Champion hurdler Bula won in 1975 and 1976 but, although a top-class chaser, he could manage only third place in the Cheltenham Gold Cup and later reverted to two-mile events. However, the most dramatic Fairlawne Chase was in 1973 when The Dikler (8/15), trained by Fulke Walwyn, met Spanish Steps (7/4), trained by Edward Courage. It became a titanic battle over the last few fences with both horses giving everything. They were still neck and neck over the last, but on the run in The Dikler, who was a huge horse at over 17 hands, began to lean heavily on Spanish Steps and took him right across the course towards the river. The rider of Spanish Steps, Bob Davies, would certainly have finished in the Thames had the race been any longer. The Dikler won in a photo finish but was inevitably disqualified. He then went to Cheltenham to win one of the most exciting Gold Cups, beating Fred Winter's Pendil a short head.

Finally, back to the Flat and an incredible day when Windsor nearly made history. Only three jockeys have ever gone through the card and, even now, with most meetings containing more races, this amazing feat becomes more difficult. In 1933, Gordon Richards was the first to accomplish this, riding all six winners at Chepstow. The general feeling at the time was sheer amazement, and that it would never be equalled. In 1957, Alec Russell followed suit and rode all six winners at Bogside. In 1996, the impossible happened when Frankie Dettori went through the card in seven races at Ascot. It was also a high-profile meeting and the wins were hailed in newspapers the following day as the 'Magnificent Seven'. Surely the bar could not be raised again – could it?

On 15 October 2012 at Windsor, Richard Hughes rode seven winners from eight rides and finished third on the favourite in the remaining race – an astounding achievement, and so close to creating history. His winners were Pivotal Movement, East Texas Red (for Richard Hannon), Embankment (Amanda Perrett), Magic Secret (Jeremy Gask), Links Drive Lady (Dean Ivory), Duke of Clarence (Richard Hannon) and Mama Quilla (William Haggas). He finished third in the sixth race on Ever Fortune (2/1 favourite).

So he did at least equal Frankie Dettori's record, and it is possible for a jockey to ride eight winners on one card – watch this space.

Richard Hughes celebrates after riding his 7th winner of the day, Mama Quilla, at Windsor on 15 October 2012.

Dunstall Park is the home of Wolverhampton racecourse and on 27 December 1993 history was made here. After over a century of racing, Wolverhampton received a complete makeover and opened an all-weather track. It was the third racecourse to use this surface but the first to include floodlights. It was not until the sixth race on that historic evening that the all-important lights were switched on for the six-furlong handicap (won by Petraco ridden by Steve Williams) and two weeks later a complete card was run under floodlights. Her Majesty the Queen officially opened the new all-weather course on 24 June 1994. Unlike the pioneers of all-weather racing – Lingfield and Southwell – Wolverhampton had completely dug up their existing turf on the original National Hunt course which had been in use since 1888.

Racing at Wolverhampton began at Broad Meadows, originally marshland known as Hungry Leas, which had to be drained at great expense before the first recorded meeting on 15 August 1825. When the lease expired in 1878, Wolverhampton was left without a course for a number of years. By chance, permission was granted to run a railway line through Dunstall Park, which persuaded the owner, Sir Alexander Staveley Hill, to put it on the market – and a new home for Wolverhampton racecourse was found. A trial meeting took place in 1886 before the purchase of the 130-acre Dunstall Park was put into motion. After a series of delays, the inaugural meeting took place on 13 August 1888 beneath a railway viaduct at the end of the home straight, just beyond the winning post, which has since become a landmark.

The first meeting was flat and the opening event, the five furlong All Aged Maiden Plate, was won by Tommy Loates riding Silver Spur, trained at Newmarket by her owner Tom Leader. Loates also rode the winner of the final race on the old course at Broad Meadows. Riding at 6st 11lb, he was one of the leading jockeys of the day and became champion the following season. He was crowned champion a total of three times, but his claim to fame was to partner the Triple Crown winner Isinglass (1893).

Many of the most vivid personalities of the late Victorian era used to run their horses at Dunstall Park, among them Chevalier Odoardo Ginistrelli ('Gini'), Lady Mabel Sievier (wife of the renowned professional gambler Bob Sievier) and Lily Langtry (actress and mistress of the Prince of Wales), whose horses ran under the owner's pseudonym of 'Mr Jersey', as Jockey Club rules at the time forbade the ownership of horses by women.

A number of good steeplechasers also ran in this period, none more famous than Cloister, who won the Great Staffordshire Chase on 19 April 1892, and from Dunstall Park went on to win the Grand National of 1893 by 40 lengths in record time, under 12st 7lb. Another future Grand National winner was beaten at Dunstall Park in January 1907 when James Daly's Jenkinstown started 3/1 joint favourite for the Staffordshire Handicap Chase. The stewards of the National Hunt Committee held strong suspicions about the running of Jenkinstown, after persistent rumours that the local stewards had agreed to his being given the run to be schooled over fences; his trainer J J Maher was summoned before the Committee but exonerated. The horse was later bought by Stanley Howard and sent to Tom Coulthwaite's stable at Hednesford. He had already won the Grand National with Eremon (1907), and Jenkinstown (1910) provided him with his second victory.

The 1915 Grand National winner Ally Sloper, owned by Lady Nelson (wife of Sir William Nelson of the Nelson Steam Navigation Company), won the Walsall Handicap Chase in 1919 and another good jumper to win here in the 1920s was Sprig, trained at Newmarket by Tom Leader, whose father had owned and trained Silver Spur, the first-ever winner at Dunstall Park. Sprig carried the colours of Mrs Mary Partridge and had been bred by her son Richard who had been killed in action in the First World War. To fulfil her son's ambition she entered Sprig in Grand National and at the third attempt (1927) he achieved his late breeder's dream, when ridden by the trainer's son Ted.

In November 1923, Major Humphrey Wyndham's Red Splash, ridden by Captain 'Tuppy' Bennet, won a novice chase by six lengths and the following year made history by winning the first Cheltenham Gold Cup, but at the Christmas meeting of 1924, Captain Bennet took a fall in the Oteley Handicap Chase, was kicked on the head and died without regaining consciousness. As a result of that fatal accident, the wearing of crash helmets in steeplechases and hurdle races was made compulsory.

More good-class jumpers were seen in action here during the 1930s. Miss Dorothy Paget's Golden Miller had already won the Grand National of 1934 and the Cheltenham Gold Cup three times prior to winning the Penkridge Steeplechase on Boxing Day 1934. The

The Wolverhampton grandstand in the 1930s.

Dunstall Hurdle, run at the March meeting, was more than once used as a stepping stone to fame during that era. Winners Reynoldstown (1933) and Royal Mail (1934) both went on to be Grand National winners in later years.

In March 1936, the 15-year-old amateur Bruce Hobbs rode his first winner on only his second mount in public when bringing Armida home eight lengths clear of the field in the Walsall Handicap Hurdle. He returned to Dunstall Park on 28 December, his 16th birthday and first day as a professional, to ride a double on Baccharis and Eliza. His only other ride that memorable day was on Mrs Marion Scott's Battleship (trained by Hobbs' father Reg), on whom he finished second. Two years later they made history together by winning the 1938 Grand National – the smallest horse to win the race and the youngest jockey to ride the winner. Hobbs went on to win the Welsh Grand National on Timber Wolf two weeks later. In June that year Bruce and Reg Hobbs accompanied the horse back to the USA to be retired to stud. A huge crowd met them at the dock, including Randolph Scott, the owner's husband. At the end of the 1937-1938 season, during which he rode

Battleship, with Bruce Hobbs on board.

35 winners, Hobbs became the first jockey to win three Grand Nationals in one year, being successful also in Long Island's Cedarhurst version. A crashing fall in 1938 resulted in injuries to the young Hobbs that included a broken spine. Although told he would never ride again, he returned to the saddle, but turned to training horses at age 25. He retired from racing in 1985 and died at Newmarket in 2005, aged 84.

Flat racing was by no means overshadowed by these fine jumpers, but you could say the five-furlong sprinters were overlooked by Three Sisters. In 1916, a strip of land beyond the five furlong start was sold to the textiles company, Courtaulds. As part of the industrial development that followed, Courtaulds built three huge chimneys, to be known locally as the Three Sisters, that dominated the course and were a well-known landmark until their demolition in 1973. They are recalled by the Three Sisters Stakes run over nine furlongs in May.

Gordon Richards paid his first visit to Wolverhampton at the age of 18 in June 1922, when he finished second in the Apprentices Stakes on Knight of the Orient, and the following day another promising young rider, Charlie Smirke, also making his debut, won the Stanton Selling Plate on Son O'Simon. Brothers Eph and Doug Smith were regulars at Wolverhampton and were often engaged in battles. In the Gunstone Plate in 1955 Eph got home by a head on Woodworm, but was promptly objected to by Doug, riding Part View, for bumping and boring. The objection was sustained.

The following day, Miss Dorothy Paget's Nucleus was ridden by Lester Piggott to a very easy success in the Merry Hill Maiden Plate for three-year-olds, with a horse called Taxidermist six lengths away in third. Nucleus and Taxidermist were to follow very different paths. Nucleus won the King Edward VII Stakes at Royal Ascot before finishing second to Meld in the 1955 St Leger. The following year he was put down due to a tumour on the brain. Three

years later Taxidermist won both the Whitbread and the Hennessy Gold Cup, plus ten other chases.

Cement City, a brown gelding foaled in 1946, may not have been the best horse of his day to run at Wolverhampton, but he was a real course specialist who became a great favourite. Trained by Stan Wright in Shropshire, he won for the first time at Wolverhampton in the Coseley Selling Handicap Hurdle in March 1952 and for the final time as a 15-year-old in 1961. From 26 appearances at Wolverhampton alone, without falling once, he won nine times and was placed ten. In five consecutive seasons he turned out for the Shrewsbury Challenge Cup, a three-mile chase, winning in 1957 and 1958 ridden by Derek Leslie, unplaced in 1959, third in 1960 and unplaced again when taking his final bow in 1961.

As part of the celebrations of the first hundred years of the National Hunt Committee, Wolverhampton staged the National Hunt Centerary Hurdle Cup in October 1966. It was won by Saucy Kit, trained by Peter Easterby and ridden by Roy Edwards. The following March, Saucy Kit won the Champion Hurdle at Cheltenham.

Saucy Kit and Roy Edwards in 1967.

A splendid feat of training and riding occurred on 11 November 1968 when Scottish trainer Ken Oliver saddled five winners, all ridden by Barry Brogan. They landed the two divisions of the Charlecoke Novices Chase with Glen Kiln and Even Keel, the Nuneaton Hurdle on Drumikill, the Beginners' Chase with Ballycurragh Lad and the Sutton Handicap Hurdle with Shingle Bay – that's what you call a good day at the office.

The 14 November 1973 meeting coincided with the royal wedding of Princess Anne to Captain Mark Phillips. To play its part in that day of national celebration, Wolverhampton staged the Cupids Novices Chase, the Wedding Bells Chase, the Royal Wedding Handicap Chase and the Bottom Drawer Handicap Hurdle. The script must have already been written because the winner of the Royal Wedding Handicap Chase was Royal Mark, owned by the former Senior Steward of the meeting, Sir Edward Hanmer – not surprisingly, there was no steward's enquiry.

Many top-class horses continued to visit Wolverhampton, few better than Night Nurse. The dual Champion Hurdle winner turned his attention to chasing and won the Astbury Steeplechase in 1978, run at the Christmas meeting. Another star to win the race was West Tip (1983), who went on to win the Grand National three years later.

Probably the most important National Hunt race to be run in the latter years was the Champion Hurdle Trial. Although run over two-and-a-half miles, it proved to be a good trial for Cheltenham and trainer Fred Rimell's Gaye Brief and Comedy of Errors were both successful before glory at the Festival. By strange coincidence, Comedy of Errors obtained the first success of his career on the flat at Wolverhampton. Trained in those days by Tommy Corrie at Shrewsbury and ridden by George Cadwaladr, he easily won a division of the nine-furlong Birches Bridge Maiden Plate in March 1971 by eight lengths. Two classy fillies on the flat to win their maidens here were Indian Skimmer (Henry Cecil) and Aliysa (Luca Cumani).

The last flat meeting to be run on the old course was on 28 September 1992, with the final National Hunt meeting on 19 March 1993, before the bulldozers moved in ahead of the grand opening of the new all-weather track, grandstand and restaurants. Many owners, trainers, jockeys and racegoers felt nostalgic about the old Wolverhampton, for over the previous century many enjoyable days had been spent watching good horseracing (and even an aviation meeting once in 1910). National Hunt racing was tried when a turf track was laid inside the all-weather on a mixed card in 1997, but it was discontinued because the course was too narrow and, on 15 July 2002, National Hunt racing was finally laid to rest when Light Programme won the final handicap hurdle. In 2004 the Fibresand track and turf were replaced with one Polytrack surface and further improvements were made to the facilities.

In September 2012, Wolverhamton saw yet another record broken when the 11-year old Dvinsky made his 218th appearance on the racetrack and his 34th at Wolverhampton which included two wins and nine placings. With Tom McLaughlin partnering him for the 27th time, they came ninth, and Dvinsky was deservedly retired in 2013.

Wolverhampton's future is entirely all-weather racing, but this final piece of turf trivia will survive.

Question: When did Good Friday last fall on Boxing Day?
Answer: When a horse called Good Friday fell in the Thorneycroft Chase at Wolverhampton on 26 December 1899.

Trainer Paul Howling with the record-breaking Dvinsky before his 218th race at Wolverhampton in September 2012.

The historic city of Worcester has a fine cathedral, is famous for its Royal Worcester porcelain and its glove-making industry, and is the birthplace of composer Sir Edward Elgar – and its racecourse is quite old too.

Worcester racecourse dates from 1718, on an area of land known as Pitchcroft meadow on the very edge of the River Severn. A horse race took place there on 27 June – a two-mile event consisting of three heats – as well as athletic races for ladies and gentlemen. It was not until 22 August 1739 that it was confined to horse racing only, and the first recorded winner was Cato, who won a 40 guinea plate for his owner, a Mr Middleton.

National Hunt racing was introduced in 1837 over a cross-country course consisting of 29 jumps, using the fencing and bushes of the adjoining meadows as part of the course. In 1844, to commemorate the 25th birthday of Queen Victoria, the Royal Birthday Stakes was run on the new course, attracting the previous two winners of the Grand National – Vanguard (1843), ridden by Tom Olliver, and Discount (1844), ridden by amateur John Crickmere, who had also ridden him at Aintree. In a thrilling contest, the race was won by Discount, who later had the distinction of being the first horse to be registered in the General Stud Book.

In 1880 a figure-of-eight course was laid down, with artificial fences replacing the cross-country course (perhaps the local landowners wanted their land back). It was not popular, however, and entries dropped, as did the prize money. Flat races could be run only if exceeding one mile and the course lasted only 20 years. In 1901, another course was laid down, oval and very flat, with sweeping bends and a long straight – a good galloping course which has been very popular with trainers, especially when introducing young horses. This is the course that exists

A different kind of sport taking place during the flooding of 2012.

the Worcestershire Plate and was won by Nimble Joe, trained by Peter Nelson.

Another champion jockey, John Francome, could well list Worcester among his favourite racecourses. It was here that he not only rode his first winner, Multigrey, to victory in his first ride in public on 2 December 1970, but he also recorded here his 1,000th winner on 29 February 1984, riding Tony Gretton's good horse Observe for his guv'nor Fred Winter, in the Sidbury Handicap Chase. Following Stan Mellor, he was only the second National Hunt jockey to achieve this milestone.

So Gordon Richards and John Francome were history-makers at Worcester, but there was a special moment for a certain 37-year-old mother of two who also managed to lift the grandstand roof off on 3 September 1987. HRH the Princess Royal rode her first winner in a steeplechase at the eighth attempt against professional jockeys.

Riding her own horse, Cnoc Na Cuille, trained by David Nicholson, in the Droitwich Handicap Chase over three miles, she had four opponents but her main rival was the favourite, Tiger Ted, ridden by Brendan Powell. Throughout the last mile the pair of them had pulled clear and it became a ding-dong battle over the last three fences in the home straight. The advantage went first with one, then the other, but with a slight lead over the last HRH got her mount home by half a length. She received a tremendous ovation from the huge crowd. While Brendan Powell was gracious in defeat, he said afterwards, "After the last there must have been 50,000 people shouting for Princess Anne and only one for me – and that was my mother in Ireland."

today. Its proximity to the River Severn has meant severe flooding at times – notably in 2007, 2008 and 2014, when the river burst its banks. Things were so bad in 2014 that the Environment Agency had to rescue a large number of enormous pike from the home straight as the floodwaters receded.

Flat racing at Worcester was on the decline after the Second World War, but it was popular with champion jockey Gordon Richards. It was here that he had passed the 2,000 mark on Fonab on 22 October 1936, but a bigger milestone was to come. On 19 May 1947 he broke the world record set by Belgium-based jockey Sam Heapy of 3,260 winners. It was a tremendous occasion for Gordon when he broke the record on Le Bosc Giard, and he brought his total up to 3,262 when he also won the last race on Overcast.

National Hunt racing was gathering momentum, as was evident on 9 January 1965 when a record 229 runners were declared for a jumps meeting. (There were no safety limits in those days). The following year, for economic reasons, Worcester staged its final flat meeting on 20 August. The final race to bring down the curtain was

Yarmouth races date from 1715, when they were run at the opposite end of the town at South Denes and it was not until 15 September 1920 that racing was transferred to a new course at North Denes, where it takes place today.

Racing had started at South Denes when a group of local innkeepers leased a piece of land from Yarmouth Corporation, but racing was irregular until 1810, when the first official meeting was recorded. However, there were a few problems as it was a tight course with two winning posts that were often mistaken, and the long distance races were run in a figure-of-eight, resulting in some horses jumping the rails and finishing in the river near the harbour mouth. The public were outraged by an advertisement for a meeting in August 1810 by the Clerk of the Course, John Buck, that requested that no person bring dogs to the meeting as they may be destroyed. Imagine that happening today – the Animal Rights protestors would have a field day!

All was not bad, though, as the old course was very picturesque. Many racegoers would arrive by boat and river steamer along the River Yare to a landing stage right alongside the course, while those by road arrived in landaus, horse-brakes and other private carriages. There were some extraordinary races in this period, with a race in August 1867 for all ages over three furlongs.

Facilities deteriorated, however, with the course subject to blown sand and shingle adding to other problems, and in 1906 the grandstand was destroyed by fire, its replacement costing £5,000. When eventually the lease expired, the land was acquired for development of the fishing industry and the course moved to North Denes – along with the new grandstand.

The new course opened with a two-day fixture on 15–16 September 1920. The opening race, the Monument Two-year-old Selling Plate over five furlongs, was won by the 9/4 favourite Sawkins, trained by George Poole at Lewes and ridden by Vic Smyth. Sawkins won again the following day, winning the Selling Nursery. The first day produced five winners from Newmarket, which has continued to be a trend up to the present day, since Yarmouth is now the closest course to 'headquarters' at Newmarket and trainers often find opportunities here for their more moderate horses.

The course at North Denes is very flat and the soil is sandy. In the early days the paddock was little more than a sandhill, but today Yarmouth is a beautifully-kept small course. One slight drawback, however, is that the centre of the course is occupied by part of a golf course, and one hole requires golfers to cross the course by the four furlong pole, leaving divots and marks from golf trolleys and, perhaps, the odd lost ball. Jockeys at this point often have to steer for the best ground.

By and large Yarmouth is well worth a visit, as many holidaymakers to the Norfolk seaside resort can confirm, and it is rather fitting that during the opening meeting in 1920 the Central cinema in Yarmouth that week was showing a play by Nat Gould, starring Polly Wyndham entitled *A Dead Certainty*.

Racecards of yesteryear.

The view from the stands in the 1960s.

Comedian and actor Leslie Crowther presents a whip to winning jockey Joe Mercer in 1969.

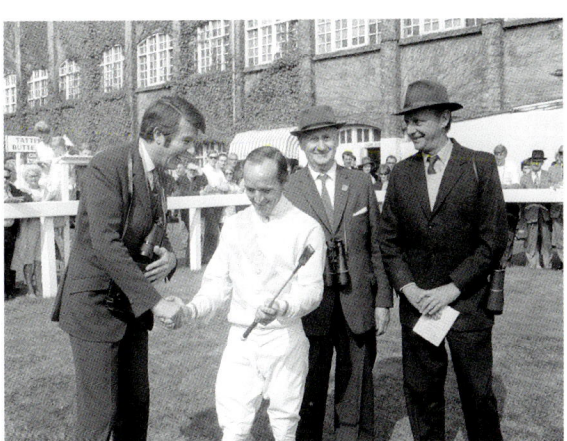

The 'Ascot of the North' is a well-known description of this magnificent racecourse but, for many Yorkshiremen, even that flatters the Berkshire course. York racecourse is situated on a piece of land called the Knavesmire, one mile south of the city centre, with arguably the most historic background to any city in the country. Horseracing may well have originated here, with records dating back to the Roman occupation during the 3rd century, during which time it would have been customary for the local gentry to match their horses against one another. According to records, York City Council sponsored meetings as early as 1530 on the Clifton Ings course in the Forest of Galtres, north of the city, close to the River Ouse. Consistent waterlogging forced it to close, and the site at the Knavesmire was far more suitable.

The Knavesmire was the location for public executions and, even on the official opening of the racecourse, a six-day fixture starting on 16 August 1731, three robbers were hanged that morning. The organisers came up with the idea that the majority of spectators for the hanging would stay around for the racing. (The hanging of Dick Turpin in 1739 – for horse theft, appropriately enough – was also on the morning of a meeting, to ensure a good crowd.)

The first grandstand was built in 1754 at the instigation of the Marquess of Rockingham and matches continued to be very popular. One young lady, Mrs Alicia Thornton, would often challenge her male counterparts, with a fair amount of success. Riding sidesaddle, her finest hour came on 25 August 1805 when she beat top jockey of the era, Frank Buckle, although she did receive a considerable weight allowance. The finest match ever staged at the

Knavesmire took place in 1851 when two outstanding Derby winners met. More than 100,000 people are reputed to have watched the five-year-old The Flying Dutchman beat the four-year-old Voltigeur by a length.

York's big meeting is the Ebor, named after the Roman name for the city of York – Eboracum. Run in August, the highlight is undoubtedly the Ebor Handicap, run over a-mile-and-three-quarters and first staged in 1843. It is the centrepiece of a three-day meeting of racing out of the top drawer. Other races include the Great Voltigeur Stakes (a St Leger trial), the Yorkshire Oaks, the Nunthorpe Stakes, the Gimcrack Stakes and the Lowther Stakes for two-year-olds and, a more recent addition, the Group 1 Juddmonte International, formerly known as the Benson and Hedges Gold Cup when inaugurated in 1972.

Even though the Ebor is a handicap, it is a high-class one. Top-class winners were Isonomy (1879) and that great mare Lily Agnes (1875). In the 20th century, three winners to savour were Brown Jack (1931), Gladness (1958) and Sea Pigeon (1979).

Brown Jack was the most popular flat horse of the century. Trained by Ivor Anthony and ridden by Steve Donoghue, he won the 1931 Ebor carrying 9st 5lb at remarkable odds of 10/1. Unusually, he started his career as a hurdler and finished his career on the flat. It all began with winning a hurdle race at Bournemouth, later winning the 1928 Champion Hurdle and the Ascot Stakes in the same year, followed by the Queen Alexandra Stakes at Ascot (six times). His career totalled 25 wins from 65 starts, both flat and jumps.

The mare Gladness landed a huge gamble when winning the 1958 Ebor by six lengths. Backed from 10/1 to 5/1 favourite, she was trained by Vincent O'Brien and ridden by Lester Piggott. Carrying 9st 7lb, she won in a canter to give those Yorkshire bookmakers a result they might wish to forget.

The loudest cheer for an Ebor winner came in 1979 when the judge announced the result of the photo finish. 'First No 1, Sea Pigeon'. Trained in Yorkshire (of course) by Peter Easterby and ridden by Jonjo O'Neill, he won by a short head at odds of 18/1 carrying the welterweight of 10st (a record that will not be beaten). Not satisfied with that, Sea Pigeon went on to win two Champion Hurdles (1980, 1981), the second of them at the ripe old age of eleven. He was the most versatile of horses, flat and jumps, winning a host of top prizes which finally amounted to 37. Astonishingly, he won his one and only race as a two-year-old, The Duke of Edinburgh Stakes at Ascot, when trained by Jeremy Tree, and even ran in the 1973 Derby behind Morston, finishing seventh before his career really took off.

The inaugural running of the Juddmonte International (as the Benson and Hedges Gold Cup) in 1972 was possibly the greatest, when Brigadier Gerard was beaten three lengths by that year's Derby winner Roberto. It was the only time in 18 races that the Brigadier suffered defeat. Subsequent winners have kept the standard very high, notably with Dahlia (1974, 1975), beating Grundy on the second occasion, Wollow (1976), Troy (1979), Rodrigo de Triano (1992), Halling (1995, 1996), Singspiel (1997), Royal Anthem (1999), Giant's Causeway (2000), Authorized (2007), Sea the Stars (2009), Twice Over (2011) and, possibly the best of all, Frankel (2012), a son of Galileo, who brought his unbeaten run to 13. Quite a roll of honour.

The Gimcrack Stakes for two-year-olds is named after a horse foaled in 1760 who won 26 times from 36 races but, oddly, none at York. First run in 1846, it has become established as one of the top juvenile races over six furlongs, but few classic winners have emerged from it. Since the Aga Khan's Bahram (1934), only Mill Reef (1970) has gone on to win the Derby at Epsom. Mill Reef's win at York was spectacular, winning by ten lengths in heavy ground. Likewise, only three 2,000 Guineas winners have won the Gimcrack as two-year-olds: Palestine (1949), Nebbiolo (1976) and Rock of Gibraltar (2001).

The Nunthorpe Stakes over five furlongs is one of the highest-profile races of the season for sprinters. A Group 1 event first run in 1922 (having previously been a seller), it has been won by some of the fastest horses ever seen on a racecourse. The filly Mumtaz Mahal set the ball rolling in 1924 when streaking home by six lengths. A daughter of The Tetrarch, she was trained by Dick Dawson at Whatcombe and ridden by George Archibald. She showed blistering speed from the gate and often had her races won by half way, and was probably the fastest filly of the last century. She was followed by one of her grandsons, Abernant (twice), and Right Boy (twice), Floribunda, Althrey Don, So Blessed, Sharpo (three times), Habibti and the flying Dayjur.

The race is also open to two-year-olds, who receive a generous weight allowance. They provided three winners in the 1950s, High Treason (1953), trained by Ted Leader, My Beau (1954), Paddy Prendergast, Ireland, and Ennis (1956), Walter Nightingall at Epsom. Since then only

Richard Hannon's filly Lyric Fantasy in 1992 (nicknamed 'The Pocket Rocket') and Kingsgate Native (2007) have won from this age group.

The Yorkshire Oaks, another Group 1 event, is usually won by fillies that have either won or run well in the English and Irish Oaks. Since 1991, the race has been open to four-year-olds and upwards. Since the Second World War those to win both the Epsom Oaks and the Yorkshire Oaks are Frieze (1952), Petite Etoile (1959), Homeward Bound (1964), Lupe (1970), Mysterious (1973), Fair Salinia (1978), Sun Princess (1983), Circus Plume (1984), Diminuendo (1988), User Friendy (1992), Ramruma (1999) and Alexandrova (2006). Of these only Fair Salinia, Diminuendo, User Friendly and Ramruma also won the Irish Oaks to complete a treble. The best of these, by far, was Prince Aly Khan's grey filly Petite Etoile, trained by Noel Murless. Over four seasons this daughter of Petition won 14 of her 19 races and finished second in the other five – an impressive record.

The Queen arrives at York for the 'Royal Ascot' meeting in 2005.

Ascot may have its 'Royal' meeting but to Yorkshire folk the 'York Ebor' meeting is its equal; indeed in 2005, while Ascot was undergoing a huge redevelopment, York was chosen to host 'Royal Ascot' and proved to be an ideal replacement. Modifications to the course were required to accommodate the long-distance races, so a round course was introduced – and has remained a permanent feature.

The three-day meeting in May, while not as busy as the Ebor meeting, is nevertheless a high-profile one, known as the 'Dante Festival'. Named after the 1945 Derby winner, it carries this title as Dante was the last winner of the Derby to be trained in Yorkshire, by Matt Peacock at Middleham. The feature race of the meeting is the Dante Stakes for three-year-olds, run over ten-and-a-half furlongs. It has proved to be the most reliable trial for the Epsom Derby, despite the fact the courses are quite dissimilar.

First run in 1958, when won by Bald Eagle, trained by Cecil Boyd-Rochfort, the first Derby victor to win the race was St Paddy (1960), followed by Shirley Heights (1978), Shahrastani (1986), Reference Point (1987), Erhaab (1994), Benny the Dip (1997), North Light (2004), Motivator (2005) and Authorized (2007).

Likewise, the Musidora Stakes for three-year-old fillies has served as an Oaks trial. Also Yorkshire trained, Musidora won the 1946 Oaks, trained by Charles Elsey at Malton. The race in her honour was first run in 1961, and was won by Ambergris, trained by Harry Wragg. The best winner to go on and win the Oaks was Noblesse

(1963), trained in Ireland by Paddy Prendergast. She was no oil painting and was bought cheaply, but she was an exceptional filly. Unbeaten at two, she won the Musidora by six lengths before winning the Oaks in effortless fashion by ten lengths. Starting the 4/11 favourite, some say she would have won the Derby as well.

Other Oaks winners to have also won the Musidora were Bireme (1980), Diminuendo (1988), Snow Bride (1989) and Reams of Verse (1997). The last three were all trained by Henry Cecil, who also won in 1987 with Indian Skimmer, who went on to triumph in the French Oaks.

York's success is owed mostly to two men. James Melrose, who became Chairman of the York Race Committee in 1875, laid the foundations of modern York and his job was well done when he died in 1929 at the age of 101. Leslie Petch became Clerk of the Course in 1955 when he relinquished his job of senior Jockey Club Judge. The course had been used as a prisoner-of-war camp for six years before racing resumed on 4 September 1945. On the second day of the meeting the substitute St Leger was run at York before packed stands, won by Chamossaire, trained by Dick Perryman and ridden by Tommy Lowrey. Leslie Petch's job was to ensure the continuance of racing, like his predecessor. York flourished under his management and in 1965 a new stand was opened by Lord Halifax. (In 2003, it was replaced by a new stand named the Ebor Stand; the original 1754 stand – the John Carr Stand – survives, though in a different location.)

Ill health forced Leslie Petch to resign in 1971, but not before he had made plans for a superb new race for three-year-olds and upwards, the Benson and Hedges Gold Cup. Petch's nephew, John Sanderson, succeeded him as Clerk of the Course and he invited Her Majesty the Queen to witness the inaugural running of the race on 15 August 1972, the first monarch to visit York for over 300 years. Leslie Petch had also laid the foundation for the seven furlong start to be moved to allow the construction of a new bypass, which eventually took place in 1973; and he persuaded the City of York to grant a lease on the Knavesmire site until 2051.

This wonderful racecourse has come a long way since the days of Dick Turpin.

COURSES VISITED

Listed below in chronological order are all courses visited, including some that have since closed, a few courses abroad and two new ones.

Epsom 19.4.1955
Lingfield Park 14.6.1956
Hurst Park 27.7.1956 (also
  final meeting 10.10.1962)
Windsor 25.9.1956
Kempton Park 20.4.1957
Alexandra Park 21.5.1957
Sandown Park 13.7.1957
Ascot 20.7.1957
Goodwood 29.7.1958
Newmarket (Rowley)
  14.10.1958
Newmarket (July) 1.7.1961
Salisbury 15.5.1963
Longchamp 6.10.1968
Cheltenham 18.3.1969
Yarmouth 10.6.1970
York 18.8.1970
Newbury 21.5.1971
Wincanton 16.11.1972
Bath 29.4.1974
Market Rasen 27.9.1974
Redcar 28.9.1974
Plumpton 14.8.1975
Towcester 20.11.1975
Wolverhampton (old)
  21.6.1976
Fontwell 14.9.1976
Stratford 18.11.1976
Worcester 24.11.1976

Ludlow 20.12.1976
Chepstow 7.6.1977
Doncaster 10.9.1977
Huntingdon 22.10.1977
Nottingham 24.10.1977
Taunton 26.1.1978
Liverpool 1.4.1978 *
Pontefract 19.5.1978
Thirsk 20.5.1978
Brighton 6.7.1978
Edinburgh 18.6.1979 *
Hamilton 21.6.1979
Les Landes Jersey 25.8.1979
Warwick 15.10.1979
Leicester 23.10.1979
Southwell 19.2.1981
Fakenham 20.4.1981
Folkestone 12.5.1981
Newton Abbot 2.8.1982
Chester 7.5.1985
Beverley 4.6.1985
Ripon 5.6.1985
Sedgefield 22.10.1985
Hexham 23.10.1985
Catterick Bridge 23.7.1986
Hereford 2.12.1986
Uttoxeter 4.12.1986
Wetherby 6.1.1987
Kelso 29.4.1987
Devon and Exeter 4.5.1987 *

Haydock 23.5.1987
Ayr 20.6.1987
Bangor 15.8.1987
Cartmel 31.8.1987
Newcastle 14.11.1987
Curragh 14.5.1988
Wexford 29.6.1988
Tipperary 30.6.1988
Punchestown 1.7.1988
Perth 19.8.1988
Carlisle 21.10.1988 (final
  course in England)
Kilbeggan 11.8.1989
Phoenix Park 12.8.1989
Roscommon 9.10.1989
Fairyhouse 3.2.1990
Killarney 8.5.1990
Tramore 10.5.1990
Gowran Park 28.6.1990
Limerick (old) 2.7.1990
Bellewstown 3.7.1990
Laytown 17.8.1990
Clonmel 20.9.1990
Down Royal 22.9.1990
Listowel 24.9.1990
Navan 24.11.1990
Leopardstown 28.12.1990
Thurles 21.3.1991
Naas 23.3.1991
Sligo 22.4.1991

Downpatrick 11.5.1991
Dundalk 17.5.1991
Mallow 21.5.1991 *
Galway 29.7.1991
Ballinrobe 16.9.1991
Tralee 31.5.1992 (final
  course in Ireland)
Wolverhampton (new)
  17.1.1994
Lanark (p-t-p) 18.2.1995
Garrison Savannah,
  Barbados 7.12.1996
Buckfastleigh (p-t-p)
  21.1.1998
Great Leighs 13.9.2008
Ffos Las 13.9.2009
Limerick (new) 11.10.2009

*The following were visited for
the first time when the meeting
was held under its original
title. The new title appears in
brackets.*

Liverpool (Aintree)
Edinburgh (Musselburgh)
Devon and Exeter (Exeter)
Mallow (Cork)

Just two examples of the author's meticulous records of meetings attended.

INDEX OF HORSES

INDEX OF PEOPLE & PLACES

PICTURE CREDITS

t=top, b=bottom, l=left, r=right, m=middle

BIBLIOGRAPHY

Books

Baerlein, Richard. *Nijinsky*. Pelham Books (1971)

Barrett, Norman. *The Daily Telegraph Chronicle of Horse Racing*. Guinness (1995)

Beavis, Jim. *The History of Fontwell Park*. (2008)

Church, Michael. *The Derby Stakes 1780-2006*. Raceform (2006)

Corbett, Peter. *Bayardo*. Rinaldo (2010)

Cottrell, John. Armytage, Marcus. *A-Z of the Grand National*. Highdown (2008)

D'Arcy, Fergus A. *Horses, Lords and Racing Men*. The Turf Club (1991)

Ellerington, Alison. *The Kiplingcotes Derby*. Highgate (1990)

Fairfax-Blakeborough, J. *Nothern Turf History (vol IV Scotland)*. Allen (1973)

Fitzgeorge-Parker, Tim. *The Ditch on the Hill*. Simon and Schuster (1991)

Francis, Dick. *The Sport of Queens*. Michael Joseph (1957)

Fuller, Bryony. *Vincent O'Brien The National Years*. Marlborough (1992)

Gill, James. *Racecourses of Great Britain*. Barrie and Jenkins (1975)

Godfrey, Nicholas. *Racing Post 100 Favourite Racehorses*. Raceform (2005)

Good, Meyrick. *The Lure of the Turf*. Odhams (1957)

Green, Reg. *The Grand National*. Virgin (2000)

Halpenny, M.R. *British Racing and Racecourses*. Holmes (1971)

Harman, Bob *The Ultimate Dream. Cheltenham Gold Cup*. Mainstream (2000)

Herbert, Ivor. *Arkle. Story of a Champion*. Pelham (1966)

––– *Red Rum*. William Luscombe (1974)

Hislop, John. *The Brigadier*. Secker and Warburg (1973)

Holland, Anne. *Steeplechasing*. Time Warner (2003)

Hudson, Noel. *Catherine the Great to Wordsworth*. Huntingdon (1985)

Lambton, The Hon George. *Men and Horses I Have Known*. Allen (1924)

Magee, Sean. *Complete A-Z of Horse Racing*. Channel 4 Books (2001)

––– Aird, Sally. *Ascot and History*. Methuen (2002)

Mahon, Jack. *The Galway Races*. Blackwater (1995)

Marsh, Marcus. *Racing with the Gods*. Pelham (1968)

McCormack, Stan. *Against the Odds*. Kilbeggan Races (1995)

McCoy, A.P. *McCoy the Autobiography*. Joseph (2002)

Morris, Tony. Randall, John. *Horse Racing Records*. Guinness (1985)

Mortimer, Roger. *The Encyclopaedia of Flat Racing*. Robert Hale (1971)

Mortimer, Roger. *The Flat*. George Allen and Unwin (1979)

Mortimer, Roger. Onslow, Richard. Willet, Peter. *Biographical Encyclopaedia of British Flat Racing*. MacDonald and Jane's (1978)

Nash, Stewart. *Plumpton 1884-2000*. Plumpton Racecourse (2000)

Oaksey, John. *Oaksey on Racing*. Kingswood (1991)

Osgood, Frank. *The Story of Newbury Racecourse*. Kingsclere (1993)

Peters, Stewart. *The Grand National*. Tempus (2005)

Pitman, Jenny. *Autobiography*.

Pitman, Richard. Cranham, Gerry. *Guinness Book of Steeplechasing*. Guinness (1988)

Plumptre, George. *The Fast Set. The World of Edwardian Racing*. Andre Deutsch (1985)

Randall, John. Morris, Tony. *A Century of Champions*. Portway Press (1999)

Scudamore, Peter. *SCU. The Autobiography of a Champion*. Headline (1993)

Seth-Smith, Michael. Willett, Peter. Mortimer, Roger. Lawrence, John. *The History of Steeplechasing* Joseph (1966)

Seth-Smith, Michael. Mortimer, Roger. *Derby 200*. Guinness (1979)

Sharpe, Graham. *Racing Almanac*. Racing Post (2009)

Smyly, Patricia. *Encyclopaedia of Steeplechasing*. Hale (1979)

Tanner, Michael. *The Champion Hurdle*. Mainstream (2002)

Thompson, Laura. *Newmarket*. Virgin (2002)

Tyrrel, John. *Racecourses on the Flat*. Crowood (1989)

––– *Chasing Around Britain*. Crowood (1990)

Ward, Andrew. *Horse-Racing's Strangest Races*. Robson (2000)

Welcome, John. *Neck or Nothing. Life and Times of Bob Sievier*. Faber (1970)

––– *Fred Archer*. Lambourn (1990)

Wilson, Julian. *100 Greatest Racehorses*. MacDonald Queen Anne (1987)

Yates, Arthur. *Trainer and Gentleman Rider*. Grant Richards (1924)

Newspapers and Racing Publications

Sporting Chronicle
Sporting Life
Racing Post
Horses in Training from 1959
Raceform